$mart-Money Moves *for Kids*

The Complete Parent's Guide

$mart-Money
Moves *for Kids*
The Complete Parent's Guide

Dr. Judith Briles

mile high
press

**mile high
press**

Books may be purchased for sales promotion by contacting the publisher, Mile High Press at PO Box 460880 Aurora, CO 80046.

Library of Congress Catalog Card # 99-75221
ISBN: 1-885331-03-7

1. Children –Finance, Personal   2. Parenting

Second Edition, First Printing October 2001   Printed in the United States of America

For Frank,

A $mart-Money kid.

Also by Dr. Judith Briles

Stop Stabbing Yourself in the Back
The Confidence Factor—Cosmic Gooses Lay Golden Eggs
10 Smart Money Moves for Women
The Dollars and Sense of Divorce
The Confidence Factor
Woman to Woman 2000
When God Says NO
GenderTraps
The Briles Report on Women in Healthcare
Money Sense
The Money $ense Guidebook
Raising Money-Wise Kids
Woman to Woman
Judith Briles' Money Book
Faith & $avvy Too!
Money Phases
The Woman's Guide to Financial Savvy
The Workplace
The Dollars of Divorce
Self-Confidence and Peak Performance

Contents

CONTENTS

Part III   The Teen Years

Part IV   The Adult Rises

CONTENTS

Acknowledgements

Books don't happen without people. *$mart-Money for Kids* was created from the demand of several of my clients for an easy to read, yet a loaded with content money-parenting book for both parent and child. The one catch was that it had to be created within an extraordinarily short period of time.

You wouldn't have this book in hand without the incredible effort of Ronnie Moore and WESType—my new heroes. Amy Hayes caught my vision for a cover that was fun, about money and said parenting. My husband John supported and cheered the effort, proofread and made sure that Ronnie and I were in sync at all times. Every time I had a question about publishing, Marilyn Ross, co-founder of the Small Publishers Association of North America generously opened the files of phone contacts to help me along.

$mart-Money Moves for Kids is the parenting money book I wished I had in my hands when I started my kids and money journey. Without my teachers—my kids and grandson Frank—and the unique skills of Ronnie, John, Amy and Marilyn, this book wouldn't have happened. I thank them all.

Introduction

Today, most kids think that money comes from the ATM. For some, they are a blessing; for others, an albatross. They're everywhere—down the street, across town, and for some, right in the house! My parenting days were birthed in the early sixties through the mid-eighties. My grand parenting days emerged in the late eighties. My kids concept of getting money was to hit Mom up for it . . . or go to the bank and write another check. Today's kid views the ATM in the same mode. If it's there, there must be cash a plenty.

I've had four kids of my own, one foster child, a fantastic grandson, a gaggle of nieces and nephews, three siblings and a father, who at eighty-eight, still believes that one does not talk about money. I suspect I share my experience curve with others throughout America.

As the decade of the nineties came to a close, family values were bantered quite liberally by both the media and institutions that catered to families. A much media hyped book surfaced in 1998 that said that families and parenting had minimal impact in the shaping of young people. I don't believe that for one second. My decades of experience, especially in the money arena has shown me that families, and parenting, play a major role when it comes to money and its value.

$mart-Money Moves for Kids is my journey through the money maze. It has involved wonderful times as well as disastrous times. There were times when

unlimited vacation dollars were available to my family; for example, we routinely spent a week, post Christmas, in Hawaii. And, each of the kids were allowed take a friend along. Then there were times when we lost everything, house, cars and many of our clothes. Ironically, the biggest leaps in money understanding and knowledge that were passed to my kids came from the disastrous times.

Two of my kids are alive today. My sons have died. As I write this, one daughter is 36, the other 33. The eldest has been money savvy since I can remember. Her younger sister is now . . . but in the old days, was a walking disaster. Was I always money savvy and as a parent, told and taught my kids the wise steps of money management? You've got to be kidding! I made tons of mistakes in learning, and teaching, about money. Remember, I grew up in a family that did not talk about money—how much we made, how much we had, nor how much we spent.

During the seventies, we had everything—big house, pool, fancy cars, great vacations—you name it, we were the consumers of the year! That all changed dramatically in the early eighties when one of my partners got into financial trouble. Her financial woes escalated and landed at my doorstep. By the time it all was unraveled, my family lost everything—home, cars, investments, savings . . . we even had to sell our clothes to feed three growing teen-agers. It was a pretty miserable time at our house. By the time it was over, we lost over a million dollars. Not fun to say the least.

Hindsight is always terrific. A plus did rise from the whole mess—a new dialogue was introduced in our family—we started to TALK about money around the kitchen table . . . and just about everywhere else. You now get to hear some of our conversations and strategies that taught us how to raise $mart-Money kids (and grand kids).

One of the things both my husband John and I have learned along the grand parenting path is that your kids' kids are far more likely to think you are brilliant and wise then your kids ever did. As a grand parent, a role that I love, I've found that grandson Frank is far more likely to seek my counsel on certain topics than his mother ever did. Somehow, my years (and gray hair) count more.

$mart-Money Moves for Kids is just not for parents—you will find that plenty of the stories and examples I use are about Frank the grandson, not just Frank, my son, who died when he was 19. We parents, and grandparents, must stick together. Next time your kid covets the $80 jeans that can barely hang on his hips and scrape the ground, you'll have a rationale game plan for which that

even he can see the logic. Not only do you get a $mart-Money Kid, you become a $mart-Money Parent.

$mart-Money Kids begin with you. What's your *$mart-Money IQ* when it comes to talking, influencing and negotiating with your kids on money issues?

$mart-Money Quiz.

1. Your son is a whiz at computers, and is only 10-years-old. He sees the latest ad for the new Think Pad and begins his campaign for you to buy him one.

   You:
   a. Tell him no, computers are for adults.
   b. Tell him to use the one Uncle George gave him that's 5 years old.
   c. Offer him a deal, since computers cost a lot (especially at a 10-year-old allowance rate), you will match whatever moneys he can save over the next six months to buy a new computer.

2. You are convinced that your five-year-old is destined for the stage. She is with you at Toys R Us and has just put on a presentation in the center aisle that convinced other shoppers that you deprived her from getting anything that is new and fun.

   You:
   a. Walk away and pretend she belongs to someone else.
   b. Shout over her antics and attempt to convince the other shoppers that she has a room full of the latest and greatest stuff.
   c. Escort her to the closest exit and end your shopping trip.

3. Your 12-year-old has a job mowing lawns for your neighbors and best friends. He's announced that he is bored and his destiny is to do more important things. He wants you to fix it for him so he no longer has to be bored with his job.

   You:
   a. Tell him that you are willing to do the lawns every other weekend with him.
   b. Tell him that it's his problem, not yours.
   c. Agree that lawn mowing can be boring, but a job is a job and he made a commitment. Just do it until the summer is over.

4. Your 14-year-old daughter gets a weekly allowance. She's decided that the work you've asked her to do around the house to "earn" her allowance is beneath her and has declared that its her right to get money.

You:
a. Hire outside help to assist you.
b. You keep paying her weekly allowance on Friday, no questions asked.
c. You eliminate all payments.

5. Your 25-year-old daughter has separated from her husband and has moved in with her two-year-old child and one-year-old pooch, "temporarily."

You:
a. Reassemble her old room so that she has "comfort" surroundings around her during this stressful time.
b. Tell her to roll up her sleeves and help out as long as she is there (and clean up after the dog).
c. Get out a pad of paper and create an agreement, in writing, as to what's the maximum time she will be there; what kind of cash contribution she will pay toward board (and food and other expenses you identify); who takes care of the adorable grandchild and puppy; and what household work she will do to help you out while you provide the roof over everyone's head.

Your answers—
As 1 point
Bs 2 points
Cs 3 points

Total # of As ___ **Total # of Bs** ___ **Total # of Cs** ___ **Your Total** ___
What your score means:

0–5 You're in trouble—your kids are raising you.
6–10 Not so bad, and not so good. Your kids know how to push your guilt buttons. It's time to keep using that wonderful two letter word—NO. You might want to read *10 $mart-Money Moves for Women*, the first book in this series.
11–15 Bravo! You are developing *$mart-Money Moves* for you and your kids. With continued fine-tuning, your kids will learn that you are not a bottomless money pit.

The Millennium Challenge

Throughout *$mart-Money Moves for Kids*, woven will be the theme of Proverbs 22:6: *Train a child in the way he (she) should go, and when he is old he will not turn from it.*

Today's world is getting smaller each year. With the incredible resource of the Internet, you and your kids have a breadth of information at your fingertips that is almost beyond comprehension. Within minutes, sometimes seconds, you and your kids can tap into information, articles, column, new books, just about anything without leaving the comfort of your home. Electronics, communications and computers have impacted how we learn, and teach.

As I finish this book, I'm in a small cabin on a 100-foot schooner sailing along the coast of Maine. Between my husband and the captain, they've figured out a way that allows me to tap into the ship's battery power supply so that I can recharge my computer batteries and continue to fine tune. Something I couldn't imagine just a few years ago.

I'm the first to admit I'm ignorant when it comes to electricity and the workings of the computer industry. I'm not, though, ignorant when it comes to recognizing a good thing that will ease my tasks and help me in the learning curve—whatever the learning process is guiding me through. And, so it goes with $mart-Money Moves for you and your kids.

As a parent, your charge is to get your kids ready for the real world. Money is part of that world—the use, understanding and implementation of it become your responsibility. It's an awesome challenge. You, being the $mart-Money Move parent that you are, will have no problem in meeting the task. You will learn and your kids will learn. A good thing for all of you.

Part One

Money Parenting 101

Chapter One

The Game Book for Parents

When I was raising my kids, Dr. Benjamin Spock was my primary resource for my babies' (and mom's) medical needs. Today, I live in Colorado, the home of "Dr. Mom" and I often read columns and articles by guru pediatrician, Dr. T. Berry Brazelton. In the old days, Dr. Spock was an advocate of a more looser style of upbringing. Today, the professionals are advocates of setting limits. They believe that not only is it possible to set limits, it's necessary.

For over forty years, I've been a reader of twin syndicated columnists Ann Landers and Abigail Van Buren. Each has written in her column that kids need discipline, shouldn't be given everything, and if they are, they will soon lose respect for money. As a parent, setting limits can be difficult, but absolutely necessary, especially when it comes to money and the things that money buys that kids want. Bad money habits start rearing their head in the pre-school years. It can be as simple as a "gimme" attack—your kid wants something NOW and expects you to instantly get it for him NOW. And, you do!

Remember the old days (or your parent's old days)—when an ice cream cone was a dime, when you could go to the movies for fifty cents (and get a soda and a bag of popcorn included), when the tooth fairy rarely left more than a dime under your pillow and the latest copy of Mad magazine cost twenty-five cents? We all remember when things cost a lot less. What we as parents must learn is to bite our tongues at times because our memories don't fit into the realties of the present day. Last time I bought a one-scoop ice cream cone, the cost was almost two dollars, not ten cents. The bottom line is this, the dollar is worth far less than it was when you and I were growing up. When it comes to talking money with kids, we need to talk in today's use, not yesteryear's.

If I asked you if there was enough time in the month to do and get done all the things that you would like to do, you would most likely say, "No," that there wasn't enough time in the day to complete all the things you have to do, much less what you would like to do. We are an over committed population. Most of us spend too little time with our kids on a daily basis; it's estimated that the average parent spends only 15 minutes each day—one on one—with each kid. The more kids, the less time.

We have become a nation of fast food and fast meals. Few families sit down together for a meal at home. There's usually someone missing, the meal is set up in a quasi-buffet style or it's, "We'll stop at McDonald's on the way." The modern family has more lessons committed to, play-overs and stay-overs scheduled and time away from home then ever before. Home sometimes feels like a place we change our clothes and sleep at.

When it comes to money talks, most parents know there should be something . . . but what? And when? And, how often? It's not unusual to get caught up in the Scarlett O'Hara syndrome—tomorrow is another day. Talking to your kids and teaching them the principles of money is almost as scary as having the "sex" talk. You know the topic/subject will come up . . . and you will stumble over it . . . and deep down, you hope they figure it all out and never ask you anything that might embarrass you. Right? I suspect so.

During the summer, my niece Torri celebrated her marriage. All the family gathered from multiple states. I hadn't seen my father since the previous Christmas and immediately noted how frail he had become. My three brothers and I compared notes and knew once again, we needed to do the "talk." My father, at 88, still would not do a will nor do any other things around the topic of money that we all felt should be addressed. I guess the good news is that my father had minimal assets, estate taxes were not an issue, but it would be nice to know what he would like us to do when he died.

In my family, at least from my parents generation, we didn't talk about money. It was a taboo topic, like sex. We were clueless about our family's money situation, how much or little was in our house. We always ate and had the appropriate clothes to wear when the new school year started. We did not know how much money my father made, how much was paid in taxes (heck, we didn't know you paid taxes) or how much we had in the bank (if anything).

In our family, money was like the wind—we knew it was around, we just didn't know where it came from. More good news is that we weren't alone—most of my friends had no idea what their parents did to bring in their money or how it was spend. And, I suspect you were probably in the same boat as we all were.

When I look at families today, I find them much more open. They talk about almost everything—sex, drugs and the perils of both, relationship problems, and yet they still hold back about money. After all, money can be a powerful tool. Some parents buy affection, others use it to cover guilt. It can be given generously or conditionally.

Parents are usually the money role model. In my family's case, none of my brothers wanted to emulate our parents benign neglect approach to money. If a parent has trouble managing money, it's not uncommon that their kid's ability to live within their means and manage their own money mimics that of their parent. Let's face it—lots of us don't like to look in the mirror of life. We'd rather be more theatrical . . . like Scarlett O'Hara.

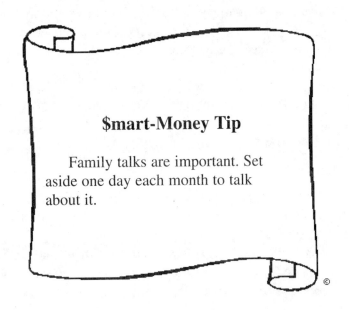

$mart-Money Tip

Family talks are important. Set aside one day each month to talk about it.

Kids spend money, mega money. The teen economy is in excess of 100 billion dollars a year—and that's just teen-agers. Don't forget the zillions of dollars the pre-teen places on store counters throughout America. With e-commerce, a whole new arena has opened for spending money in cyberspace. Traditionally, teens had bought stereos, radios, CDs, CD players, headphones, and video games.

In the early nineties, a small percentage of homes had computers. With the new Millennium, over half of all households have computers, probably on its way to a percentage that will match the number of homes that own televisions. The regular feature of a computer in a home means that kids access them. In fact, most kids are far more knowledgeable about them then their parents are. Kids have created their own personal libraries of computer and video games, something that we didn't even have an option to spend money on. The software available to computer owners is quite extensive. A recent program purchased for grandson Frank was a typing program designed for the at home user. Remember when we all went to Typing 101? Now you can do it at home for $20.

Kid's and Money

Kids spend a lot of money. Over $100 billion is spent by teens every year according to Teenage Research Unlimited. Girls and boys don't outspend each other, they are fairly equal in their spending habits. Kids are most likely to spend money on food, clothes, movie tickets, electronic equipment (videos, games, software) and for girls, cosmetics. Once a car arrives on the scene, it becomes the money pit.

Younger kids (under 12) are more inclined to yield to parental influence in money matters. A greater percentage is saved, I think primarily because Mom and Dad are more included to cover everyday type purchases, even though allowances should be spent on some of them. Another $12 to $15 billion is added to the spending pie.

Then, there's indirect spending—all those moneys that get spent that are influenced by your kids (or, as one of my friends said, manipulated by the kids). According to *Consumer Reports*, more that $180 billion of purchases each year are influenced by kids.

So, what does all this mean? It means that several million dollars is spent everyday on candy, sodas, snacks, toys, games, movies, sports, live entertainment; video arcade games, CDs and telephones. A lot of money and a powerful segment to market to.

There's no doubt about it, money brings incredible power to kids. Power that enables them to purchase items they think they need, and items they want. As a parent, you are in control of your children up to about the age of three. After that, most kids are given choices such as what type of ice cream cone they want or which toy they wish to play with. Or buy.

Post age three, kids are recognized as a consumer force. Just look at the commercials on children's TV programming, and for that matter, at the ads designed for family viewing slots. By the time kids are eight, it's common for them to make unassisted purchases when they are out shopping with adults—you or another.

One of the recognized experts on kids and their influencing/spending habits is James McNeal, a marketing professor at Texas AM University. For years he has studied them and estimates that kids between the ages of 4-12 influence adult purchases in over sixty product categories; everything from pasta to bicycles and athletic shoes. Children's spending tripled in the nineties.

What's the bottom line? If you don't take an active, and early, interest in your kids' money training, there's a gaggle of folks who will. Their friends and peers and the media will top the list. Your parents probably told you that money didn't grow on trees. If you were a smarty, you might have responded that it did too—the paper that bills are printed on came from trees. Kids today have a different view or cliché. They believe that money grows out of an ATM or a plastic credit card. The reality that you initially put money into a bank account to seed future withdrawals never dawned on them. Most kids today believe that credit cards can satisfy every need and whim, which include but are not limited to:

- at least one VCR and video game
- two CD players—one portable, the other permanent in their bedroom
- the latest fashions in clothing (grandson Frank didn't think much of paying $42 for a pair of board shorts when he accompanied us to Hawaii for a vacation—he did pay with his own money that he brought along)
- the most recent fad item

It's their perceived birthright, or so they think.

The TV Ad Monster

Frank is my twelve-year-old grandson. In school he struggled with math when he was eight. During the same, "I don't get it Grandma" times, I was fascinated at his ability to memorize all the infomercials and their corresponding (800) numbers that flash on the TV. During one month, he called to tell me about the benefits, costs and respective phone numbers for a variety of products. He especially thought I should immediately order a Smart Mop, Power

Foam and Abflex unit.

With the billions of dollars that kids spend annually, you can't ignore their buying power. You are literally zinged and zapped from multiple sides to buy this and buy that. Commercials are designed with one purpose—to motivate the viewer to buy. When your kids watch their favorite shows on TV, the commercials bombard them with the message to buy, buy, buy. If you tune into the Saturday offerings of cartoons, it's not unusual to find that the production of the show is actually less than the creation of the ads.

Next time you are at the grocery store, shop it versus just buying. Note the type of items that are kept on the lower shelves (kid eye level), especially in the cereal, candy and snack aisles. Also note the amount and variety of frozen foods. When Swanson introduced it's first TV dinner in the fifties (it was turkey with mashed potatoes and peas), I suspect they had no idea how big the "already cooked/heat 'em up" industry would be one day.

In our parent's time, it used to be a chicken in every pot and two cars in every garage, now it's at least one VCR and two TVs in every home. With the VCR, a whole new industry evolved around videos: from decades old movie (*The Wizard of Oz* and *ET* were played over 90 times for Frank before the tape broke and we bought a new one), to the latest Disney classic or movie that played in your local theater just six months ago.

Reproduction of videos became a billion dollar business that create a new industry that in turn created the video giant in every city, Blockbuster! These videos are not viewed once, they are seen dozens and dozens of times just like *The Wizard of Oz* and *ET* were in our house. The distributors of such have tuned into this savvy fact and preface the feature film with several commercials about upcoming or already distributed films. After all, they have a captive audience with popcorn and sodas set up and viewers settled in. It's frequent viewer time.

Sexism Sells

Don't leave sexism out, it sells and it sells well. The Zandl Group is a New York City research company that specializes in studying the youth market. They found that, over the years, boys are far more likely to respond to commercials and ads that are sports oriented and aggressive; girls respond to commercials that are cute and sentimental. Nothing new—muscles and sweat versus kittens and cuddles.

Shoes are a very hot item. Nike and Keds have learned that boys like Nike and girls buy Keds. When it comes to the huge soda market, girls preferred diet sodas and flavored filtered water and boys preferred root beer and Classic Coke. When it comes to reading, *Seventeen* and *Jane* are still favorites with girls and boys look for *Sports Illustrated* and car and motorcycle magazines. It's no secret that kids like TV and when *Beverly Hills 90210* debuted, it quickly became #1 with teenage girls; boys preferred the camaraderie of sports bar *Cheers*. When *Melrose Place, Dawson's Creek* and *Friends* entered the TV seen, they found the teen-age audience.

Now that your kids are hooked, what's a parent to do? Start by watching. Sit down and watch TV with your kids, no matter what their age may be. American kids watch two to three hours of TV each day. Within a 30 minute program, commercial time can ranges from eight to twelve minutes. A great majority of those commercials are specifically targeted toward your kids. Advertisers are not dummies, they know that kids have money of their own (billions!). With the use of the Internet, more commercials and ads are coming their way. Get on-line with your kids and check out what their favorite sites are. It's not uncommon to have commercial banners flow across the screen.

Kids are masters. They know that they can influence, and manipulate, what their parents buy. And, you know that they know, they know that you know and the advertisers know it too! So, should we ban all advertising in children's programming as some would like to do? No, I don't think that's a realistic approach and you are now on the doorsteps of the First Amendment folks.

I've watched plenty of commercials in my fifty plus years and have marveled at the cleverness of many. When we get together with friends for our annual Super Bowl viewing, there's always plenty of chatter about the uniqueness, humor, or stupidity of the program's many million-dollar spots. Viewing the shows your kids like with them offers you an opportunity to learn how the commercials pitch to the viewer—your kid. It opens the door to a discussion about the product, how the commercial presents it, distorts the pitched benefits (if you think it does), the necessity of it, and if appropriate, how it ties in with your values.

When Frank was younger, about eight, here's a game that we played with him. He loved cereal and had developed an expertise in getting me to buy every brand that he saw on TV. I confess that as a doting grandmother, I did it, but then I got smart. Try playing our TV Commercial Comparison Test in your home. Not only will it teach the strategy of being a $mart-Money consumer to your young one, but also it will introduce some refreshingly new and interesting dialogue between you and your child about truth in advertising and which product is the best deal.

TV Commercial Comparison Test

Your goal: To teach your kids to be a $mart-Money consumer.

Tools you will need: Any kid show on TV, preferably an afternoon or Saturday morning program. A pad of paper and a pencil. A visit to the grocery store before and after viewing the show.

For the test: Three "testers" work well—friends or family members. All testers should be potential consumers of the product.

Rules: Watch a TV program with your child with specific emphasis on commercials. During the show, there should be no interruptions. Ask the child if he or she can remember what kinds of products are on the rows in the grocery store. If he or she remembers, explain that, because there are so many different product choices, the people who design and make commercials try to convince you both that their product should be in your home. Ask your child to select one of the products shown in the commercials for a test.

The Prize: The "winning" item from your test will be stocked in the cupboard.

How to Proceed: I did this with the cereal. Fruit snacks, cookies and sodas are also ideal candidates. We went to the super market and Frank found the product he had selected for our test (it was Cocoa Pebbles). The grocery we go to has rows that are 6 shelves high. Our test product was found on the second shelf from the bottom. This is a good time to explain product placement on the shelves; i.e.: what can little eyes see at their level compared with the adult level? After all, whom are they trying to pitch? We purchased one box each of Cocoa Pebbles, Cocoa Puffs, and a similar store generic brand. When we got home we did a taste test.

Three bowls of cereal were poured, milk was added and each of our three testers was blindfolded. The taste testers then picked the product that they liked the best.

In your test, if it was the one that was promoted in the commercial, your kid wins. You will buy the product for regular family consumption. If the product flunks the test (the majority of our testers didn't rank it #1), then you won't buy it. After you do this a few times, your kids will learn that what is seen in the commercial is not necessarily as good as it appears and that getting what you ask for is not always satisfying.

As an added note, you can ask: How did our product comparison go? (substitute your test product)

Cocoa Pebbles cost _____ , Cocoa Puffs cost _____ , and the generic brand _____ .

Our taste test put the generic brand in the lead, which allowed me to take the lesson one step further. Assuming that two boxes of cereal were eaten every month for twelve months: twenty-four boxes would cost _____ .

If Frank had insisted in staying with his preferred Cocoa Pebbles at _____ , the yearly cost would total _____ . The yearly difference in the cost between the Cocoa Pebbles and the generic brand totals _____ . I told him that since we were going to buy the generic brand, we would put the cost savings into his bank account, his reward for being a $mart-Money consumer.

At twelve, Frank does his comparisons with a pad of paper that he makes columns on and labels Item #1, #2, #3 etc. He has learned to look closely at labels, is very vocal about rip-offs and can tell you why he wants to get a certain product. Not bad for a twelve-year-old.

Money Stores for Kids

When I was a kid, we had bank days at my elementary school. Every Wednesday, I deposited 25 cents in my bank savings envelope. The school then delivered the deposits to the bank, which in turn posted the deposit to the bankbook. Granted, 25 cents was worth a lot more in 1952 than today. Yet that weekly deposit introduced a concept to me that my accumulated pennies, nickels, dimes and quarters could add up to a tidy sum by the end of the year. I could add more or withdraw my money whenever I wanted. School banking programs were everywhere in the 50's and then disappeared. Today, some schools have re-introduced them—a good idea.

I didn't get an allowance when I was a kid, but I was able to earn my share of nickels for jobs around the house. I had a bonus too. My father said I could keep any pennies I found lying around and I collected bottles from all the neighbors. Back then, a soda bottle yielded a two-cent return deposit, the big quart bottles, five cents. So, sometimes my twenty-five cent deposit per week was all I had, at other times it was a fraction. I thought I was rich until I discovered these huge dill pickles that cost a nickel. Once a month I withdrew a nickel from my growing savings account and treated myself to a pickle (my reward for saving money). Encouraging kids to save is part of developing a $mart-Money strategy.

In the nineties, The American Express Company and Consumer Federation of America sponsored a nationwide test of the consumer knowledge with high school seniors. The results were embarrassing. Only eighteen percent knew that the annual percentage rate (APR) is the best indicator of the true cost of a loan. Teens think they know plenty about cars. Well, they missed out on the insurance side. Only eighteen percent knew that rates for car insurance offered by different companies to consumers (them) in the same area and with comparable driving records could vary in different amounts in premiums charged.

At the same time, the National Council for Economic Education did a survey that included the general public as well as high school and college students. Their results weren't so terrific either. Only thirty-six percent of those knew what a profit was. If only one-third of the general population has any $mart-Money awareness, the pass down of knowledge to the next generation is not promising. These statistics stress the importance of teaching your children all you can about money. Your $mart-Money Moves need to be as sharp as possible to meet the challenges you have ahead with your children.

Kids are gullible, and are easily roped in by the TV commercials that bombard them on a regular basis. One way to turn their light bulbs on is to subscribe to *Zillions: Consumer Reports for Kids*. *Zillions* appeals to the 10-14 year old crowd and routinely does comparison tests on items that kids spend their money on—from hamburgers to sneakers. It follows the advice and reputation of its well-known parent, *Consumers Report*.

My style in communicating with you will be on a common sense approach. You will find throughout this book a series of $mart-Money Tips that are meant to enhance the common sense approaches you already have in place. That, and being consistent with your children, will dramatically enhance the $mart-Money Moves you are developing.

Repeated studies and dialogue with parents shows that when kids are given information and the incentive to learn about money, they are quite astute. In my hometown of Denver, CO, the Young American Bank birthed several years ago. Customers come from every state in the country and range up to 22 years of age, with the average age being 9. The bank offers banking by mail, checking and savings accounts, credit cards and loans. It also offers a variety of newsletters and summer classes. Kids learn to work in the shops of Young AmeriTowne® and the Girls Can® programs at regularly scheduled times.

The Young American Bank carries over 17,000 savings accounts with an average balance of $357. The most common reasons their customers give for saving are: to buy a car or computer games. The bank has over 300 certificate of deposit holders with an average balance in excess of $2200, the average CD

$mart-Money Tip

Zillions: Consumer Reports for Kids
Encourage your kids to develop $mart-Money consumer
habits by subscribing to *Zillions*—6 issues per year—Call
914-378-2000

Young Americans Bank
The ideal bank for young people, started in 1987, is
Young Americans Bank, 311 Steele Street, Denver, CO,
80206, 303-321-2265. Write or call for information.

The Kids Market Myths and Realities
by James McNeal (Paramount Marketing Publishing, 1999)
A great resource for latest facts—*www.newdream.org*.

holder age is 15. The most common reason for saving is for college funds.

When it comes to checking accounts, the bank carries over 1000 individual accounts with an average balance of $390, average depositor age of 16 and the average check written for $35. The most common reason given for having a checking account was "experience." The experience comes when checks are written for pizza, shopping articles in local stores and mail orders.

Peer pressure surfaces when kids hit twelve. You are no longer the key factor in their decision making, their pals and schoolmates are. That means the primary years are yours to create and make your kids smart with their money. One of the most important things for you, as a parent, to do is to develop a type of strategy that fits with your personal family values and lifestyle. Not your neighbors or your kids' friends. What works for them may not work for you. Think about your income level, your characteristics and traits, as well as spending and savings habits that you practice. Your next part is a big one—you must commit time to your kids in sharing and teaching your principles and values.

Chapter Two

Being in the
Spot Light

Most kids like money, especially yours. The environment in your home will be a key factor in your kids' attitudes and behaviors when it comes to money. Let me probe a tad and ask a few questions. If you are married, do you and your spouse talk about money? If so, is it positive or negative? Do either of you scold the other about spending too much or not enough? Do you put each other down for making mistakes with money? Is money a taboo topic, or do you talk about it openly? Does having money, or the lack of money, create tension? Do you buy new things because your neighbors have acquired them or do you buy them because you need them? Have you thought about how you spend money and how your spending might influence your kids?

When adolescence and hormones kick in, your kids take on personas that sometimes seem alien. They routinely turn to their peers for advice. Unfortunately, it doesn't matter how good the advice is or how bad. If you had practiced sound parenting attitudes in the pre-teen years, it rarely is lost. As your kids transition through their teens, maturing into adults, your earlier attitudes and practices will resurface.

Not All Parents Are Alike

If you had your druthers, would you rather spend money or would you rather save it? Let's find out. Below is the *$mart-Money Parent Quiz*. Part 1 is for you and Part 2 is for your kids (You will answer about them).

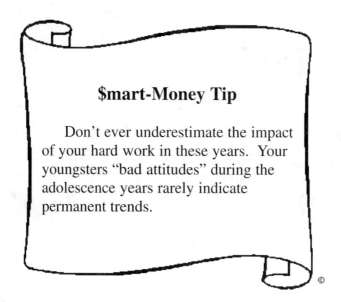

$mart-Money Tip

Don't ever underestimate the impact of your hard work in these years. Your youngsters "bad attitudes" during the adolescence years rarely indicate permanent trends.

$mart-Money Parent Quiz

1. Is it important to own lots of things?   Yes ___ No ___
2. If Uncle Bert left you $200,000 would you put most of it in the bank?   Yes ___ No ___
3. Do you have ongoing credit card balances?   Yes ___ No ___
4. Are you afraid of being poor when you are old?   Yes ___ No ___
5. Do you say, "We can't afford it," when your spouse says, "We need it?"   Yes ___ No ___
6. Do you think about money a lot?   Yes ___ No ___
7. Do you max your credit cards out?   Yes ___ No ___
8. Does having money give you a feeling of power or being liked?   Yes ___ No ___
9. Do you know how much money is in your purse or wallet, within 10% of the total?   Yes ___ No ___
10. Do you reward yourself for a good day or an achievement by going shopping?   Yes ___ No ___
11. Do you feel inadequate financially in comparing yourself to your friends?   Yes ___ No ___
12. Do you love watching investments and bank accounts increase?   Yes ___ No ___
13. Is it hard for you to make decisions about how to spend your money?   Yes ___ No ___

14. Do you use a shopping trip to make you feel better? Yes ___ No ___

15. Do you have stuff hanging in your closets with price tags still on them? Yes ___ No ___

Transfer your *Yes* answers as X's to the table below and total.

How to score:
If you answered: *Yes* to #'s 1, 3, 7, 10, 11, 14, & 15 indicates you are a ***Spender***
  Yes to #'s 2, 4, 5, 6, 8, 9, 12, & 13 indicates you are a ***Saver***

Spender: 1 ___ 3 ___ 7 ___ 10 ___ 11 ___ 14 ___ 15 ___
Total ***Spender***   *Yes* Answers _____

Saver: 2 ___ 4 ___ 5 ___ 6 ___ 8 ___ 9 ___ 12 ___ 13 ___
Total ***Saver***   *Yes* Answers _____

So, how did you do? How do you think your child might answer those questions as an adult? To get a peek, answer the 15 questions from the *$mart-Money Kids Quiz* and see what may be in the future.

$mart-Money Kids Quiz

If you have more than one child, make extra copies, as needed, of the quiz or answer for each child with a different colored pen or pencil.

1. When given money, does your kid save most of it? Yes ___ No ___

2. Does he routinely save his money for those special things he wants? Yes ___ No ___

3. When you go on trips, does your kid want to buy souvenirs or trinkets for friends? Yes ___ No ___

4. Does your kid routinely misplace or lose money? Yes ___ No ___

5. Does your kid like to put money in his bank account? Yes ___ No ___

6. When you say "no" to a stop for pizza or hamburger, does your kid offer to pay for it? Yes ___ No ___

7. Is "Frank has one" a reason your child uses for buying something? Yes ___ No ___

8. Is he hesitant about spending any of his money? Yes ___ No ___

9. When shopping, does your kid begin a lot of sentences with "I want?" Yes ___ No ___

23

10. When your kid has a bad day at school, do you suggest
a shopping trip?   Yes ___ No ___
11. If your kid sees money on the ground, will he pick it up? Yes ___ No ___
12. Does your kid often ask for merchandise related to the
latest "hot" movie?   Yes ___ No ___
13. Does he like to collect things?   Yes ___ No ___
14. Does he pay attention to sale ads or coupons
in the newspaper?   Yes ___ No ___
15. Do you think your kid is "too" generous?   Yes ___ No ___

Transfer your *Yes* answers as X's to the table below and total.

How to score:
Yes answers to 3, 4, 6, 7, 9, 10, 12 & 15 indicate that you have a ***Spender*** on your hands.
Yes answers to 1, 2, 5, 8, 11, 13, & 14 indicate that you have a ***Saver*** in the making.

.

Spender: 3 ___ 4 ___ 6 ___ 7 ___ 9 ___ 10 ___ 12 ___ 15 ___
Total ***Spender***   *Yes* Answers _____

Saver: 1 ___ 2 ___ 5 ___ 8 ___ 11 ___ 13 ___ 14 ___
Total ***Saver***   *Yes* Answers _____

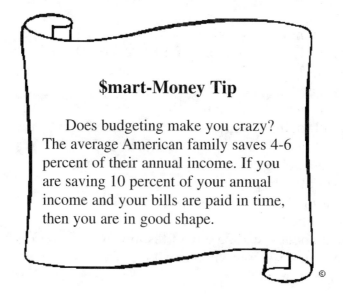

$mart-Money Tip

Does budgeting make you crazy?
The average American family saves 4-6
percent of their annual income. If you
are saving 10 percent of your annual
income and your bills are paid in time,
then you are in good shape.

If either you or your kid(s) scored extremely high in any one category, it doesn't mean that you will be either tightfisted or a spendthrift for the rest of your life. Ideally, what you'd like to be is a careful and prudent spender as well as a consistent, committed and disciplined saver. Throughout *$mart-Money Moves for Kids*, you will find quizzes and games that can be used as examples for teaching money behaviors, plus some modifications of existing behaviors. Not only will your kids learn some things, but you might too.

It's well documented that disagreements (and sometimes war) about money are one of the top three leading causes of divorce in the U.S. The others are sex and kids. Knowing whether you are a *spender* or *saver* is important.

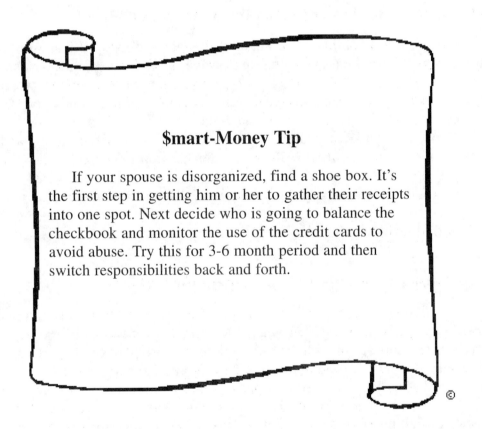

$mart-Money Tip

If your spouse is disorganized, find a shoe box. It's the first step in getting him or her to gather their receipts into one spot. Next decide who is going to balance the checkbook and monitor the use of the credit cards to avoid abuse. Try this for 3-6 month period and then switch responsibilities back and forth.

If you feel that things are seriously out of control, there is always help available, whether it's with mounting debt or just spending too much. In the first book of this series, *10 $mart-Money Moves for Women*, I identify several sources for help and credit counseling assistance.

They include:

Consumer Credit Counseling   800-388-2227
8611 Second Avenue, Suite 100   *www.nfcc.org*
Silver Spring, MD 20910

Christian Financial Concepts   800-722-1976
601 Broad Street SE   *www.cfcministry.org*
Gainesville, GA 30501

Do You Do as You Say or Do You Do Something Different?

Kids need to hook into your chain of thought and logic. It makes no sense for you to lecture them about their extravagance and wastefulness when they want to replace their Nintendo video systems with the latest version, when you borrow to buy a new car every year. When it comes to money and your kids, a critical $mart-Money rule is to be consistent.

If you pay your kids an allowance—and I think this is a good idea—and you have made a rule that there will be no advances on next weeks allowance—Hang Tight!

Your kids must learn that they must live within their own spending plans. If you regularly give into their pleas for advances, wait a few years and see what they will do with credit cards.

The Puppies of the Yuppies Believe that Love = Things

I'm not quite sure how it all began, but I believe a key factor in a kid's belief that love equals things started when both parents went to work. Perhaps, because of less time spent with the kids, guilt came into play. Some parents found that one surefire way to temporarily relieve guilt is to buy something.

So, what do you do when your kids badger you for more and more things? Or, how do you deal with the issue when your kid *must* have a $100 pair of sneakers—all the other kids parents bought them? I can remember when a pair of Keds, the only sneakers available in my growing up years, was under $5.

Believe it or not the best answer is so simple, that I'm embarrassed to say it: *Just Say No!* No doubt about it, your kids are going to be ticked at you, but in

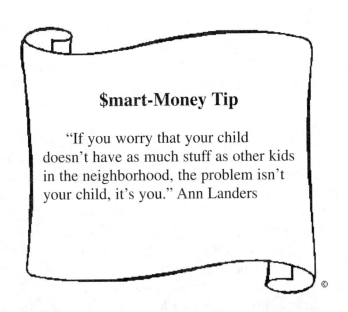

$mart-Money Tip

"If you worry that your child doesn't have as much stuff as other kids in the neighborhood, the problem isn't your child, it's you." Ann Landers

the end you're still Mom and Dad and they are going to love you despite your refusal to give in to every whim they have. Remember, you are the adult, and it's your house and you pay the bills. Therefore, you're supposed to be in charge.

Most people think that $100+ for any pair of shoes is extravagant. However, if just plain No doesn't appeal, you can offer a compromise. Tell your son or daughter how much you allocate toward their shoes and tell them that you will contribute that much to the overall cost. They had better start working and saving. It's interesting how individuals of all ages often reevaluate a financial situation, when they realize that their own money must go into the pot to make it work. It wouldn't hurt to remind your kids that their feet are still growing and they may not be able to enjoy wearing their $100 investment in a few months.

When my youngest daughter was 14, she was obsessed with brand labels. It was designer this and designer that—from the name on the back of her favorite designer jeans to the coveted $100+ purse she felt was essential to carry to school. My answer was a resounding NO! Today, when Frank wants something he has seen on TV or something his friends have, she looks at me and rolls her eyes and says "It's pay back time."

Kids are astute in deciphering who is the easier mark, Mom or Dad. For the parent who is the soft touch (and it's usually Mom) it might make sense to say something along this line: "That's an interesting idea to spend money on; let's talk to Dad and see if we agree that this will fit our spending plan." After they hear that a few times, it's most likely that they will back off with their external hand out. If you are a single parent, try "Let's get our calendar and mark-off two weeks. If, at the end of two weeks, you and I *both* feel that you need this, then we will make a plan on how to budget for it."

Mistakes to Avoid

Above all, be candid with your kids about money. When they ask questions, answer them. It doesn't mean you have to tell them the exact family income. Most kids who are mid teens and younger can't comprehend the difference between $40,000 and $240,000. Either way, it sounds to them like a lot of money and with that much money you can buy whatever they want. If money is tight in your home, let them know it. Explain why you can't buy the new roller blades and why you can't spend the money to go to Wendy's and Taco Bell a couple of times a week like their friends do.

One of the smartest things I did with my kids was instituted when they were in their teens. When each one hit the age of 16, they got to be one of my personal assistants. They did all the shopping with me and they helped me pay all the bills. For the three-month summer period, they wrote checks for the mortgage, cleaning, insurance, gasoline, entertainment, etc. Anything that demanded a check, they wrote it. This hands on experience showed them the reality of how much money was required to operate our household. They never forgot that.

In the early eighties, our family went through a financial disaster that impacted us for the next ten years. As soon as I recognized the depth and the seriousness of it, I called a family meeting. I told the kids what was going on—that, in the end, we could lose our home, cars, even our business. We wouldn't be taking vacations, going out to dinner—good times and "things" that cost money would be deleted from our lifestyle. As it came to pass, we lost everything.

What happened? I had a partner who got into trouble and drew money against a credit line that I had personally guaranteed through our business. When it was over, we lost in excess of a million dollars. It was a devastating time, but it could have been far worse if I hadn't called our family together and explained the circumstances. I made the upside and the downside of our new life together perfectly clear. The kids all pitched in—Amazing! Demands ceased and help was overflowing. They knew we were fighting for our lives; mentally, physically, financially and even spiritually.

Tell the truth to your kids; if you are in trouble with money, let them know. If things are okay; they need to hear the good news too. It's amazing what young minds can construe to be a problem in the household when there is none. Keep your children posted. Sharing with your kids about how much things cost and how to use money, brings you closer to each other. Soon, you will see your values growing in them. Values that they will, in turn, seed in their own kids.

The *$mart-Money* Parent's Creed

Teaching youngsters about money in their formative years can promote their intellectual development. It also helps adults rethink the basics of the value of money and the importance of making it grow. Children need to understand that we seldom receive anything for free. We work for what we receive. But if we work, and we work hard, we have a right to expect to benefit.

The $mart-Money Parent's Creed reads:

Parents provide their child with a hands-on learning experience while maintaining an atmosphere of trust and communication that is critical to the learning process. The parent teaches through experience, and the guiding principle is clear: Learn by doing, not just by talking.

If your kids function as responsible, cooperative, giving family members, and if they understand and accept the "game rules" that you set up, they should participate in the benefits.

Chapter Three

Your Insurance IQ

Contrary to popular belief, life insurance is for the living—the living that are left behind if you die (which you will, someday). There are three key reasons why you buy life insurance:

1. To replace income if you die prematurely and family members depend on that income.
2. To provide money to buy out a business partner, repay business loans, or hire a successor in case of an owner's death.
3. To provide immediate, liquid money to pay estate taxes.

As a parent, the first reason should flash blinding lights at you. Unless you have huge amounts of money that are easily accessible, you family needs some financial protection if you were no longer in the picture. It doesn't matter if you are the primary breadwinner, secondary breadwinner or a homemaker. Either role, and all the ones in-between, has a significant financial value to them.

As you begin to probe the maze that is insurance land—and believe me, it is—keep two rules in mind:

♦ *Keep it simple.* It is easy to go brain-numb when considering insurance. If you don't understand what an agent is recommending, don't buy it.

Remember, you are the purchaser, if you don't like the style and quality, there's another policy out there.

◆ *Frugality wins.* Buy the lowest cost insurance you can. Stretching your dollar to get the most for the least is your recommended guide. Insurance products and prices (premiums) change all the time. The policy I owned just five years ago has already been replaced with more coverage for fewer dollars . . . and I'm older.

Life insurance is death protection—protection for those you love and care for. Other types of insurance that go beyond pure death protection, with savings and investments attached to the policy as part of the deal, may have a hefty price tag attached. More later...

Who Needs It?

Not everyone. But, if you have kids, most likely you. Below are a few scenarios. See where you fit:

You're married, with children. You need insurance, lots of it. Those kids have to be raised and educated, and it's not cheap. But you probably need the coverage only until they're on their own (this is one of your parental goals). Most people think that a couple of hundred thousand dollars in life insurance is quite ample. Think again. In the olds days, it was assumed that the husband would die first and that the wife would remarry, thus having a regular paycheck coming in. Not so today. Many don't remarry and those that do often keep their finances separate. A common guesstimate is to multiple your annual income by seven—that's the amount of life insurance you should carry on your life.

 Get ye to the phone at once and set up an appointment with a Certified Financial Planner or a Chartered Financial Consultant to go over your insurance needs.

You're single with dependents. Dependents come in all ages: babies to elderly parents. Red alert! What happens if you die . . . tomorrow? If you are divorced and you have children, the kids may go to their father. Would he need to pay for childcare, housekeeping, etc. services if you weren't there? What about college costs that you agreed to split in your divorce? What about the elderly parents? Who will provide care and supplement their income if you currently do it—the supplemental income fairy? Some type of coverage is a $mart-Money move.

If you have dual responsibilities—kids from a previous marriage and kids from your present marriage—it can get complicated, even messy, when you haven't set up adequate financial coverage for their upkeep. A life insurance policy could be placed in a trust that would designate what disbursements are to be made to whom, when and why—your lawyer, agent or financial planner will help here (after you tell them what you want).

If relatives will become guardians, do your kids *and them* a huge favor by having insurance proceeds to fund education needs. Don't assume that your brother and his wife are going to open their checkbooks to your kids as they would to their own. Talk about what happens "if" and then plan for it now.

 If you are under 50 years of age, and a non-smoker, you can get a term insurance policy for less that $200 a year—that's $16 per month!

You own a business. Most companies carry policies on key employees—that means you. It gives your family the cash to pay any debts that you may have incurred on behalf of the company. It also creates the cash to fund a buy-out of your ownership share if you have partners.

Here's a twist. When you are self-employed, you are the moneymaker. What happens to your moneymaking capabilities if something happens to one of your kids? Here's what happened to me. My son was 19 when he died in an accident. I became non-functional. Oh, people on the outside thought I was doing OK. But inside? —I wasn't. There were times that I couldn't remember to pay bills.

When you work for someone else, your co-workers cover for you and you get a regular paycheck—everyone understands you need to grieve, it's normal. When you are self-employed, you need to be present to continue making money. The pain that comes from the loss of a child is immense. I wasn't present and I couldn't function fully. The end result was that less money came to take care of our needs.

My solution was to purchase $100,000 policies on each of my girls. The cost was $105 per year—a peace of mind. The last thing I would want is to have something happen to them, but if it does, I can take time off and grieve and heal.

Don't assume your partner will take care of your family with future cash distributions or dividends. If you are self-employed, insure your kids for a nominal amount to give you healing time. Get coverage.

You have been married before and receive alimony or child support or have moneys due from a divorce settlement. By carrying a policy on your ex's life, you have coverage for moneys due you—an added safety net.

Calculate how much child support or alimony you are owed over its lifetime, then purchase insurance to offset the balance owed.

You're rich. You may need money to pay estate taxes. If your investments are illiquid, meaning you can't get your hands on needed cash within seven days (real estate and privately owned companies fit here) you need money—ready cash.

If you're in this category, make an appointment with an estate-planning attorney to set up an irrevocable trust to keep the insurance proceeds out of your estate.

If your job (or your spouse's) pays into Social Security, you have extra coverage. When Social Security was started in 1937, no one foresaw that kids would be covered... but guess what, those under 19 are. Here's more. Social Security will pay an income to:

- ◆ Surviving spouses age 60 and up.
- ◆ Disabled spouses age 50 and up.
- ◆ A spouse who remarries a Social Security recipient. She or he can still collect on the first (or any previous marriages of 10 years) spouse's account if it pays more.
- ◆ Un-remarried, surviving spouses caring for a child under 16 or one who was disabled before 22.
- ◆ Unmarried dependent children under 18.
- ◆ Unmarried dependent children under 19 if still in secondary school.
- ◆ Parents at least 62 and older who got at least half their support from the worker who died.

Don't forget—there's a lump-sum death benefit of $255 to the surviving spouse.

Check your Social Security record every few years. The form PEBES—for Personal Earnings Benefit Estimate Statement—is quite easy to read. Call 800-234-5772 for Form SSA-7004.

Life Insurance 101

There are two types of insurance and a zillion hybrids. *Term* and *Whole Life* are the most common. *Universal Life* was introduced several years ago which combined the two—kind of—and then there are variations of each.

Term insurance answers most needs when it comes to replacing lost income. The key parts of term are:

♦ You pay premiums every year (monthly, quarterly or annually). Insurance stays in force until you stop paying. There is no cash build up—so, there are no savings.
♦ With ordinary term, your premium increases slightly each year. You can buy a level term, which keeps the premium fixed for several years.
♦ Costs are determined by age, whether you smoke, and by gender (although some insurance companies use unisex rates).
♦ Companies vary in what they charge—the same policy and amount can cost twice as much at another company.
♦ It should be renewable—which means you don't have to requalify with a physical every year.

Whole life insurance has a savings account attached to it. The longer you are in it, the more savings you will have. In order to achieve this, whole life's premiums are greater than term's in the early years of the policy. When whole life is proposed it's always accompanied by illustrations—the "What-ifs." Projects for growth in the savings side are *always* inflated—they are *never guaranteed*!

It's easy to be misled on interest rates. Insurance companies routinely announce high interest rates to keep policyholders at bay, and then they increase their operating expenses and charges for mortality (the death benefit). These expenses are deducted from your cash value before any interest is paid.

The result: you do get a higher interest rate, but it's paid on a smaller amount of cash. You, therefore, earn less than the promised rate.

Universal Life offers some flexibility. You can get a guaranteed policy amount for when you die; you can accumulate tax deferred cash; you can pay extra premiums early on so that extra cash will build up (theoretically), so that your extra cash will pay future premiums. Here's the catch: if the interest rates projected in your illustration are not achieved (after all, rates do vary—in the eighties, they were high; in the nineties, low) you may have a problem—your cash won't build up to pay the premiums down the road.

Once into a Universal Life policy, it can be quite expensive to cancel it. In fact—you can lose 100 percent of the money you put up on the savings side. Read the small print! If you decide on a universal type of policy, go with one that does not have the fixed-interest option. Why? —Overall, the stock market has outperformed the interest-related markets for growth.

 If you like the universal approach, consider the *variable universal life*—its success is determined by the success of the mutual fund that the insurance company manages.

Replacement Income

In the table below, you will notice, under the columns headed 25 years, 35 years, etc. that there are two percentage numbers—75% and 60%. These are your replacement goals and they refer to the actual percentage of current earnings that you would like to have available to your spouse if you were to die. In using the table, multiply this factor by your current gross earning. The result will tell you approximately how much life insurance you need.

If earnings and/or age of spouse fall between the indicated figures, you can determine your multiple by averaging the difference between the age span and the earnings. The replacement percentages refer to the percentage of income that is represented by your spouse. If, however, you make more than your spouse does, he should carry the amount of coverage on you that the loss of your earning would represent.

For example, let's assume that you make $30,000 a year and your spouse makes $22,500 a year. $22,500 is 75 percent of $30,000. Let's also assume that your spouse is 35 years of age. If you were to die tomorrow and your objective was to leave him with replacement dollars for your lost earnings, you would multiply 8 times $30,000 and arrive at $240,000. That would be the recommended amount of insurance coverage for you to carry on yourself.

Multiples-of-Salary Table

Your Present Gross Earnings	Present Age of Spouse							
	25 Years		35 Years		45 Years		55 Years	
	75%	60%	75%	60%	75%	60%	75%	60%
$ 7,500	4.0	3.0	5.5	4.0	7.5	5.5	6.5	4.5
$ 9,000	4.0	3.0	5.5	4.0	7.5	5.5	6.5	4.5
$15,000	4.5	3.0	6.5	4.5	8.0	6.0	7.0	5.5
$23,500	6.5	4.5	8.0	5.5	8.5	6.5	7.5	5.5
$30,000	7.5	5.0	8.0	6.0	8.5	6.5	7.0	5.5
$40,000	7.5	5.0	8.0	6.0	8.0	6.0	7.0	5.5
$65,000	7.5	5.5	7.5	6.0	7.5	6.0	6.5	5.0

Paying the Piper

How much should you pay for life insurance? The amount you pay each year is called a *premium*. After you decide how much life insurance you need in your particular situation, the amount of your annual premium is based on four calculations:

1. Your age;
2. Status of your health;
3. The insurance company's expenses (commissions to agents, costs of sending you annual statements and bills, etc.);
4. How much money the insurance company can earn on the money you pay in premiums.

How Much Cheaper Is Term Insurance?

Picking only from lower-cost companies, the table below shows dramatically how much more coverage you get for your money with term insurance. The premiums quoted are for a $100,00 policy for a nonsmoking male. Women will be slightly less. The term premiums rise every year; those for cash-value policies can stay level for life. But in terms of what's affordable at any give age, term insurance wins hands down.

How to Find Cheap Insurance

There are two ways to find the companies that lower your insurance costs.

1. *Check out the National Insurance Consumer Organization (NICO).* In the nineties, it set out the following *maximum* rates that consumers ought to pay for annual renewable term insurance. If your coverage costs more, it's too expensive. You can probably find lower rates than these, however, by checking the insurance-quote services indicated below.

   Write NICO at:
   121 W. Payne ST.
   Alexandria, VA 22314

2. *Locate a computerized price-quote service.* All you need is your age, gender, health status and the computer starts to crunch. It's a good idea to recheck every three to five years—who knows what "deals" will be out there. There is no obligation to buy and *no salesperson* will call you to sell you a policy. In other words, you are in charge.

TermQuote
800-444-8376
www.rcinet.com/~termquote

SelectQuote
800-343-1985
www.selectquote.com

InsuranceQuote
800-431-1147
www.iquote.com

Quote Smith
800-431-1147
www.quotesmith.com

Yearly Premiums For a $100,000 Policy			
Age	Term Insurance	Universal-Life Insurance	Whole-Life Insurance
30	$136	$ 590	$ 875
35	140	746	1,095
40	163	950	1,391
45	205	1,217	1,776
50	320	1,583	2,311
55	440	2,078	3,038
60	610	2,741	4,717
65	980	3,665	5,376

Source: National Insurance Consumer Organization

Caution—price quotes are accompanied by brief descriptions (not with great details) of the policies. Usually, five different policies are offered. Make sure you ask for *annual renewable term* quotes. Many will give a re-entry or revertible term which means you have to re-qualify in a few years (as in health).

Two groups that will connect or refer you to individuals who sell low-load or no-load policies are:

- *Fee for Service* 800-874-5662. This service is located in Tampa, FL and will direct you to financial planners who sell low-load cash value insurance. The fees for consultation or analysis of current policies run about $100-$150 an hour. The policies they offer typically charge less than 20 percent of usual agent's commission on similar policies.
- *Life Insurance Advisors' Association* (LIAA) 800-521-4578. LIAA is a national association consisting of fee-only advisors. Members' objectives are to offer unbiased life insurance, low cost, non-commissioned insurance and independent reviews of policies currently held. Any policy recommended is not commission motivated—you will pay the advisor an independent fee. Remember, there is no free lunch.

As a guideline, the following is a table of rates supplies by NICO:

The Most You Should Pay For Term Insurance

Nonsmokers			Smokers		
	Annual premium *			Annual premium *	
Age	Male	Female	Age	Male	Female
18-30	$ .76	$ .68	18-30	$1.05	$ 1.01
31	.76	.69	31	1.10	1.05
32	.77	.70	32	1.15	1.10
33	.78	.71	33	1.21	1.15
34	.79	.72	34	1.28	1.20
35	.80	.74	35	1.35	1.25
36	.84	.78	36	1.45	1.31
37	.88	.82	37	1.56	1.38
38	.92	.86	38	1.68	1.45
39	.97	.90	39	1.81	1.52
40	1.03	.95	40	1.95	1.60
41	1.09	1.00	41	2.12	1.73
42	1.17	1.05	42	2.30	1.89
43	1.25	1.10	43	2.50	2.05
44	1.34	1.15	44	2.72	2.22
45	1.45	1.20	45	2.95	2.40
46	1.59	1.29	46	3.22	2.59
47	1.74	1.41	47	3.52	2.79
48	1.91	1.53	48	3.85	3.01
49	2.10	1.66	49	4.21	3.23
50	2.30	1.76	50	4.60	3.50
51	2.49	1.90	51	4.97	3.79
52	2.70	2.06	52	5.38	4.10
53	2.96	2.22	53	5.82	4.44
54	3.40	2.40	54	6.29	4.80
55	3.40	2.60	55	6.80	5.20
56	3.66	2.79	56	7.31	5.58
57	3.94	3.00	57	7.87	5.99
58	4.23	3.22	58	8.46	6.43
59	4.55	3.46	59	9.10	6.90
60	4.90	3.70	60	9.80	7.40
61	5.43	3.98	61	10.83	7.95
62	6.02	4.28	62	11.98	8.54
63	6.67	4.60	63	13.25	9.18
64	7.40	4.93	64	14.65	9.86
65	8.20	5.30	65	16.20	10.60

* Per $1,000 of coverage, per year. Source: National Insurance Consumer Organization

Notes to the table:

♦ The table shows the premium rate per $1,000 of coverage. If you're buying a $100,000 policy, multiply the cost by 100 and add $60 (for the insurer's fixed policy expenses) to see the most that you should pay.

♦ Policies smaller than $100,000 cost a little more. Policies written for $500,000 and up cost a little less.

♦ Nonsmoker rates are for preferred health risks.

♦ The relative rates for smokers keep rising, as insurers see how fast the smokers are dying.

♦ Rates and companies may have changed by the time you read this. For an update, check the latest NICO guide: *Taking the Bite Out of Insurance*: *How to Save Money on Life Insurance*, available at book stores or by contacting NICO, 121 N. Payne St., Alexandria VA 22314.

Finally, one other way to cut out the middleman (agent) is to buy a no-load policy directly from the insurance company. No-load means no commissions are paid, which becomes attractive when whole life or cash value insurance are your choices. Three of the best are:

♦ *Southland*   800-872-7542 x 6518
Rates are very competitive. Southland offers policies through fee-based financial planners and advisers.

♦ *USAA Life*   800-531-8000
Individual representatives—not commissioned salespeople—will answer your questions and send you policy quotations based on your individual needs.

♦ *Ameritas*   800-552-3553
Individual representatives, not commissioned salespeople, of Ameritas Life Insurance respond to your questions. Note: Ameritas offers other policies that are sold by agents, but to get the direct sales office you must use the toll-free number listed above.

Who's the Fairest in the Land?

Most insurance companies quote their A. M. Best rating when queries are

$mart-Money Tip

The Individual Investor's Guide to Low-Load Insurance Products by Glenn Daily is a great guide to saving dollars in buying life insurance. You can order it by calling International Publishing at 800-488-4149. Cost is $22.95 plus shipping.

made about safety. When Executive Life failed in 1991, A. M. Best was still rating the company "A+"! Go ahead and fake a yawn if you get the Best rating—what you want is the Weiss Research rating.

Weiss Research is the newest rating kid on the block. And, the most conservative. Before Executive Life went belly up, Weiss' rating of Executive Life had been reduced to "D."

To date, libraries don't carry Weiss. You can contact Weiss directly at 800-289-9222. Their ratings aren't free; your cost will be $15.

Agents won't tell you if the insurance company they are illustrating/promoting is unsafe. Nor will they tell you that any investment projections are unrealistic. You may get a low quote for future premiums—they may be dependent on the company making a 15 to 20 percent profit on its investment portfolio. Forget it. And, it is a rare agent who will tell you that you can get a better deal some place else. After all why should he?

To protect yourself, *you* must be informed and take responsibility. Insurance moneys are very serious dollars. If I were in your insurance shoes, here's what I would do:

- ◆ Use low cost insurance.
- ◆ Buy annual, renewable term insurance. In the majority of your key

years for insurance, it will have the lowest cost.

♦ Stop smoking (If you are weed free for two years—you are considered a non-smoker—you save big on premium dollars each year). I don't, and I do!

♦ Check out what Social Security will pay. Whenever I recheck my accumulated "earnings," I'm amazed at how much I'm supposed to get when I retire.

♦ Buy insurance from a Weiss rated company and/or a company rated A+ for a minimum of 10 years. This would have saved thousands of policyholders the grief of loss of money from the Executive Life fiasco.

♦ When the kids are gone and financial responsibilities decline/disappear, you retire and your spouse is self sufficient, and money is available for estate taxes, cancel your policy. And congratulate yourself.

Most Need It . . . Few Have It

Of all the insurances available, disability is the one that is the most ignored. Too few carry it; those who do, often don't carry enough. No matter what your occupation is, if you get a serious illness or are in an accident that prevents you from doing your work, where's the money coming from to pay your bills? Rents and mortgages have to be paid. And your family would appreciate it if the heat stayed on and there was food on the table.

Insurance companies have three definitions of "disabled." They are:

♦ Totally incapacitated and confined to bed
♦ Unable to work at any occupation
♦ Unable to work at a specific occupation

As a rule, the sooner the benefits of a policy begin, the more costly it would be. According to data, people who are temporarily disabled, return to work after an accident or illness within 21 days of the onset of the disability. With that in mind, explore policies and their costs that commence 90 days after a disability versus a 30-day wait.

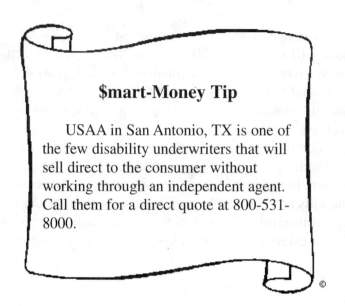

$mart-Money Tip

USAA in San Antonio, TX is one of the few disability underwriters that will sell direct to the consumer without working through an independent agent. Call them for a direct quote at 800-531-8000.

What It Says, Is What You Get

Contract language is critical—especially when it comes to insurance. Any disability policy that you purchase should have a *non-cancelable clause*. As long as you pay the premiums on time, the insurance company cannot cancel it.

A *guaranteed annual premium* is a must. It means that the insurance company cannot increase the premium that has already been declared within the policy. As a rule, the younger you are when you purchase your policy, the less the premium costs will be.

If you become disabled, a *waiver of premiums clause* is most welcomed. It says that you if you are disabled, you don't have to pay the ongoing premiums to keep the policy in force.

An excellent disability policy also includes *a residual benefit disability payment*. This means that the policy will pay the difference between the income that you are able to earn after you are disabled and the original amount of your guaranteed monthly payment.

What You Don't Need

There are two insurances that you probably don't need. The first is children's insurance. Unless you have a movie-musical star under your roof or are self-employed, pass on life insurance here. And if Gramma tells you that she is going to buy her favorite grandson a policy to pay for his college education, tell her to pass on it. She would be better off putting her money into a passbook savings account and get a better return. Encourage Gramma to buy a growth mutual fund.

The other insurance deals with school. It is quite common to have your child come home with information on student polices at his school. Pass on this if you already have adequate health insurance coverage.

Insurance—life, disability, health and others—must be purchased with $mart-Money awareness. If it isn't, you will overpay, buy the wrong type at the wrong time, and not know until years have passed. Not good. Having the right insurance coverage for your particular needs is imperative in building you financial security. This is one area where it makes sense to "hurry." The appropriate insurance is a must for today's family.

Chapter Four

The Will of Your Way

In my most recent financial book, *10 $mart-Money Moves for Women*, I wrote about my friend Nicole who had come for dinner and spent the night. In my kitchen is a large unframed oil painting of geraniums. She loves it and asked me if I died before she did, would I leave it to her? "Absolutely," was my response. Knowing that I wouldn't be rushing to my attorney the next day to change my will—I immediately wrote a note to give it to Nicole if I died and taped it on the back of the canvas for my family. I then told my husband that it should go to Nicole. Until I get it done properly, my family was told that this is what I wanted done with the painting.

How about you? What if you were to die tomorrow—does your family know what you want with your stuff, all your assets, treasures, and most importantly, your kids? During the fourteen years I did financial planning, numerous tragedies happened to young families I worked with, families that were so sure they would live out normal life spans. These families were sometimes irked at me for pushing life insurance coverage, wills and trusts, but were grateful they were in place.

Your daughters may love your jewelry. If you leave your jewelry to both of them, what happens if one moves 1000 miles from the other, who decides who gets what or how do they share?

Few people can reach perfect accord over what to do with mutually owned property. Anything that can't be divided should either be left to one person or

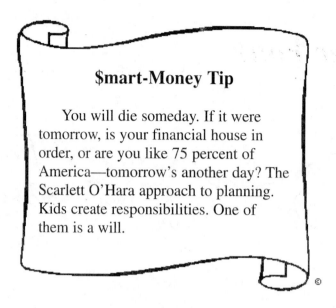

$mart-Money Tip

You will die someday. If it were tomorrow, is your financial house in order, or are you like 75 percent of America—tomorrow's another day? The Scarlett O'Hara approach to planning. Kids create responsibilities. One of them is a will.

sold and the proceeds split. When it comes to death and dying, few really plan for it or for those they leave behind. If no planning is done, those who are left behind may end up living with a monster.

Years ago, I came across this column by Judge Sam Harrod III, of Eureka, Illinois. He has given me permission to reprint it so that your wake up call comes now, not later.

IF YOU DON'T HAVE A WILL, YOUR STATE HAS ONE FOR YOU

The Statutory "will" of John Doe.

I, John Doe, make this my "will," by failing to have a will of my own choice prepared by my attorney.

1. I give one-half of all my property, both personal and real estate, to my CHILDREN, and the remaining one-half to my WIFE.

2. I appoint my WIFE as Guardian of my CHILDREN, if she survives me, but as a safeguard, I require that:
   a. My WIFE make written account every year to Probate Court, explaining how and why she spent money necessary for the proper care of our CHILDREN;
   b. My WIFE file a performance BOND, with sureties, to be approved

by Probate Court, to guarantee she will properly handle our children's money;

c. When our CHILDREN become adults, my WIFE must file a complete, itemized, written account of everything she has done with our children's money;

d. When our SON and DAUGHTER become age 18, they can do whatever they please with their share of my estate;

e. No one, including my WIFE, shall have the right to question how our CHILDREN spend their shares;

3. If my WIFE does not survive me, or dies while any of our CHILDREN are minors, I do not nominate a Guardian of our CHILDREN, but hope relatives and friends may mutually agree on the one, and if they cannot agree, the Probate Court can appoint any Guardian it likes, including a stranger.

4. I do not appoint an Executor of my estate, and hope the Probate Court appoints someone I would approve.

5. If my WIFE remarries, the next husband:
    a. Shall receive one-third of my WIFE'S property;
    b. Need not spend any of his share on our CHILDREN, even of they need support, and
    c. Can give his share to anyone he chooses, without giving a penny to our CHILDREN.

6. I do not care whether there are ways to lower my death taxes, and know as much as possible will go to the Government, instead of my WIFE and our CHILDREN. In witness whereof, I have completely failed to make a different will of my own choice with the advice of my attorney, because I really do not care to go to all that bother, and I adopt this, by default, as my "will."

(No signature required)

Sounds pretty bleak doesn't it? Without writing one, everyone has a will. If you don't choose one on your own, you get the one your state picks for you. Would you choose the one that Judge Harrod framed? I think not.

As this stage progresses, and assets build up, you must begin to consider that you are mortal. Rarely do I see people under 40 with a will that is properly put together and I do believe that wills should be written as soon as you begin to acquire any assets or *if you have children.*

The average working person spends over 10,000 days making money. It seems shortsighted not to spend one day making a determination of where your assets should go when you die. Unfortunately, over 80 percent of those who will die today leave no will. When you leave no will, the state in which you reside will step in and assist you in determining exactly where the assets will go. Just as the Judge wrote.

Make It So

Wills are critical, and they should be written now. If you don't have an attorney, or you are shopping around for one, by all means sit down and make a holographic will until you can get a formal document drawn up. A holographic will is merely one that is handwritten by you. In it, you will recite who you are, your permanent address (and, if applicable, a secondary address), your place of birth and your marital status.

Your spouse should do the same. If there are any previous marriages, make sure that information is included, and include the names and addresses of your immediate family, which would include your sons, daughters and parents.

If you have ever created a trust, make sure you indicate the appropriate title for that. If you are entitled to any pensions, profit sharing or other things, include that information. If you have an insurance policies, include the numbers and beneficiaries—both primary and secondary—and, if you are covered under any group policies.

Have a complete list of all your assets, as well as current market value. If any of your assets are held under a name different from your present one, make sure that it is specified. If you have any safe deposit boxes, state where they are located.

You should indicate the name and address of an executor or executrix of your estate, as well as a guardian if you have children under 18, and a trustee if that is appropriate for the management of your assets until your beneficiaries reach the age in which the actual distribution will be granted.

If you have any stocks, bonds, limited partnerships, retirement accounts, passbooks, time deposits or any other marketable assets, make sure they are included, as well as the location of your previous tax return for the last three years.

Finally, make sure that you spell out exactly what your plans are for your beneficiaries.

Then sign it.

This document acts only as a temporary instrument. It is much preferred that you have an attorney who specializes in estate planning look it over, and make whatever changes are necessary. If you have already gone over the location of your various assets and listed them, this should reduce your bill substantially. Remember, changes can be made as the circumstance warrant, and an addendum, or codicil, can be added to your new will.

If you have made any previous wills, state in your new one that it revokes any previous testaments. In addition, to be safe, destroy all copies of any old wills. If you have out-of-state assets, make sure you deal with them accordingly. Some states will demand that you go through a separate probate in their state. It might be wise to liquidate your assets and bring them into the current state in which you reside and/or set up a separate will that covers that state's laws.

If you have any personal belongings of sentimental value, do yourself a favor and attach to the will a letter of intent that states exactly who gets which belongings. If the majority of your property is divided by percentage, the items covered in your letter of intent will be excluded from a distribution of the primary estate.

You are probably wondering—if you have done all this, why you would need an attorney. For two reasons: First, the tax laws that deal with estates and trusts keep changing. Unless you are in the legal profession, it is highly unlikely that you are going to be up-to-date on the current laws.

When should you update your wills? One time to do so is when you move from one state to another. It is important to check whether the probate laws are comparable in your new state. If you have moved, play it safe and have a local attorney check your will.

Another reason to update your will would be that the executor you have selected is no longer acceptable or has died; in this case you should name a new one. (It is often a good idea to choose an executor or executrix who is younger than you are.) In addition, if you have divorced or remarried or if the number of children you have has increased or decreased, this should be noted in your will. And, if your family size has increased with grandchildren and in-laws, you may desire to include them.

If the value of your estate has risen or substantially declined, it may make sense to look over the details of distribution you previously stated. Or, if you have disposed of any real property listed in your previous wills, you should readjust the document accordingly. I recommend an overhaul of your will approximately every three years. With the way our laws keep changing, as well as our own personal objectives, it makes sense. If you have a few changes, it is not necessary to have the whole will rewritten. It can be handled with a codicil. A codicil is merely an afterthought and is added on to the will and then initialed or signed separately.

No Excuses Please

People come up with plenty of excuses for not having a will. From, "I'm not dying this year," to, "I have nothing to leave anybody," to, "It's too morbid to think about death," to, "Tomorrow is another day."

- You can/should have a will even if your financial affairs are a mess.
- When you do yours, only you (if its holographic) and the attorney who writes it up will know the contents. Everyone else finds out when you die (unless you tell before).
- You don't have to have any of your assets appraised—just say which person you want to have it (note: I said "which person" as in singular. Don't do sharing with your favored folks . . . it just doesn't work).
- No one has to know what you own—again, unless you tell them.
- If you change your mind about who you want to have what, change your will—the only time it becomes permanent is when you die.

Doing a will can be fun. Now you are thinking, this woman is off the wall. Let's do a little visionary work. Imagine how grateful your niece is when she receives the treasure she has always told you she loves. This is your chance to have the last word . . . a tactic many love and rarely get to act on.

When I wrote *10 $mart-Money Moves for Women,* I knew that I was long overdue in doing another will. My excuse . . . tomorrow was another day. When my friend Nicole said she would love one of my paintings, I ended up calling several close friends and asking if them was any item I had that they might like if I died. After the initial shock at my question, we would brainstorm about my various treasures. From my book library to my pearls, to the lead toy soldiers to an afghan I made. Each found a home. What homes do you want your memories and treasures to go to?

To recap, without a will, here's how the courts deal with your former life:

- Depending on state law, not all of the property may go to your spouse.
- Your grown children may get some of the money that was meant for your spouse, leaving your spouse with too little to live on.
- A court will choose your children's guardian.
- Stepchildren usually get nothing.
- Your friends get nothing.
- Your family might battle with the courts.
- Your family will battle with each other.
- A fight might break out among your relatives over who gets the kids and who runs their inheritance (if there is one).
- A bigger fight breaks out over the kids if there is no money.
- There probably won't be a trust to take care of your young children's money (if there is any).
- Part of the money that you meant for your spouse may go to your young kids. Your spouse, as guardian, can use it only for their support. The court will have to approve certain expenditures, and will require an annual accounting. Read Judge Harrod's article again.
- Part of the family might be cut off from the family business.
- A closely held business will have to be sold fast, because the estate might not be permitted to run it; or, you need money to pay estate taxes.
- You can't leave your favorite things to your favorite people.
- Your unfavorite people could end up with your favorite things—this is a bummer!
- The state bends over backward to keep money safe for young children—then hands it all over to them when they reach majority, usually age 18. If they're not ready for the responsibility, too bad.
- You can't leave a contribution to a church or charity.
- Your retarded or handicapped child may inherit money, disqualifying him or her from government aid.
- Everyone will be mad at you.

Some people have the view that if they are married, their spouse gets everything . . . so why bother with one. What happens if you both die in an accident? Now, who gets your property, your treasures, and your kids? If you have childcare for your kids when you are alive, why wouldn't you want to select the childcare provider—now called a guardian—for when you are not alive?

$mart-Money Tip

If you have a handicapped child, get a copy of *How to Provide for Their Future.* Contact the Association for - Retarded Citizens, PO Box 1047, Arlington TX 76004. Your cost is about $8—well worth it.

Most of you think that even without a will, property passes to the person who most ought to own it. Wake up. What's "right" under your state's law may be all wrong for your family and friends. Laws vary, but the following scenarios give you a general idea of what could happen if you die *intestate.* This means you left no will—at least, no one could find one.

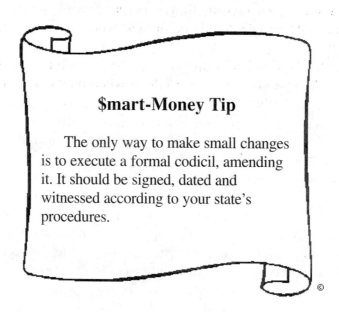

$mart-Money Tip

The only way to make small changes is to execute a formal codicil, amending it. It should be signed, dated and witnessed according to your state's procedures.

Here's what's in store for you if:

You are:	And *die without a will, your property will go:*
Married, with children.	Depending on the state and size of the estate, all to the surviving spouse, or part to the spouse, part to the children. The spouse may get one-third of one half of your separately owned property, part or all of the community property, and all of the joint property you held together.
Unmarried, with children	Assets go to your children but probably not to step-children, if any. The court appoints a guardian for your minor children and their funds.

Why Bother . . . ?

You may have thought—if I told my friends and relatives who get what, why bother with the will stuff. Here are a few good reasons:

- ◆ To name a guardian for your children and your children's inheritance.
- ◆ To give away property you didn't expect to own. This especially affects married couples. This usually happens with accidents. If your spouse dies and you die a few days, months, even a year later—your property and the kids now have the state deciding what's what.
- ◆ To dispose of any property you get after your death. You actually can get rich when your dead. If you die in an accident, a court might bring in a big judgment payable to your estate. What do want done with the money?
- ◆ To avoid family uproar.
- ◆ To avoid all the problems of joint ownership and named beneficiaries. Single people should have wills.
- ◆ To dispose of your half of jointly owned property, if both you and the other owner die in the same accident.
- ◆ To make sure that your probate avoiding tactics work. If you set up a living trust, you need a so-called "pour-over will." It guarantees that

55

any property you forgot, or that comes to you after your death, will be added to your trust.

I know that a lot of this sounds fatalistic, but let's get real. People die, from diseases, accidents, even brutally. You read about them in papers, hear about them on the news, even know them or about them through friends. Things happen and they can happen to you.

Do It Yourself vs. Paying a Lawyer

Previously, I wrote about the do-it-yourself model of wills—the holographic will. To me, it should be used as a temporary solution—you can't get into the attorney until the end of the month. The holographic will covers most of the things you want until you can get an official, attorney-drawn one done.

Homemade wills may be quite clear to you, but vague to others. A trip to the local court may be necessary to determine what you really meant (Mary is to get all my jewelry—is that Aunt Mary or niece Mary?).

In a fairly simple will, an attorney should charge from $150 to $300—you can pay big dollars if you are complex. Here's why an attorney, who specializes in wills, makes money sense:

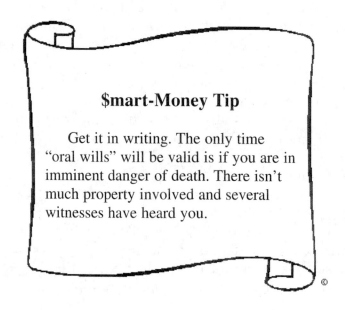

$mart-Money Tip

Get it in writing. The only time "oral wills" will be valid is if you are in imminent danger of death. There isn't much property involved and several witnesses have heard you.

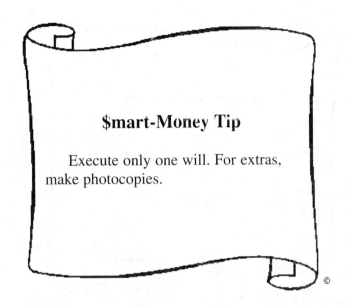

$mart-Money Tip

Execute only one will. For extras, make photocopies.

♦ To say exactly what you mean: is it niece Mary or Aunt Mary who gets your jewels?
♦ To advise you on how to hold property.
♦ To reduce death taxes. If your estate is under $650,000 (in 1999)—you owe Uncle Sam nothing; but, not all states match the federal $650,000 floor for exemption.
♦ To advise you on any twists in the law—i.e., if you leave Aunt Mary your home and there is a mortgage on it, your estate may be required to pay off the mortgage, thus leaving niece Mary out of getting the cash you thought would go her way.
♦ To ask you questions you might not think about. Such as, do you want a beneficiary's share to go to her children or her spouse if she was to die before your treasures got to her . . . or would you want it to not pass to her family members at all if she wasn't alive—instead go to a battered women's shelter?
♦ To make your will challenge proof. And believe me, challenges arise. You need the right number of witnesses (varies state to state), who could testify you signed it, you were in sound mind, etc.

For the do-it-yourselfers, one of the best guides is Nolo's *Simple Will Book* by Denis Clifford. It's available in many bookstores or you can contact Nolo Press at 950 Parker St., Berkeley, CA 94710.

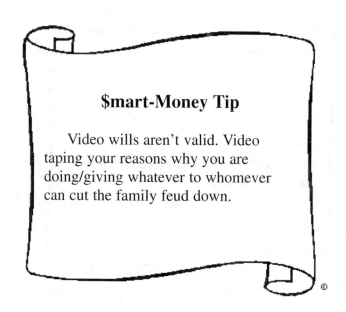

$mart-Money Tip

Video wills aren't valid. Video taping your reasons why you are doing/giving whatever to whomever can cut the family feud down.

Who Should Get the Children?

The first response is usually Gramma. Certainly, grandparents want the best for their grandchildren. But if Gramma is 75, this is not such a hot idea. First she's raised her family—no parent in their right mind covets raising kids through the teen years again. Second, you are setting your kids up for losing their new parents in a fairly short period of time again. Gramma could easily die naturally within the next five to ten years.

Now, if Gramma is young, under 55, that's another story. Your better bet is a sibling. Or, if you have a "second family," an older married child, even a close friend who shares your values and way of life.

If your kids are old enough to understand the question, ask them where they would want to live with, if something happened to you. The older your kids are, the more critical it is that they be involved in the decision.

In addition to the "care" guardian, you need someone to handle the money side. Usually, the care guardian does both. But, if she or he is not great at handling money, it may make money sense to get someone who has common sense in the money department.

If you are divorced, the kids usually go to the ex-spouse, if he wants them. Courts rarely step in if the other parent is fit (unfit could be an abandonment, no contact or financial support for at least two year, drug addicts, etc.).

Put in your will why you chose the person you did, to be the guardian of your kids. Spell it out clearly so that your kids are protected. The last thing they need is to be a Ping-Pong ball.

How to Leave Money for Your Kids

1. *Name a legal guardian for the children's funds.* State law determines what can be spent on the children and what investments can be made. The guardian makes an annual accounting to the court. When the child comes of age—at 18 or 21, depending on your state—he or she gets the money.

2. *Use the Uniform Gifts to Minors Act (UGMA).* In most states, you have to make the gift during your lifetime, rather than by will. The funds are left to an adult who acts as custodian for the child. The law determines how the money can be spent and invested. A custodian usually has more flexibility in handling money than a guardian does, such as not having to go to court every time something is bought or sold. The funds go to the child when he or she comes of age, usually at 18.

3. *Use the Uniform Transfers to Minors Act (UTMA),* if your state has adopted it. UTMA allows transfers by will, as well as gifts during your lifetime. The custodian can hold the assets until the child is 18 or 21 (25, in California). This is much better than the UGMA—a few years extra in maturity can do wonders in preserving a nest egg.

4. *Leave the money in trust.* This is the best solution for sums over $20,000 or so. Your trustee—a relative, friend, attorney, or bank—manages the inheritance and pays it to the child according to your instructions. Money can be doled out as needed for the child's education and living expenses. The remainder is turned over to the child at the age you set—it could be 25 or 30.

You can state that the child gets the money all at once or in installments—say, at ages 25 and 30. You might want to give the trustee the power to withhold payments, if it seems to be in the child's best interest. (Young people have been know to join cults—is this where you want money to go?) You might make the child co-trustee in the early 20s. By sharing in investment decisions without yet having to handle the money solo makes sense. It's a good learning tool for their future.

Set up a single trust for all the children. If one child has big medical bills, they can be paid out of common funds without looting that child's basic inheritance. Or, if you have already financed two kids through college, you may want to designate a greater amount to your third one for college costs, then do a split. Typically, all the money stays in trust until the youngest child reaches an age you specify. Then the trust dissolves and everyone gets his or her appointed share.

Changing Your Will

You should change your will when:

♦ You have kids—either by birth, adoption or marriage.
♦ Your net worth takes a jump, or a dive.

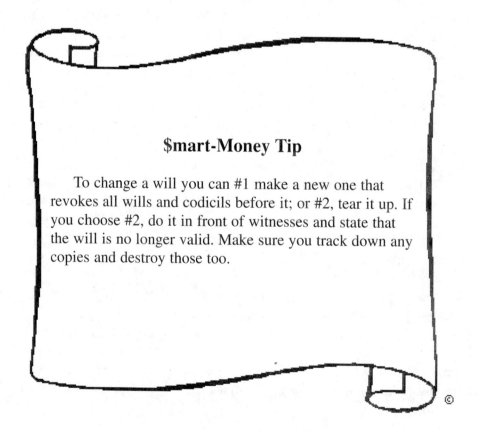

$mart-Money Tip

To change a will you can #1 make a new one that revokes all wills and codicils before it; or #2, tear it up. If you choose #2, do it in front of witnesses and state that the will is no longer valid. Make sure you track down any copies and destroy those too.

- Your child(ren) marries, separates or divorces.
- One of your heirs dies.
- You have a child who has an illness that may go on forever.
- There are any changes in the inheritance or property laws—Federal or the state you live in.

If you have only one child, do a will, and then have another, what happens? Without being specifically mentioned, the second child will get something. It could be the same . . . or different. The deciding factor is dependent on what state you live in and what its laws are. Both birth and adopted children are treated the same. Stepchildren aren't. Unless you specifically say your stepchildren are to have something, they won't.

$mart-Money Tip

Whenever there is a new tax law, ask your attorney if the new laws impact you. Don't assume they don't.

You probably feel that assembling all those bits and pieces are a tedious and time-consuming chore. They are. But you can be assured that it will be time well spent, should the unforeseeable occur. Do yourself a favor, as well as your heirs, and make sure you have this base covered.

Any woman, any man who cares for their spouse, their kids, their parents, their friends, their church and their community will not put off any longer this critical document. There is only one time that will work. *It's called now.*

Nothing Is Free

When an attorney prepares your will, you will sign it in the presence of witnesses. You receive a copy and your attorney keeps a copy in his or her "vaults." That's the one service an attorney offers free of charge—vault storage for your will. Granted, your will won't take up much space, but there's a reason behind the freebie.

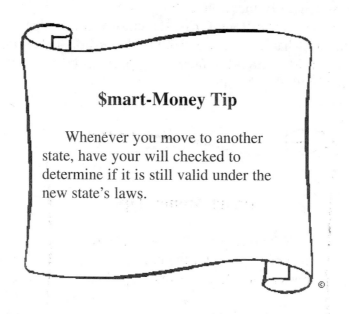

$mart-Money Tip

Whenever you move to another state, have your will checked to determine if it is still valid under the new state's laws.

Your attorney bills you for the legal expenses of drawing up your will. When you die, your heirs will need an attorney to take your will through the court process of *probate*—changing the names on all your assets as directed by your will. Who best to do it but the folks who drew it up? Aha! A method behind his/her madness!

The legal fees for handling an estate through probate can be many times the fees charged for writing the will. In many states, probate fees are based on a percentage of the gross value of the estate. If you have a young attorney, he or she will hope to outlive you and earn the probate fees. An older attorney will have shelves of wills in the "vault," just waiting to be probated by a younger partner.

Alas, there's never a free lunch. Your attorney may have a breakfast on what he made preparing your will. When you die, he takes/gets a vacation!

Probate

Probate has nothing to do with taxes. It is the legal process of changing the title on assets you own into the names of your heirs when you die. The probate court resolves disputes, pays off creditors, inventories your estate and distributes your assets. If there's no will, it distributes your assets according to state law. Now, this can be scary.

This process presents a double whammy:

1. It's expensive—legal fees can be as much as 10 percent of the total value of your gross estate. In states where the gross valuation of assets is the basis for determining legal fees, the court does not deduct the amount of any loans—including mortgages—from the asset side. Ouch!

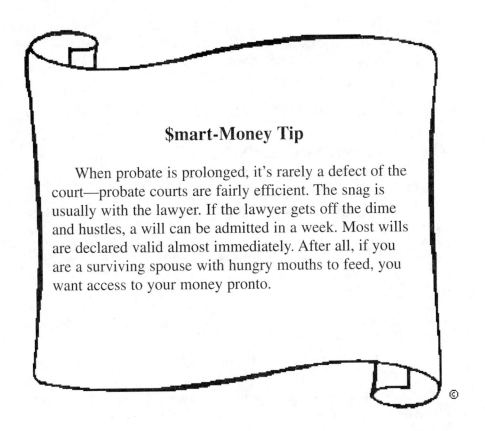

$mart-Money Tip

When probate is prolonged, it's rarely a defect of the court—probate courts are fairly efficient. The snag is usually with the lawyer. If the lawyer gets off the dime and hustles, a will can be admitted in a week. Most wills are declared valid almost immediately. After all, if you are a surviving spouse with hungry mouths to feed, you want access to your money pronto.

2. It can take a long time (it shouldn't, but it often does). It's not uncommon for many estates to take over two years to process. If you own property in states other than your residence, the process in repeated in each state you own real estate in.

The Living Trust (a.k.a. Inter Vivo Trust)

A trust is a legal entity that can own, buy and sell assets. When you personally transfer items to a trust, you no longer own them. The trust does. Have you lost control? Nope. Name yourself trustee and you are in charge. A Living trust is like a will—it's revocable, meaning that you can change it as often as you want.

Here's what a trust can do in a nutshell:

1. It allows for continuity of your personal finances and business.
2. Privacy is maintained after you die. Wills are public documents; trusts aren't. This is why very wealthy people are rarely reported to have zillions of dollars at their deaths. The great majority of their assets are buried in trusts . . . for their, their families' and attorney's eyes-only.
3. All assets in the trust bypass probate.

The cost of creating a living trust can range for $500 to $2,500, depending on your needs . . . and the attorney's fees.

The living trust is not the answer to all estate planning issues, but it certainly does create flexibility in managing estate issues. The living trust, by itself, *does not* save Federal or state death taxes. But it *does* save all the costs of probating your will, while giving your estate a high degree of privacy both in death and during your lifetime should you become incapacitated and require a conservator to look after your financial affairs.

Leaving Money in Trust

A *testamentary trust* is set up by your will. Instead of leaving money directly to the beneficiary, you leave it in trust, to be managed by a trustee. Funds can be paid out for various purposes. At some point, the trust dissolves and the money is distributed. You get to decide when.

A trust can hold money until a child grows up. But don't try to control from the grave. By the time he or she is 30, the child should be able to get the money

$mart-Money Tip

Work with a lawyer who specializes
in estate plans, not business plans.

and swim . . . or sink.

A trust can save estate taxes. If your net worth is over $650,000, talk to a lawyer about how to cut Federal taxes. Often, you can do it without using a trust. The state may levy taxes on net worths less than $650,000—not all match the $650,000 federal exclusion. This exclusion will increase in increments to $1,200,000 in 2006. In the latter part of 1999, several proposals were in Congress to further increase the exclusion. One even had all taxes eliminated. Your CPA and estate-planning attorney will be the best source for what is current and what's not. Ask.

A trust can manage money left to a spouse. A trustee runs the money. Your spouse receives the income and, if needed, payment out of principal. When your spouse dies, the remaining money goes to whoever is named. A family member, bank, or investment advisor is usually the trustee.

The spouse should be able to change trustees if the relationship isn't working. Again give the option—many surviving spouses do a better job than the friendly bank. Don't lock up *all* of your money in trust. Your spouse may have ignored managing money when you were alive, but could thrive when you're gone. Allow some flexibility.

A trust can provide for retarded or disabled children. State and federal programs cover basic medical and residential care, but only if the child has almost no money. This presents parents with a Catch 22: Money left to the disabled child will be consumed by the institution, guaranteed. If there's no money, the child will get only bare-bones support. A definite parental nightmare.

Middle income parents may feel that they have little choice. They leave their modest assets to their healthy children and let the handicapped one get government aid. If this is the case, you should specifically disinherit the handicapped child (and tell your relatives to do likewise). You hope and pray that your healthy children will provide the extra comforts that their institutionalized sibling needs.

Do your entire family a huge favor and call a powwow. Be blunt about the situation and get their commitment that they will be there for their sibling. Promises made at times like these usually glue for life. Don't assume—tell them what you expect. If they can't commit, you know who to leave your money to.

If you have money, set up a trust. The disabled child (having little or no money) can usually qualify for government aid. The trust supplies extra maintenance and support, not dependent on siblings' generosity. For advice on how to do this, call your state or local Association for Retarded Citizens. Ask for the names of lawyers experienced in your state's public-assistance laws.

A trust can assure that the children of a prior marriage will inherit. If you leave all your money to your new spouse, he can do anything with it, including cutting your children out. A trust prevents this. If you want, you can give your spouse an income for life while guaranteeing that your children will ultimately inherit when he dies.

As you have read through this section, you may have thought, "Well, this doesn't sound too overwhelming." One of my missions in writing *$mart-Money Moves for Kids: The Parents' Complete Guide* is to demystify the money maze. Wills and trusts are loaded with potholes. Please, please get legal advice and use an estate-planning attorney to guide you.

Part Two

Kids—
From Preschools to Preteens

Chapter Five

Preschoolers—
Sesame Street & Barney

Quick, what do preschoolers do that their older siblings usually don't do? Answer, they get to watch more TV. Advertisers are in heaven because they know they have a captive audience—TV is often put in a baby-sitter role. Your preschooler is blitzed; TV advertisers know how pliable young minds are. They can pitch just about anything and your youngster can, and often does "parrot"—verbatim—much of the verbiage dedicated to commercial messages.

When Frank was 3-years-old, we discovered the Berenstain Bears' book series. This series covers a variety of topics. Among them, we read about baby-sitters, doctors, Mom going to work, and sibling rivalry. One of Frank's favorites was about the "gimmes." We all know that scene; if you haven't personally experienced it, you have seen and most definitely heard such an episode.

The stage is most often set at any retail or grocery store. Children learn quickly that they have a big audience to play to. Your own home works too. Ever notice how they act up when company arrives? Usually, it begins innocently enough with "please Mommy." A negative response accelerates the loudness of the young one's voice, and even the number of his demands. Birthdays and holidays seem to inspire peak performance. The message from the Berenstain Bears rings true for just about every adult; it says clearly that preventive medicine is your starting point.

Lay Out the Rules

Before you go on any outing, discuss the agenda for this event with your child and be clear about the possibility of a treat (if there is one). The treat could be edible or it could be material. I've found that it made sense with Frank to be specific about the range of choices and dollar amount (he knows in advance, what I will *not* buy). In the 3 to 4-year-old range, he first discovered the Ninja Turtles. Later his interests evolved to the X-Men, Batman, Power Rangers and anything from the Star Trek series. This past summer, we came through Star Wars and now we are heading to music as in CDs.

When I laid out the ground rules before we left on a store adventure—and believe me, they were often adventures—*and* the "gimme" song began, I could easily say that these weren't items that I had agreed to buy. Frank has always liked gum, and when the agreed upon item for the outing was a pack of gum, it was amazing how easy it was to direct his shopping time to the selection of the most perfect pack of gum. Happily, most stores have several brands.

The same thing happened with cereal and fruit snacks; he loved to look over all the boxes. Again, if a box of cereal was the treat, this was all we took home with us—no more. If he acted out, with a pushy attitude, nagging or whining, he was told No! If any of the undesirable behaviors continued, he was told that he would not go on the next outing and—he didn't. Kids really do keep a careful ledger of what you say, so be consistent.

Big Isn't Always Better

Kids like to handle money and they love coins. When they evolve from putting them in their mouths to putting them in their pocket or on the counter to pay for something at the store, you're ready to take their hand to start them through the money maze. Until kids really grasp numbers, paper currency doesn't have much significance to them. They do, though, LOVE coins: the sizes, shapes and colors fascinate them.

If you were to set out a penny, a nickel and a dime, most likely they would select the nickel—why? Simple, it's bigger. Kids have no trouble discerning value when you put out a quarter, a half-dollar and a silver dollar. They go for the bigger and heavier silver dollar—size and weight speak loudly. Think about it, when you were a kid, which gift package did you go for first at birthdays and holidays? I suspect that it was not the one that was shaped like a ring box.

When Frank was eight, he was enthralled with the Mighty Morphin Power

Rangers. His Mom's best friend bought him one of the Power Ranger action figures he dearly wanted and wrapped it in a huge Barbie dream playhouse box. The box was beautifully wrapped and strategically placed under his Christmas tree. He drooled as he looked at the biggest package under the tree, counting the days, even hours, until he could rip into the wrappings. On Christmas morning, we could barely hold him back until everyone was in place for the big event.

Frank's first choice—you guessed it—The Big Box. When he unwrapped it, and saw what the box was, he assumed that it contained a Barbie, he was literally crushed. He couldn't believe that Aunt Becky would give him such a thing. Tears started to well up. We encouraged him to continue opening the box and not to judge the gift by the wrapping. He reluctantly forged ahead. Eventually, he found the treasured action figure.

Frank learned several lessons: 1. Aunt Becky has a sense of humor; 2. Don't judge what's inside by what's on the outside; and 3. Most important of all, bigger is not always better. Since that time, we have a Christmas tradition, everyone wraps treasured things in goofy boxes—and Frank laughs the loudest.

There are plenty of books out there that focus on activities to teach kids. Anything that Bonnie Drew publishes is a good bet. I wish she had been around when I was teaching my kids. The good news is her work is readily available for you to enjoy. Below are a few ideas for games and activities that we used with our kids who are now in their thirties. They are just as good today for teaching basic shapes, sizes and meanings of money with your preschoolers.

The Coin Game

Here is a game you can play with your child to begin to teach him about coins. Gather one each of the different coins; yes, even track down a silver dollar. Give your kids paper and pencil and you can begin to teach them math by using coins. Have them outline the coins as follows: first, outline the penny five times, put in an equals sign and outline the nickel (five pennies equals a nickel), next have them outline five nickels, add and equals sign and then outline a quarter (five nickels equals a quarter); have them do the same with dimes, half dollars and so forth.

I can't emphasize enough, the need to imprint the concept of the value of money in your preschooler's mind. Be prepared, they will ask why a dime is smaller than a penny and is yet worth more. Please play this game often, so they will be comfortable with the inconsistencies of the U.S. coinage. You might also want to take this a step further. Have them outline the number of coins it takes

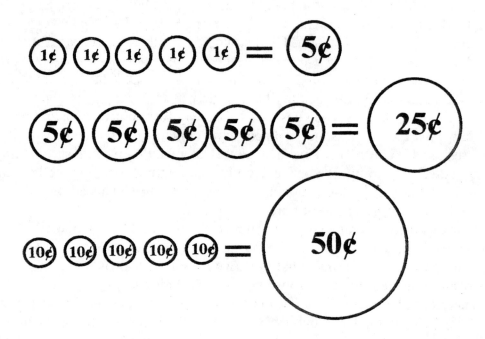

to buy their favorite edible treat and have them complete the game by drawing the treat after the equal sign.

Once they learn which coins are which, The Treasure Chest Game introduces exchanging pennies for nickels, dimes and quarters—that one coin may actually be worth less than a smaller number of another type of coin.

The Treasure Chest Game

For eight years, my daughter Sheryl worked with me. When Frank's preschool had teachers' day off or he had a fever or a case of the sniffles, it wasn't uncommon for him to come to work with Sheryl. My offices are in my home, so we have all the creature comforts he needed. We usually receive deliveries, for our business, on a daily basis.

One day, Frank's route and the UPS man's route converged on the same point—the front door. A very large package arrived that day full of the packing peanuts that are so commonly used in shipping. Frank wanted to keep the box for his own because he was fascinated by it's size and most of all, by the peanuts. He was also just learning about coins, their sizes and their values.

So, we turned this box with its gallons of peanuts into the Mystery Treasure Chest. I dropped a handful of coins, pennies, nickels, dimes and quarters, into the Chest and gave the peanuts a stir. Then I challenged Frank to dive his hand into the box. Each time he came up with coins in his hand he had to identify the name of each coin, its value and then total them all up.

At this point, he began to learn that he could switch five pennies for one nickel and ten of them for a dime. Those shiny little dimes had greater value than the bigger brown pennies. This fun, but educational, game kept Frank busy and happy that day and made work possible for the working members of The Briles Group, Inc.

Shopping Alert

My younger brother Terry has 3 kids, Christen, Jimmy and Patrick. When Christen and Jimmy were 3 1/2 and 1 1/2 years old (Patrick was yet a gleam in his parents' eyes), my brother wanted to surprise his wife with an anniversary weekend getaway; my husband and I agreed to keep the kids as our anniversary gift to them. Under the pretense that they were coming for dinner, the four of them arrived at our doorstep late one afternoon. Then a limousine arrived.

As we all waved good-bye, it dawned on me that, my brother's enthusiasm didn't match his prior planning. He hadn't brought much of the necessary kid hardware—T-shirts, diapers, toddler food items and the like. It had been quite a few years since I had the 24-hour-a-day responsibility of little ones, and our larder was devoid of wee kid necessities. So, off I went to the grocery store with the two very active youngsters in tow. What a fiasco!

I had totally forgotten about busy little hands and the distance a grocery cart, loaded with two toddlers, needed to be from the shelves. As I was getting diapers and T-shirts for Jimmy (yes, they do carry everything at Safeway), I glanced down. To my dismay, I found the two of them sharing a purloined box of chocolate cookies. Most of the cookies were gone, some to their tummies and lot to their faces, hair, clothes and even toes.

What a MESS! Chrissy and Jimmy didn't agree—going to the store with Aunt Judy was great fun! Unfortunately, with young ones, too much of a good thing proves out the old saying—what goes in, must come out. The cookies were running through little Jimmy by the time we got home.

The moral of the story might be to leave the kids at home or come with a suitcase; but that is not always realistic. What to do? If I had had my wits about me, I would have made a game of going to the store (Rule #1: stay in the center of the aisle so little hands can't reach anything). So, the next time I had to take them to the store with me, I told Chrissy that I would pay her a nickel—remember it's a *big* coin for a 3 year old—for sounding out if Jimmy grabbed anything off the shelves. Indeed, she truly earned her pay.

You can extend this game by taking advantage of the terrific recall system kids develop early from the TV bombardment of commercial images. I also told Chrissy, that for another nickel, I needed more help. When we got to the cereal aisle, I told her that I was in pursuit of Captain Crunch. I described the Captain Crunch cereal box a little bit and sure enough her face lit up. She began to scan the aisle, looking for the desired package. Since there were several types of this brand of cereal, Chrissy got to choose.

When she dropped the box in the basket, little did I know that this was just the beginning of her talent of putting what she wanted in a "basket". It would pave her way to college as star female hoopster. When she graduated from high school, she was a very hot item with several college coaches.

By allowing her to have choice, we avoided any "gimme" episodes, plus she felt like she was part of the shopping trip. Also, if you have the time as you shop with preschoolers, you can point out items (unbreakable only) you need to buy and let them take them off the shelves and put them in the basket. Take it a step

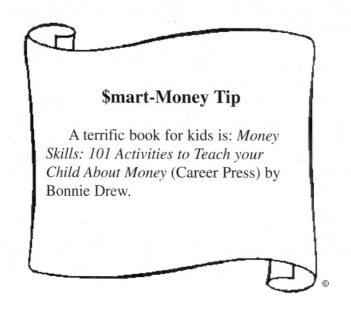

$mart-Money Tip

A terrific book for kids is: *Money Skills: 101 Activities to Teach your Child About Money* (Career Press) by Bonnie Drew.

further. Encourage them to build on their math skills by having them count the number of items they put in the basket.

A good way to introduce kids to the savings that coupons offer is to turn over kid related coupons to your 4-year-old (only for those products that you would normally buy). When you get to an aisle that has one of the coupon items, hand her the coupon and tell her to spot it for you. If possible, have her walk, not ride. Most of the kid oriented products are placed on shelves at their eye level, not yours and not above basket level. I was surprised to find that my grandson's favorite frozen penne pasta and chicken dinner was even found at kid eye level.

TV Pitch

Programs that are targeted at the preschooler contain commercials with a lot of flash and glitz—dancing peanuts, stars, raisins and cute animals. It's all there and kids love it. In the cartoon venue, it's often difficult for a preschooler to recognize the difference between the program and the commercials and his recall of the program will show that it has all blended together.

Take the time to sit down with your child and watch a half-hour program and ask questions when it is over—you will probably be amazed. There's an excellent guide entitled *A Parents Guide: Advertising and Your Child* published by The Children's Advertising Review Unit (CARU). The guide recommends

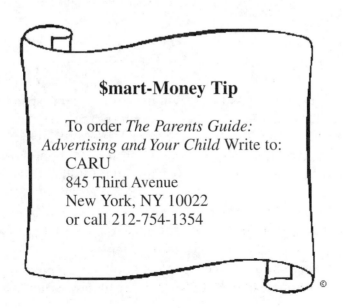

$mart-Money Tip

To order *The Parents Guide: Advertising and Your Child* Write to:
CARU
845 Third Avenue
New York, NY 10022
or call 212-754-1354

ways that you can monitor, interpret and explain the different advertising that is directed at your kids.

Allowing Allowances

From a very early age kids learn that there is only one way for Mom and Dad to take things out of the store—and that is by paying for it with money. At the age of 3, kids began to grasp this concept, so this is the time to begin to introduce the concept of saving. It's quite difficult to save, if there isn't a source of income (there aren't many Help Wanted ads for 3 to 4-year-olds). Outside of grandparents, you are their primary income source. This may be the time to introduce a small allowance, but not before the age of 3 and, not a large amount of money. Generally, allowance is paid weekly, but you can tie it to your pay periods if this works best. When you decide to start an allowance program, you need to ask yourself some questions:

♦ Long term, what can you reasonably afford? Watch what you spend on your kids for incidental goodies for a few weeks and base the allowance roughly on this amount.
♦ Should you tie the performance of household chores to an allowance? Good idea if you will be consistent about monitoring.
♦ How much of the allowance do you want your child to save? Be reasonable.

With the allowance in place, you can begin to step away from instant gratification (the gimmes) and reinforce with the concept of why saving money is essential to the $mart-Money kid. You will have the answer when he sees something on TV that he wants NOW. The answer is—"Let's see how we can help you save for this treasure." You have to be realistic about savings with the 3 to 4-year-old because they don't understand the difference between wanting a $2 toy and $20 toy. With patience from you, how far a dollar stretches, will sink in.

Here's another use for the coin drawings: have your daughter outline the coins that relate to the amount of her allowance, then explain to her how many of these drawings it will take to buy a desired item.

Play on the young child's fascination with coins by supplying a clear plastic container (easy to open and close) to bank the money at home and so he can

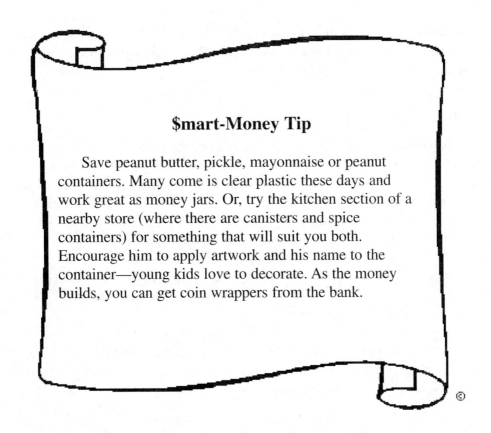

$mart-Money Tip

Save peanut butter, pickle, mayonnaise or peanut containers. Many come is clear plastic these days and work great as money jars. Or, try the kitchen section of a nearby store (where there are canisters and spice containers) for something that will suit you both. Encourage him to apply artwork and his name to the container—young kids love to decorate. As the money builds, you can get coin wrappers from the bank.

visibly see the coins and bills multiply. Resist the cute piggy bank. With most, he can't see his money or handle it without the danger of hurting himself when he wants to handle or play with his money (kids like to touch and feel it).

There is a debate about whether or not an allowance should be tied to household chores. Some believe that a regular allowance in and of it self will begin to teach a child about money and it's usage. Others believe that allowances should be tied to the performance of specific chores. I am a member of the latter school that believes in the work ethic—if you work, you are rewarded. I also firmly believe that a clear line has to be drawn between those chores that need to be done as a responsible family member and the performance of chores that are to be rewarded with money.

If you choose to give an allowance with no strings attached, don't get yourself in the position of being overly generous. And, it may make sense to offer chores that they can choose to do for extra money—this is far more likely to occur with older kids.

If you choose to tie allowance to performance of chores with your preschooler, be sure that they are simple and reasonable tasks. You don't want to knock them down and out when they are just beginning to walk the money maze. More on allowances in Chapter 7.

The Big 3: Saving, Sharing and Spending

If the point or price tag system doesn't appeal because of the bookkeeping, and you decide on a fixed rate allowance, you need to determine how much. Again, your spending plan is the first consideration. If you are considering allowance for the older child, you will do well to determine how much you shell out to each child, over a month's time, before you make a final decision. With the 3 to 4-year-old, the range of $1 up to $1 times the child's age in years per week ($4 for a 4-year-old per week) works for most. Granted, giving a 4-year-old $4 per week might appear to you to be going overboard. So let's open the door to what kids do with allowances. This is the time to introduce the concepts of saving, sharing and spending.

Savings   Most kids love to spend money. When you let them know that they will *always* get to spend a portion of what they receive, you are on solid ground. Telling your young kids that they are saving for their college education

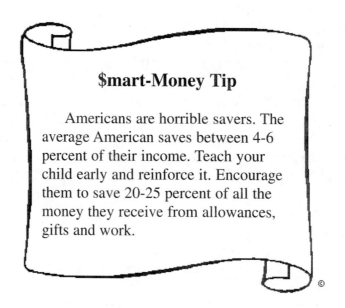

$mart-Money Tip

Americans are horrible savers. The average American saves between 4-6 percent of their income. Teach your child early and reinforce it. Encourage them to save 20-25 percent of all the money they receive from allowances, gifts and work.

will be probably get a 0 to 1 rating out of a possible 10. If you tell them they can save for a desired toy, game or outing, you are playing their tune. Preschool age kids can only think short term. The bigger ticket items (cars and college) can't be dealt with successfully until the middle years of 12 and up.

Sharing   A child doesn't need a Ph.D. degree to learn that there are people that are destitute out there. They may not know what the word destitute means but they have seen commercials for Save the Children, TV broadcasts about disasters, such as the September 11th Terrorist Attack and the Oklahoma City bombing, and homeless people on the street—children are very observant. Adults tune in to such things. There is no reason why your kids shouldn't. Kids know when someone is down and out. Encourage them to allocate some of their money on a regular basis to an individual or group that is less fortunate.

For families who are connected with churches, synagogues and the like, moneys that are collected and donated for missions fit into this category. Check with yours to see what the children's ministry is supporting.

Generally speaking, a child is not born with a charitable nature when it comes to his money; thus charitable giving will require some nurturing from you. When you both see something that touches the child, ask him what he would like to do with his money to help the situation. Two excellent child oriented charities are The Ronald McDonald House and The Wish Foundation—helping kids and their families through difficult health issues and realizing dreams and wishes that their families couldn't afford.

After the September 11th Terrorist Attack, I made money donations to the Red Cross, Firefighter, the United Way and the Salvation Army. I felt, thought that I could do more. After a week of probing, I discovered NASAR—the National Association for Search and Rescue . . . the dogs that are so vital in the search and rescue around disasters. Now, I donate a portion of all my book sales plus part of my speaking fees to this incredible group—their website is *www.nasar.org.* When kids see and hear about disasters, they want to help. Encourage yours to allocate 5 to 10 percent of their moneys to help others.

Spending   This is discretionary money and your child should be allowed to spend as she sees fit. Every household has limitations on what money can be spent on. In our house, one X-rated item is cotton candy and no money can be spent on it. This is something Frank wants at the Rockies baseball game and the answer is always—No!

If your son spends all his money and then begins the begging, whining and badgering, be firm and continue to say NO! Many times, young kids experience "buyers remorse." They have blown their spending money on what you always considered to be junk. Now, he agrees because he has spied what he *really* wanted all along.

Remind him he had his choice on how he spent his money. Then you could involve him in a discussion of the enjoyment, or lack of it that resulted from his spending. Follow up with encouraging him to save his money so he can buy something that may give him more lasting enjoyment. Maybe, with time, his periods of dissatisfaction won't occur so often.

Often a parent gives in to a tantrum. This only reinforces the kid's belief that he knows how to push your button and turn you into his personal ATM. Don't get into the habit of giving in, especially when you are out in public, or this will be something you will have to deal with for years to come, perhaps as long as when your "child" has passed his 30th birthday.

Your preschooler catches on fast to your concepts about money, your beliefs and disbelief. As your kids' primary role model, this is the time to help them start building sound money habits that will be successful for them the rest of their lives.

$mart-Money Resource Center:

Books for Younger Kids

There are lots of books and specially designed software programs for computers that can help you in your efforts to educate your child about money. Consider adding some of them to your library.

Books:

The Berenstain Bears Get the Gimmes by Stan and Jan Berenstain (Random House)

Trouble with Money by Stan and Jan Berenstain (Random House)

Mama's New Job by Stan and Jan Berenstain (Random House)

Meet Santa Bear by Stan and Jan Berenstain (Random House)

The Berenstain books are part of an ongoing series and new titles are added on regular basis. Check with your favorite bookstore for the new additions. These books can also routinely be found at garage sales.

Freckle Juice by Judy Blum (Dell)

This is a story about a young boy who uses several weeks of his allowance to buy a secret freckle formula and learns a valuable consumer lesson.

Neale S. Godfrey's Ultimate Kids' Money Book by Neale S. Godfrey (Simon & Schuster)

A visual assortment of topics from where money comes from (you'll learn that some money is 12 feet long), bartering, saving, into investing and credit cards. Some of this doesn't apply to young kids, but the cartoons are good and will encourage them in the areas you deem right for them.

Chapter Six

Beyond Barney—
The Middle Years

A great learning tool for kids age 6 and beyond is the American classic—the garage sale (or tag sale in some regions). Several years ago, Frank burst into my kitchen with the announcement that, just around the corner, one of my books was on sale for $1. He insisted that I drop everything and get right over to pick up the bargain. After plunking down my $1 to pick up a book that sells for $23, but is impossible to find at any price, we scouted the other tables at the sale for other great finds.

Garage sales are a terrific environment for you to introduce your kids to a comparison of buying *used* versus *new*. There is another plus factor—you can teach them about bargaining on the price. Garage sales offer a potpourri of merchandise. Kid's toys and clothing are usually a staple, but the range of items for adults is almost limitless.

Granted there's going to be a lot of junk that the seller seems to value beyond reason (I have seen things I would trash without a second thought). But, with a little probing, some joyous bargains can be found. Haven't you seen a news item pop up that recounts the purchase of a dirty old painting at a garage sale? Subsequent removal of the grime of years of neglect and the result—the face of a masterpiece shines back.

Frank has trooped to many garage sales and tag sales with his Mom and me. And, he has astutely realized that he too could participate in such entrepreneurial events. So, he decided to sell his ho-hum Power Ranger stuff at his Mom's garage sale that have been in the back of his closet for several years. The next step for him was to price the items he planned to sell; and since they were his toys, when they sold, any money would be his.

The light bulb of understanding about bargains lit his face when I emphasized that his expensive ($30-$40 original cost) toys would bring in only $5 to $10 each. He didn't like it much, but he learned that the bargains flow both ways—if you can buy something you absolutely love that has only a few hours of wear and tear on it for $5, so can someone else. We both agreed that bargains are great fun but there is always a price to pay.

After Power Rangers, Frank became interested in Star Trek and all the related memorabilia for the Next Generation, Deep Space 9 and the latest in the series, The Voyager. He realized he could have the treasured items from this multiple series, and at a fraction of their retail price, if he was patient and diligent in his scouting at garage sales.

Comparison Shopping

From the ages of 6 to 10 you can have a tremendous impact on your kids. They are at their peak of receptiveness to your guidance. Post 12, peers have a great influence on their spending. From age 6 on, kids know that 10 dimes are one heck of a lot better than 10 pennies or even 10 nickels.

This is a great time to teach them about pricing. Show them what unit pricing is all about (source: the item labels on grocery shelves) and have them help you determine whether 2 for the price of 1 is really the best bargain. Have them point out an item in the store that they saw pitched on TV and see how it compares price wise to similar items. This age group is prime for learning about the differences between brands: their cost, size, quality and quantity.

The middle years' kids are readers now, and they are anxious to show you what they can read to you. Encourage them to read labels, ads, etc. to you. Kids are very visual. This is a good time to include them in the stocking and restocking of household needs. Their interest goes beyond their needs and the obvious—food. You may be surprised to find out that they are interested in what is needed in the bathroom, the kitchen in general, and even for household maintenance, like vacuum cleaner bags and light bulbs.

A fun project for a rainy day is to put together a list of the "necessity" items that are used around the house; start with the kids area to get them going.

- *The Kids' Bathroom:* the most logical inclusions would be toothpaste, soap, shampoo and, for some, bubble bath would be considered a necessity.
- *Your Bathroom*: to the first 4 items above, you most likely will add deodorant, hand lotion, Q-tips, dental floss, conditioner, razor blades, etc.
- *Kitchen*: offer suggestions such as sugar, flour, cereals, coffee, tea, spaghetti, rice, raisins, cocoa, spices, canned goods and so on.
- *House*: dish washing soap, garbage bags, light bulbs, vacuum bags, washing machine soap, fabric softener, etc.

The purpose of these lists is to help identify the basic necessities needed to run your family's household. The kitchen and house in general are primarily your domain, but don't exclude the kids input. You will be surprised at their interest in learning about what is needed. Favored foods should be included—for Frank, penne pasta with chicken was at the top of his list for four solid years.

A final note to compiling the lists with the kids. Work with them on the difference between: do we *need this* versus do we *just want it*, but really can live without it for now. As you look over the list and ask those questions (do you need, or do you want?), your kid may respond—no, I don't need the bar of soap versus I need the chocolate—remember you are the adult and get to give the final yea or nay on all items listed.

Once you have established what is essential and what is not, your shopping will be made much easier. So now let's turn your kid's attention to the food advertising supplements from the newspaper that come mid-week and on weekends. Grocery stores spend a lot of advertising dollars putting these coupon sections together to get your attention. Use them, they can be a wonderful resource for you and you child.

These supplements often contain terrific pictures that will snag your visual 6 to 10-year-old's interest. And, they contain pricing in general, notations on cents off pricing, and most important—the dates for the sale. They are a terrific way to introduce your child to comparison-shopping. Now, it's time to put the kids to work.

With the help of the ads, they can scout them to see what fits with your already prepared "necessity" list. You can also let them search for what fits the—if we have "extra money," it would be nice to have—list. If you live where there are competing grocery stores, the comparison shopping opportunities are even more challenging for your kids. Using more than one store's ads could, however, create more of a challenge for you at shopping time than you bargained for.

With scissors in hand, your assistant(s) are ready to go to work. Have them clip coupons or price quotes for items from the necessity list (later you can work on the "extra money" list). Then, have them put the clippings in alphabetical order using the general name for each—not the brand name. For example: put an ad for Oreo's in the pile for the letter C – cookies—not under the letter O.

The next step is to put the alphabetized clippings into general categories: fresh fruits and veggies in the produce pile, soaps and cleaning needs together, etc. Then proceed to compare prices to see what coupons win the price competition and discard the rest. The same steps can be taken with the "extra money" list.

Most adults are familiar with the stocking procedures of the nearby stores and know what aisle to go to for a particular item and so are kids (at least for those things they like). You might want to further organize the coupons according to the store's general topography. If several kids are involved, you might want to assign them an area and it's respective coupons to avoid total pandemonium at the store. When kids have done this several times, they can probably rid you of this chore for years to come.

Now we're ready to go to the store (But is the store ready for all this efficiency in comparison-shopping?). Appoint yourself the captain of the grocery cart, direct the traffic and put the kids to work. Have them hunt down the items for you. It is essential that you emphasize the necessity of sticking to the shopping list. It's easy to get off target and be swayed by impulse buying.

As the kids pick up each item that has a coupon, have them note the regular price and the coupon price on a pad of paper. When you get home, tally the differences so all can see what the total savings were for the shopping trip. If you think the kids will tire of doing this, here's an incentive to keep them going. Put the savings total in a kitty for a special family outing such as miniature golf, the latest kid movie or pizza. Or, you could reinforce the $mart-Money kid, by putting the money in their savings account.

A few summers ago, Frank took his friend A.J. along with us to see a Rockies baseball game. When the invitation was issued to the boys, they were told that we would have a ball park type dinner—translation: hot dogs, sodas and most likely some other gooey type of concoction. Upon arrival at the stadium, the boys were told that they had some choices for food that evening. They could

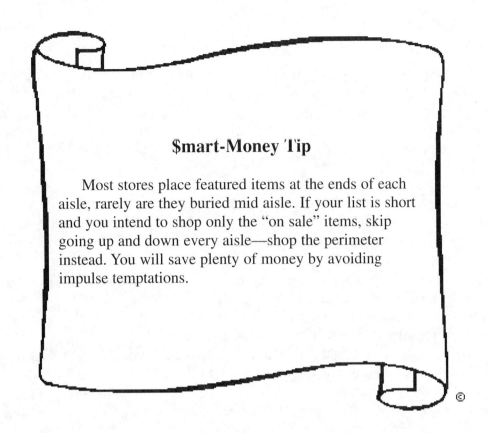

$mart-Money Tip

Most stores place featured items at the ends of each aisle, rarely are they buried mid aisle. If your list is short and you intend to shop only the "on sale" items, skip going up and down every aisle—shop the perimeter instead. You will save plenty of money by avoiding impulse temptations.

pick from the food booths we passed on our way to our seats (purchases to be made later, after several innings had been played) or take a chance on pot luck by selecting from the concessionaires, who pass through the stands.

They were each given a budget of $10 for the evening. They added up the cost of items they thought they wanted, as they filled their bellies. Between the two of them, they made it a game—how much could they get with their combined pool of $20? By the end of the game, the boys had spent approximately $18. We liked it because they weren't hounding us for money all evening—it was their problem to spread it out, not ours.

Instead of just doling out dollars whenever they ask you for money, put a few strings on the "gift." Tell them that there is just so much money allocated to a particular event and to attend, and they must work/live within the proposed budget. As an incentive, you can offer to put the difference in their savings account, if they come in under budget. We were open to that, the kids gave us back the change at the end of the evening—to go toward parking!

Spending Plans and Kids: A Lifetime Road Map

Kids and spending plans go hand in hand. Most people call them budgets, I prefer spending plans. You can help your kids by devising a simple method of keeping track of their expenditures: what they spend their money on and how much (if any) is left over at the end of the week (for older kids, usually the month). Here's a spending plan that we put together for Frank when he was 8.

This is the first step in establishing a life long habit of planned spending and as well as dealing with expected income. It's a simple spending plan, but you can expand or contract it to meet you child's needs. Just make sure that you take into account that, like adults, children have fixed and variable expenses and income.

By the time your kids hit 6-years-old, their allowance should include the provision for some "walking around" money that can be spent on whatever he or she desires. As your kids approach the age of 10, the ability to match income with expenses should become evident. Your son or daughter should have a good grasp of the sources of his or her income and outgo.

Your 10-year-old should understand what expenses are fixed—such as school lunches and supplies; a grasp of amounts to put toward savings and donations to charities and the church should also be evident. Your shining hour as their top role model is here. Kids at this age are very tuned in to how you save money—do you need to start saving now for next summer's vacation? and how you spend it— ongoing family expenses.

The key here is to give your kids a road map to designing their spending plan. Discuss your family's spending plan: the how and why of the income and outgo, the successes and the failures in keeping to the spending plan. A monthly family spending plan session is an excellent tool to use for regular reinforcement for the concepts you are teaching your kids.

Star Wars, Tarzan and A Bug's Life Too!

By the time your kids reach age 8, they have some inkling about phony TV commercial promises, what rings true in them and what doesn't. When I wrote the first edition of this book, TV blitzed kids with commercials relating to Tarzan, Star Wars and A Bug's Life, all new movies in 1999. Any movie that cost multi-millions of dollars to produce also had a handsome advertising budget. Watches, cups and toys beckoned youngsters—some were free, but most had to be purchased.

Frank's Spending Plan

Month _____ **Week** _____

Money Received	Mon	Tues	Wed	Thur	Fri	Sat	Sun
Allowance	___	___	___	___	___	___	___
Gifts	___	___	___	___	___	___	___
Odd Jobs	___	___	___	___	___	___	___
Other	___	___	___	___	___	___	___
TOTAL	___	___	___	___	___	___	___

Money Spent	Mon	Tues	Wed	Thur	Fri	Sat	Sun
Art Lessons	___	___	___	___	___	___	___
Books	___	___	___	___	___	___	___
Candy	___	___	___	___	___	___	___
CDs	___	___	___	___	___	___	___
Charity	___	___	___	___	___	___	___
Church	___	___	___	___	___	___	___
Clothes	___	___	___	___	___	___	___
Crafts	___	___	___	___	___	___	___
Gave to Friends	___	___	___	___	___	___	___
Gifts	___	___	___	___	___	___	___
Lunch Money	___	___	___	___	___	___	___
Movies	___	___	___	___	___	___	___
Parties	___	___	___	___	___	___	___
Pets	___	___	___	___	___	___	___
Savings	___	___	___	___	___	___	___
School Events	___	___	___	___	___	___	___
Snacks	___	___	___	___	___	___	___
Sports	___	___	___	___	___	___	___
Toys	___	___	___	___	___	___	___
Videos	___	___	___	___	___	___	___
Other	___	___	___	___	___	___	___
TOTAL	___	___	___	___	___	___	___

Total Money Received $ _____
Total Money Spent $ _____
Over / Under $ _____

All of this marketing was directed toward your youngster; reaching you, other than through your kids, was never a part of the equation. Since the "hype" of these advertising blitzes is directed solely at your kids, it opens an important window of opportunity for your joint investigations of the truth and fiction in a TV blitz.

Most kids are inexperienced and naive about advertising. Thus it is normal for your daughter to expect that a product will perform exactly as it does on TV. This brings up the subject of enhancers. If you don't know what an enhancer is, the nauseating details of some follow. Enhancers are used to demonstrate a product, to make it look better or more accurate (such as perfect). You have a great opportunity to discuss how they're done and more importantly, WHY.

Don't forget celebrity endorsements (how could you miss them?). One of my favorite all time commercials that uses enhancers is the one made by McDonald's a few years ago. When Michael Jordan joined the Chicago Bulls, basketball history was made. Basketball is one of the hottest sports in our country. McDonald's paid millions to Michael Jordan, Larry Bird, and Charles Barkley for a series of commercials that shows all three taking a shot (a TV game of horse) with a basketball, including one from the earth to the moon. The prize for the winner—a McDonald's Big Mac.

Use ads like these as examples of how ridiculous or impossible some feats portrayed on TV really are. To get the dialogue going, ask you kids a few questions, such as:

♦ How did Michael Jordan and Larry Bird get on the moon?
♦ Can Michael Jordan really shoot a basketball from the moon to the earth?
♦ Why do you think these players want to be in the commercial? Money or fun?
♦ Do you think any of the players did the commercial for free? (Some give money to charity, and pointing this out is an opportunity for positive emulation of a celebrity).
♦ Do you think they would have done the commercial even though they might not like McDonald's Big Macs?
♦ For the older child, you can even open up the values drawer. If Michael Jordan got into "trouble", would McDonald's still use him as an endorser? If your kids understand what the "trouble" was, would this information impact their decision to buy the product?

Ask your kids if they can remember how the Big Mac hamburger looked on the TV spot and then ask them to compare this image to the next one they bite into. It's rare that the TV burger looks anything like one in real life—why? As a rule, the meat in the burgers in commercials is basically raw. The burger has been seared for only a few seconds on each side (this is done to avoid the shrinkage that occurs when the meat is cooked well done, as it should be). Those terrific looking barbecue grill marks are painted on by hand. You have seen the sesame seed buns—well, those seeds are glued in place, one by one and the more the merrier. Ask your kids if they have ever gotten a hamburger with a soggy bun, and most of them will respond with a big yes. In the commercials, the buns have cardboard slipped into them for stability so they won't collapse from the moisture that accumulates during the shoot. After all, those filming lights are hot!

The *Consumer Reports* folks have produced three "behind the scenes" videos that expose what really goes on when a commercial is produced. The best resource to go to is their website at *www.consumersreport.com* for a menu of their products that are available to the public.

Zillions: Consumer Reports for Kids publishes it's annual ZAP awards. A panel is made up of 12 of its readers and they evaluate all the nominations from other readers. ZAP means to zap it off the air. What are they zapping? Various commercials and pitches that don't live up to their promises or are downright misrepresentations.

Every season will bring on a new crop of commercials that stretch your imagination. Whether it's the Taco Bell dog that speaks and dances or the electronic miniature pets that promised to teach kids how to be responsible (one 12 year-old told me that she and her friends had a race to see who could kill theirs' first!), the folks in advertising will find a variety of ways to enhance their products to attract buyers. You and your kids—as the beacon of truth, you get to spot (or at least listen to what your kids are chatting about, then spot) advertisements and gimmicks that are merely that.

Dealing with Peer Pressure

When your kids are between the ages of 8 and 12, they are most aware of their friends and peers inventory of things as well as the degree of "in-ness" that is attached to each one of these things. Every parent has felt the subtle pressure or has been subjected to the outright demand to buy something because a friend has one. You might hear one of these statements: "I'll just die if can't have that" or "What will the other kids think." Once in a while, there can be a legitimate reason for yours wanting to "keep up with Jones kid," so don't tune him out as a matter of principle.

Once you have determined whether a need is real or imagined, give your son an answer. It is very important to make your value system—what you think about the acquisition of things—clear to him, as well as what you can afford and not afford to do. It's not uncommon for kids to think that money comes from the ATM. They either forget or they may not be aware that it takes your hard work, and sometimes pressure induced sweat, to provide them with the lifestyle they are presently enjoying.

If they want something that's inappropriate (whatever the reason) or because of it's cost and you are categorically opposed to having such a thing in your home, let them know why. Examples of responses could be "I don't have the money to spend on this right now" (also make clear when or if the money

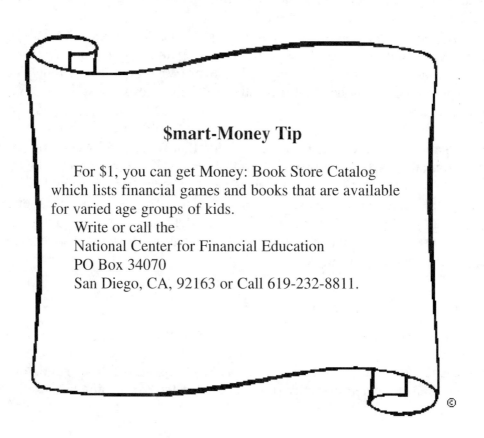

$mart-Money Tip

For $1, you can get Money: Book Store Catalog which lists financial games and books that are available for varied age groups of kids.
Write or call the
National Center for Financial Education
PO Box 34070
San Diego, CA, 92163 or Call 619-232-8811.

will be available) or "I believe this is dangerous . . ." whatever your rationale may be. Beware—parents often do their kids a disservice when they either give in to or actually foster the duplication of what their peers have, so they will "fit in." You might want to try out a toy swap with your kids' friends so that this need for duplication diminishes.

Have you ever said—everyone is different and being different is definitely okay? If your kids learn early on that they don't have to be like everyone or do what everyone else is doing, they will have an easier road to travel. As a teen, they will find that saying the important word, "No," comes naturally. Most kids can accept their financial status in life, if you have been clear in stating the facts to them. An excellent resource on this topic is the book *What Makes You So Special?* (Dial Books) by Edna LeShan. LeShan deals in a common sense manner with the subject of giving your child the resources to deal with peer pressure.

There are two classic games that teach children about money: *Monopoly,* the old stand-by and the *Game of Life.* It takes much more time to complete a game of *Monopoly* than it does to play a *Game of Life.* A few years ago *Monopoly, Jr.* was introduced and this game can be completed in an hour or less. Even though this game was designed for middle aged kids, adults like it too.

$mart-Money Resource Center

Newspapers and Magazines

> *Zillions: Consumer Reports for Kids*
> Subscription Dept., PO Box 5177, Boulder, CO, 80321
> Encourages kids to be savvy consumers.

Mini-Page
Many newspapers include the once weekly Mini-Page. A mini newspaper for kids can include riddles, games, experiments and money tips. Check your local paper out. If the paper doesn't carry one of these, crusade for it or check out-of-town papers at your local newsstand.

Books

Henry and the Paper Route by Beverly Clearly (Dell)
Young boy faces the problems of starting his own business. Excellent fun for your budding entrepreneur.

If You Made a Million by David M. Schwartz (Lothrop, Lee & Shepard)
A magician shows the reader what money looks like and introduces the concept of a million dollars.

Making Cents: Every Kid's Guide to Money by Elizabeth Wilkinson (Little Brown)
Lots of moneymaking ideas for the middle year's child.

The Money Book: The Smart Kid's Guide to Savvy Saving and Spending by Elaine Whatt and Stan Hinden (Tambourine Books)
Lots of good tips about budgeting, saving, banking and earning.

Money Doesn't Grow on Trees by Neale S. Godfrey (Simon & Schuster)
A good all-around book that looks at savings, spending and being responsible with money.

The Monster Money Book by Loreen Leedy (Holiday House)
Shows young kids how to manage and spend their Monster Club dues and also how to be a good shopper.

The Totally Awesome Book for Kids and Their Parents by Adrienne Berg and son Arthur Berg Bochner (New Market Press)
Berg has written several financial books. This one focuses on kids, with a strong voice from her son throughout. Anything Berg comes out with will be a good addition to your personal library.

Software

We are now in the age of personal computers and most schools and many families have them. New games and educational programs are being created as you read this. Stores, such as Blockbuster, rent computer games. *A $mart-Money* parent should "test" (rent) the product before buying. Don't forget your local library as an additional source for testing before buying books, tapes, computer games, etc. With the Internet, you may be able to download them for free—a $mart-Money move for sure.

Chapter Seven

Allowances—Do You . . .
Or Don't You?

Contrary to the belief of many, an allowance doesn't make your kid spend more money. Now hear this: when you give your kids an allowance, it doesn't make them spend money frivolously. And, it doesn't mean that you spend more on them. I'm a strong proponent that giving a regular allowance teaches them responsibility and accountability.

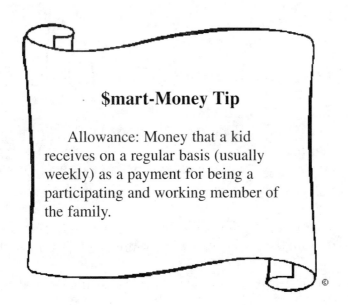

$mart-Money Tip

Allowance: Money that a kid receives on a regular basis (usually weekly) as a payment for being a participating and working member of the family.

The debate among child experts on the wisdom of giving a child an allowance continues. Those that agree on the allowance concept cannot agree on whether an allowance should be tied to the performance of jobs around the house, or whether it should be given with few or no strings attached. I believe the right answer is—allowance should be tied to jobs.

Most parents want their kids to be self-sufficient. Let's not forget that they will go out in the world one day and work for pay. In the gentle environment of your home, you have the opportunity to show your kids that if they do the job right they will get paid *and* keep their job. Another step toward becoming a successful $mart-Money adult is the "salaried and employed kid." Which usually means starting employment with an allowance in the picture.

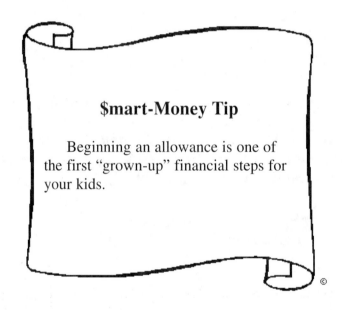

$mart-Money Tip

Beginning an allowance is one of the first "grown-up" financial steps for your kids.

Statistics show that the "unemployed" kid (one who doesn't get an allowance) has access to, and spends the same amount of money, as does the "salaried" kid. But the big difference is: the "salaried" kid is empowered—through control of their money. Let's look at what allowances can introduce and achieve to you and your child:

♦ For *You*: control of the amount of money your child gets from you.
    For *You Both*: reduces the stress of "gimme" attacks for both of you.

♦ For *You*: an easy way to open the door of the money taboo cupboard.

For *You Both*: Discuss healthy money concepts—money is part of the work/reward system and not a cure all for being sad or to be used in place of spending quality time together or to purchase things that create status with peers.

◆ For *You*: a perfect place to begin serious dialogue about what a specific amount of money does and does not do.
For *You Both:* the concepts of spending plans and saving flow naturally for you both through the discussion of allowances—you can share your successes (failures too).

◆ For *You:* a terrific opportunity to discuss the realities of your child's spending needs.
For *You Both*: quickly identify what is needful and what is wishful thinking.

◆ For *You*: a starting point, a springboard for laying the foundation for your child's attitudes toward spending and saving.
For *You Both*: less friction about money issues—you both know the rules—what the allowance is based on.

◆ For *You*: a great way to create and foster the responsible $mart-Money Kid.
For *You Both*: he completes jobs that create cash flow for him and you pay him regularly—a new word—accountability (and it does go both ways).

Finally, allowances cannot be a money cure all, especially when emergencies arise. You may have to dip down in your pocket once in a while, so be flexible but firm in your approach.

Being Part of the Family is Worth What?

I'm for starting a very simple allowance for mature 3-year-olds. Your child may not be ready until age 4 or 5. Here are some tips to identify that perfect moment in time.

◆ Does your daughter understand that a nickel is the same as five pennies? Or that a quarter is the same as five nickels?

99

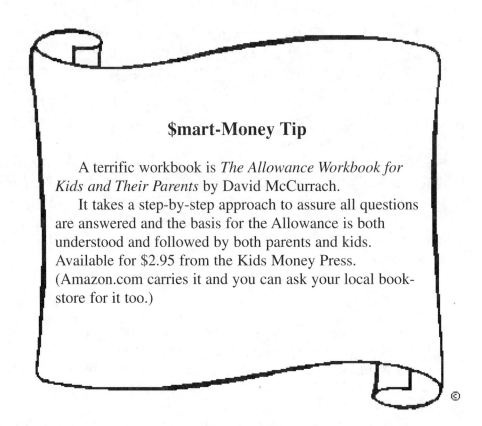

$mart-Money Tip

A terrific workbook is *The Allowance Workbook for Kids and Their Parents* by David McCurrach.

It takes a step-by-step approach to assure all questions are answered and the basis for the Allowance is both understood and followed by both parents and kids. Available for $2.95 from the Kids Money Press. (Amazon.com carries it and you can ask your local bookstore for it too.)

- Most preschoolers think that bigger is best, and so their logic tells them that a nickel has more value than a dime. Once they grasp that there is a difference, they're ready.
- Does your daughter understand trading? When you take her to McDonald's and she orders a Happy Meal, does she expect to give money to receive it?
- Do a test allowance. If you give her twenty-five cents, does she understand that this money needs to last for several days (young children often have trouble grasping the concept of an entire week)?
- Does your daughter understand that the grocery store will not take Monopoly play money or those chocolate coins covered in gold foil? If the answer is yes, she's ready.
- Has you daughter started the "gimme" phase or does she expect you to buy something? If the answer is yes to either, she is ready to start an allowance (then she can save and pay for own "gimmes").

If your child meets all the criteria above, it's time to start talking money. First, make sure that you take charge of the amount given for an allowance. They can choose how they receive it. For example, they can have fifty cents in nickels or dimes or they can have $1 in 2 quarters, four dimes and two nickels, etc. Then, talk with them about what they will use the allowance for and when they will get it. It is normal to tie the child's pay periods to yours. Make a commitment to be being consistent—your child needs to know she can count on having her allowance whatever the amount or timing.

Once you agree on the amount of the allowance and when it is to be paid, be fully aware that the money is not yours anymore—it belongs to your child. They get to decide what they will spend the money on and believe me, they will make mistakes (don't chide them too much at first). Also, don't be surprised if they lose the money a few times (little children don't have any idea how to keep

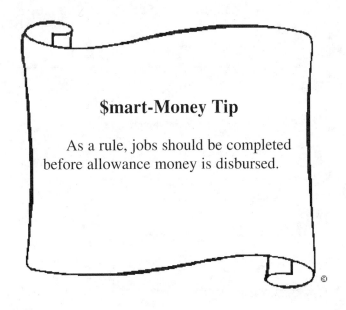

$mart-Money Tip

As a rule, jobs should be completed before allowance money is disbursed.

their money safe at first—let them know about holes in their pockets. All of these new experiences will give both of you opportunities to discuss their first money successes and failures. And, make sure praise is given so they will know what you like about their spending practices. At this age, your child delights in pleasing you by being a big girl or boy, a la exhibiting responsibility.

We had a job check list on our refrigerator door when my kids were 11 (Shelley), 10 (Frank) and 8 (Sheryl). It looked something like this:

Job Check List—Week of _____

	Water garden	Feed Gillie & Sam	Dirty clothes to washer	Clear Cat Box	Scoop dog poop	Unload groceries	Dinner dishes	Take out trash	Unload dish-washer	Set table	Clear table	Sweep back-yard
Shelley			X		X	X		X		X		
Frank	X		X				X					X
Sheryl		X	X	X					X		X	
Complete on/by:	Tues., Sat.	AM & PM Daily	Sat. AM	Wed. Sat.	Wed., Sat.	As needed	Each day	Each day	Each day	Each day	Each day	Sat.

In order for my kids to get their allowance (pay time was Saturday morning and was based on the preceding week), each task they were assigned had to be marked "Done". The "Done" box had to have as many X's as days required to complete the individual tasks. If not, they would be docked a portion of their allowance. As time went on, jobs were added and deleted. Assignments were based on age and ability.

The older child will need more money because they are more active outside of the home—they are in school now. When hot lunches were introduced at my school, I begged my mother to let me buy my lunch (I admit to an ulterior motive). Trading or bartering items from school lunches goes way back in kid history, and my usual lunch from home, a peanut butter and mayonnaise sandwich, had no value in this market place.

Success—I got my way and I was given lunch money—I became a budding entrepreneur. I discovered, that with cash in hand, I had choices: 1. Buy a portion or all of someone else's lunch; 2. I could purchase the cafeteria offering for the day; or 3. I could bank all or some of my lunch money—I would eat a couple of apples I brought from home.

Every parent wonders how much allowance really is enough. Studies have shown that as a rule, family income has little bearing on the amount given out (especially to the preschool child). Age is one factor and parental education level is another.

$mart-Money Tip

Two great books to give you more info on allowances are:
Kids' Allowance-How Much, How Often & How Much by David McCurrach (Kids Money Press-2000) and *Kids' Allowance Book* by Amy Nathan and Debbie Palen (Walker & Co-1998)

Some parents tie the amount of allowance to either the age of the child or the grade in school. For example, a second grader would receive $2 per week or a seven-year-old could receive $7 per week.

In our home, we had a list of chores that were rotated by the kids that had to be completed prior to the disbursement of allowance. If they didn't arrange for a substitute or just plain skipped doing the chore, they got no allowance at all. It was as simple as that—all or none. Granted this policy created some grumbling but only took a few skips to understand the responsibility tied to their allowance pay out.

Other ideas that can work include a point system. You and the kids identify chores around the home that can be accomplished (to *your* satisfaction) and the pay rate for each. Make a chart or use a bulletin board (the kind that accepts push pins—reusable) with the kid(s) name at the top and the chores/rate of pay down the side. When the jobs are completed, use a star or pin to designate completion. Tally them up at the end of the week and pay for what has been done satisfactorily.

Some households like to use price tags instead of points. For instance, feeding and watering the dog is worth ten cents, bringing dirty clothes to the laundry is worth fifteen cents. Again, at the end of the week, a tally is done and pay is issued.

Be clear with your child that, if his allowance must cover some expenses, he knows what those expenses are. Most parents take the responsibility of covering the costs of school clothes and supplies. You might want to plan ahead, and decide when or if your kids will receive a clothing allowance. Older children should be allowed to exercise some of their preferences in clothing styles (a good opportunity to teach them about the extra cost of brand name clothing). It is totally reasonable to expect kids to pay for: snack foods that are not part of your normal pantry stock, recreational games—including the video arcades, movies, CDs, tapes, etc.

Frank's Spending Plan, from the preceding chapter, includes money being spent on charity, crafts as well as savings. One way to set an early habit of portioning out money is to get one of those checkbook size expandable files for coupons. You can make labels for each "envelope" in the file to include all the items from his personalized list of budgeted expenses—toys, movies, gifts, Halloween costumes—don't forget savings, church and charity.

It's Saturday and let's suppose that today is allowance payday and your child expects his $3. Instead of giving three $1 bills each Saturday, give him a combination of bills, quarters, nickels and dimes. This way your son has the change he needs to disperse his allowance to the budgeted "envelopes." Encourage him to put in 10 percent for your church, another 5 to 10 percent for a charity of his choice, and 20-25 percent to savings. The rest? Well the rest is his to spend in any way he wants.

Most kids are very visual and they want to see where their money goes. By placing the money in a holder, they can have the pleasure of counting and recounting their moneys. You can also use clear jars (plastic please) that are labeled as follows: Spending, Savings, and Sharing. These were referred to in the previous chapter.

In talking with most allowance paying parents, the most accepted way is with age—your 10-year-old would get $10 per week.

When is it Time for More, or Less?

Most adults like to be paid more when they do a good job. Kids are no different. So, count on it, they're going to ask for a raise, sometime. Revisit the allowance issue several months down the road from the time you start it—this is especially important for the preschooler. For instance, if your 5-year-old has been a little Trojan and completed her work the way you want her to do it—give her a raise. Every dime counts. For older kids, an allowance evaluation is appropriate about every 6 months or so. When you re-evaluate the allowance for your 11-year-old, be realistic about what you expect you son or daughter to spend their funds on—tune in to *their* cost of living. Bite your tongue if you are thinking, "When I was a kid..."

When do you know that you are paying your child too much allowance? If your child spends or gives away the greater portion of their allowance, it doesn't mean that you are giving them too large an amount. You must respect your child's choices. Simply devote a little more time to guidance, if you feel that you have a budding spendthrift on your hands. If, however the assigned jobs are not done satisfactorily and/or not on time, you have a problem.

Let's look at an example: Each week your daughter is supposed to dust the front room, collect the dirty clothes and empty the trash. She has decided that once a month is adequate for dusting, dirty clothes can be worn wrong side out so the dirt doesn't show and the trash doesn't really smell that bad. Does this sound familiar? If so, it's time for a combo meeting of parent and daughter. In fact, call it what it is: a business meeting. This is salary review time—employer meets with employee.

You may have to consider docking your kid's paycheck (allowance) or even go so far as to put him or her on leave without pay if your meeting doesn't result in better level of performance. Sometimes, kids get bored with the "same old, same old." Try being creative by varying the job description (new jobs and chores for a while). But above all, be firm. I come from the philosophy that a bargain made is one you must keep. If your child isn't keeping up his part of the bargain, you don't pay the allowance.

The Case of the Missing Buck

Today is Wednesday and allowance is paid on Saturday. Your sports fanatic daughter's allowance is already gone. She doesn't know where it went and claims it disappeared to "Allowance Heaven." This could be the opportunity you've been waiting for, to involve her in an assessment of her spending habits. You have discovered that she has the niftiest and most expensive collection of baseball cards in the neighborhood. You find out that she is spending lunch money, which is included in her weekly allowance allotment, to expand this collection. You decide that it's definitely time to call a halt to *this* spending practice.

If she is using her lunch money to buy baseball cards, she's still a hungry at lunchtime with no money to ease the hunger pangs. The possible results: her friends are sick and tired of her attempts to mooch their lunches, and she too may soon be so sick and tired that her attention in afternoon classes will be nil. A solution to this problem could be to call the school and see if you can prepay for her lunches. Or, send the money with her each day if prepayment is not possible. And of course, reduce the allowance paid to her by the amount allocated weekly for lunches. One thing is for sure, kids need to eat to stay healthy. If she persists in redirecting her lunch moneys and refuses the cafeteria route, you could tell her to be creative—pack her own lunch and then bag it.

It's a rare parent that hasn't been approached with "I lost it and I can't find it" or "Someone must have taken my money, it isn't where I left it." What to do? Do you sympathize? Do you join the hunt? Or do you say "Tough." Possibly, you respond with one or all of the above. Trust me, there will be a time, and perhaps many, when your kids will approach you for an advance. It's one of those skills that are mastered early.

Here are two of the more common reasons for needing an advance: he may have simply overspent and payday is several days out; or, there could be a legitimate event coming up that requires prepayment. In either case, you will have to trust your son—that he is giving you the complete scoop—then put on your fair judge's robe.

In the case of a legitimate need to prepay without much advance notice, advance the money against next week's allowance, no strings attached. If you find that the child has known about the event for quite a while and failed to do some prior budget planning, take the time to work on this concept and deal with the advance as outlined for lost money and overspending:

Lost money: If this becomes a frequent occurrence, some detective work is required. Does your child use good methods for carrying and storing his money? Help develop these skills if not.

Overspending: Help your child develop budgeting skills.

Now, do you pay or not? Sure, but with the understanding that the "extra" money is an advance on next week's paycheck/allowance. Try not to advance against more than one week's allowance.

In Their Interest?

And, if you really want to try out a sophisticated lesson, go ahead and add interest to the advance. They will have to learn about loans someday, and it's never too early. Use the example of your mortgage or car loan. If you borrowed a portion of the proceeds to complete the purchase, explain that you didn't have enough in savings to pay all cash. You were able to arrange a loan at the bank, but that loan had strings attached—interest.

The bank agreed to give you the needed money, provided that you paid back a part of the money each month plus something extra—interest. Explain that interest is the price you pay to get money that you don't have but want or need. I suggest that you keep your interest low, at about five percent. Calculate how much a day his loan will cost him by multiplying the loan amount by the interest rate and then divide by 365 days in year. If he hasn't learned multiplication and division, avoid confusing him with your calculations. Or, you could charge from 5¢ to $1, depending on the amount of the advance.

I know I'm talking pennies, but there's a lesson in life here. Loans to kids should only be for week or two. Every kid should understand that money isn't free. The price to pay immediately happens when an allowance is reduced by the amount borrowed *plus* interest.

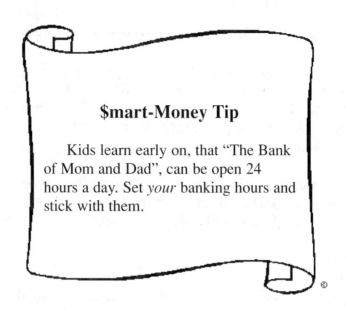

$mart-Money Tip

Kids learn early on, that "The Bank of Mom and Dad", can be open 24 hours a day. Set *your* banking hours and stick with them.

If your kids run short of money week after week, it's time to get out paper and pencil. Remember Frank's Spending Plan from the preceding chapter? Have your son or daughter keep track of each expenditure on a daily basis— give a pad of Post-It notes and have them detail each transaction—one per Post-It. Next, provide a piece of poster paper with a line drawn down the middle from top to bottom and label the right side **Wants** and the left side **Needs**. The next step is to apply the sticky labels on the board each day in its proper category.

At the end of the week, the two of you should evaluate the board to see what is gobbling up your kid's cash. Almost without exception, you both will probably see that Post-Its in the **Needs** column are fewer than the **Wants**.

Here's the $64,000 question. Ask him if he thinks he might be *bypassing* **Needs** and *spending* too much for **Wants**. Have him carefully evaluate his **Wants** Post-Its, to identify which things he really wants most and help him find ways to trim back. At some point, a candle of understanding has to be lit in his mind. You can gently guide him to the revelation that *needs must be met* before *wants can be addressed*. One of the real *Ahas!* of life.

The middle year kids will probably see that their wants list has grown longer and longer and that the cost per want is more expensive—roller blades and CD players come to mind. We sure saw this with Frank. His wants became fewer, but the cost factor was significantly greater. If this is the case, you both can consider some additional household jobs. Or consider creating income from odd jobs done for friends, relatives and neighbors or possibly the old favorites—the paper route, lawn mowing, pet care, bringing in newspapers, mail and watering gardens for vacationing neighbors.

Grades: The Good, the Bad and the Ugly

If there ever was a "hot potato" in parental money guidance, paying for good grades is one of them. Should you pay them for good grades? Most psychologists say no. One school of thought says that kids are far better off for good performances at school to be rewarded with sincere and detailed praise. Or a non-cash treat reward, such as stickers for a young kids, a CD or pizza outing for a middle kid or movie passes or a clothing gift certificate for a teen.

Some parents think cash for grades is a great idea and they will do anything to get their kid's grades up. Then there are the parents who are appalled that any money for grades would pass hands. Before you decide where you stand and give a black or white "no" to either side of this issue, consider a compromise.

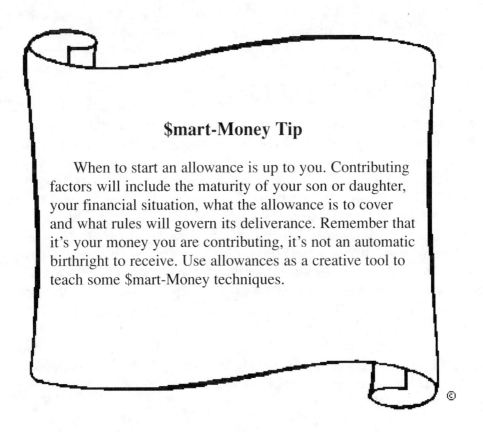

$mart-Money Tip

When to start an allowance is up to you. Contributing factors will include the maturity of your son or daughter, your financial situation, what the allowance is to cover and what rules will govern its deliverance. Remember that it's your money you are contributing, it's not an automatic birthright to receive. Use allowances as a creative tool to teach some $mart-Money techniques.

When a child is young and it is improbable that he or she will be looking for after schoolwork, paying for grades doesn't make a lot of sense. There is an exception. If your child shows vast improvement in a particular subject, a reward might be appropriate. It can be either cash or non-cash—it could be a coveted treat, a special movie or outing. When your kids stretch themselves and achieve beyond their normal capabilities, applause and recognition is in order.

If your older child is doing some heavy duty studying in lieu of picking up the extra income lawn-mowing job, consider giving him a "Bravo" by increasing his allowance. After all, some adults get paid for using their brains; others are paid for using their brawn.

Cut Backs and Bonuses

When your kids are lagging in their responsibilities, don't fully meet their commitments or go on strike—don't ignore it. If you have more than one, your reaction or lack of it will not escape the sibling's ever-watchful eye. If you don't react promptly and definitively, you have sent a clear message that dereliction of duty is okay. In fact, they think are you condoning it.

Your first statement, loud and clear, needs to be "Everyone in this family is expected to chip in and do his or her fair share of the work. You are no exception." If you are ignored or get a response like "Billy (the brother or friend) doesn't have to work as hard as I do," you classic parental response could be, "Because I said so." You are the adult, it's your house and you are in charge.

In reality, taking that position has far greater impact with the preschoolers and the early middle year child. When kids are in their teens, they are most likely exercising every bit of independence they can muster. In our household, my youngest Sheryl, was a master of the "The Look." When she heard a statement she didn't like or was asked to do something she considered beneath her, she had a look that could "kill."

Parents respond, out of frustration, to this type of kid rebellion by saying "If you don't do this, you won't get that." "That" could be an eagerly anticipated outing with friends (even family), shopping, movies, a slumber party, you name it—all kids have a long laundry list of events that they would hate to miss out on.

The bottom line is, that if you draw a line such as this, commit to the announced action/reaction scenario. Then stand firm. If the lawn isn't mowed and the dog isn't walked, the shopping mall trip is history. For teens, withdrawing driving privileges inflicts exquisite pain. Wonder of wonders, your wish becomes their command.

When kids repeatedly shirk their job responsibilities, some parents reduce the allowance accordingly. That may work, but look before you leap and be sure you reduce the allowance fairly. One way, is to determine how many chores are required to do for his or her allowance. Divide the weekly allowance by this number to determine the pay rate for each job. Don't be tempted to evaluate the job by the length of time each job takes or it's degree of difficulty, or you will be quickly drawn into an esoteric debate that will result in a no win situation for both you.

With the pay rate determined, you could then simply add up the jobs not done, multiply by the rate and deduct from the next allowance due. Usually, after a few deductions, your daughter will discover that her newly adjusted economic status is no fun at all. If you have an eager beaver on the sidelines, you could offer this (these) job(s) and the pay to them for a given period. Your "partially" employed kid may actually seek other jobs to make up for the hole in her pocket...even her pride.

Every parent wants their kids to do well—to stretch and succeed at their tasks. When they do a *great* job, reward them. When your kids understand the "no-work, no-pay" ethic, they will also understand a "superior-work, better-pay" ethic. I assume you do, so will they.

It only takes a little bit of effort to be above average. Telling your kids that work that produces superior quality is above average. If they are willing to commit themselves to reach that level, you are willing to "bonus" them—their earned reward.

Pitch the Penny Reward Wheel Game

When a task is done in an above average manner, bonuses can be treats, events out, money, etc. The reward selection can be a fun event too. Make a *Pitch the Penny Wheel Reward Game*. All you need is paper, pencil and a penny. Make a wheel of prizes—perhaps like the one on *Wheel of Fortune* TV show. You may have to censor some of the prize choices your child presents for the wheel—her zeal could overwhelm your pocketbook.

When the wheel is satisfactory to both of you, lay the wheel on a table or the floor. The prizewinner stands back and tosses a penny at the circle. Wherever it lands, the designated reward is theirs. A wheel for each child in your home might be appropriate. Here's what Frank had on his wheel when he was 8:

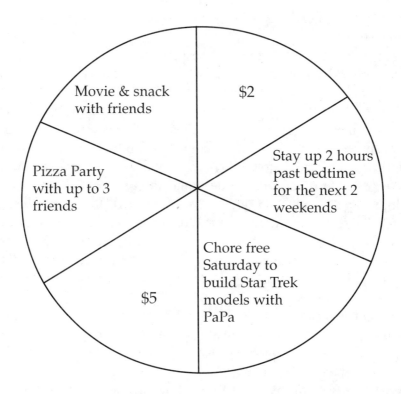

Pitch the Penny Reward Wheel

Be prepared to change the prizes every few months. Kids' interest change quickly with their age—not in years, in months.

Your Emerging Teen

When most kids hit their teens, they begin to actively pursue income opportunities outside their homes. They soon recognize that their allowance is not meeting their financial needs and wants. An outside job could mean that the teen wouldn't have time to fulfill her allowance job commitment. If you don't want your teen to take on an outside job, you may want to increase their allowance base. Or, encourage and cheer her on but with this string attached—require that a large portion of the new income go into a college fund savings account. Extra income should not be kiss-off money.

Outside of owning a car, the most coveted teen possession is a phone line of her own. A second phone line may make a big difference in your life, too—your friends and business contacts can actually reach you—busy signals will be a thing of the past. A friend used the "kid" phone line as a dinner bell. Instead of hollering up the stairs, she dialed her teen's number. Assuming the line wasn't busy, she knew it would be answered.

Before adding a kids' phone line, it's important for you to lay out the ground rules. Specifically, what hours the phone can be used (we had a 10 PM curfew) and who pays for what. All charges, other than the flat monthly rate for the additional line, must be paid for by the teen. *Don't pay for anything that you didn't agree to pay*. Believe me, one disconnect, plus the cost to reactivate the line, does wonders for teen financial responsibility.

It is not uncommon for a teen to have a checking account. A small reminder here, there are special accounts for kids at The Young Americans Bank, Denver, CO, call 303-321-2265 for information. Although this bank has plenty of checking and savings customers under the age of 13, your may want to introduce checking accounts in some form of trial run at your own bank. We did this when our kids hit 13—their name was printed on the check (it became a cherished status symbol for awhile) and my name was on the account. Although my banker knew it was not my account, as a parent, I was legally responsible in the end.

No matter what amount of allowance you decide upon, your child will learn a variety of positive lessons that she will carry throughout the money maze of life. By setting a good example with what you spend, budget, save, give and tithe, you will instill a deep-rooted value system with each child. Your legacy to the next generation.

Chapter Eight

Savings—
Creating a Habit for
the New Millennium

Most people will agree that saving money is not a genetic quality; it is a learned habit, which in some case has to be relearned. The simple fact is that America has one of the lowest savings rates among the industrialized countries. There are three primary reasons for saving. Two of the reasons can be categorized as *"Needs"*: *retirement* (a "non-word" for young adults and kids) and *back-up funds* for tough times and emergencies. The third reason for saving is: to accumulate funds for the presently unaffordable *"Wants."*

Kids' emergency *Needs* are usually covered by parent funding. Retirement? Kids are still very much in that immortal stage of life and won't waste a moment of thought to *this Need*. But, *Wants* are something kids know quite well. How do you spark your kids' interest in saving? Tie saving money into something he or she really, really *Wants*.

Jump Start for Savings

Here's a three-step program to get your child up and running with a regular savings plan that should work.

♦ *Identify Sources of Money for Savings*
   Birthday and holiday gifts of money are good sources, but erratic in their

$mart-Money Tip

Kids confuse **needs** and **wants**. A parent's job is to "un-confuse" them.

timing and amount. An on-going and routine source for your kid's savings program is most desirable. Allowances are the #1 candidates.

♦ *Create A Safe Storage for Their Money*
Possibilities for storage range from the plain and simple: shoe box, jar, bottle, to the ornate: piggy bank or toy safe. Kids must have a "bank" of their very own; they will need to make deposits, withdrawals and they really enjoy viewing and counting their growing hoard. For kids under 12, those wide-mouth plastic jars are ideal—hands and wrists easily fit in. Kids like to keep "in touch" with their money.

♦ *Cheer Lead Them On—Empowerment Through Goal Setting*
Talk with your child about her goals for saving. Are these goals within her grasp: is the timeline reasonable and is the dollar amount feasible? At first you may need to direct her interests. As the program works for her, acknowledge her efforts and lavish her with praise.

Simplicity is the byword for kids under the age of five. *Savings* is a process. When Frank was saving for his Ninja Turtle Action Figures, we made sure that saving for his targeted treasure would take him no longer than two weeks time—a reasonable timeline. Prior to the age of five, Frank kept his money in a colorful crayon shaped bank. It was easy for him to open for his periodic

$mart-Money Tip

Keep savings goals *very simple* for young kids.

counting of the coinage of his progress. Frank is like all kids, he liked to look and feel the money he had saved. Then, we switched to large plastic jars.

Children between ages of 5-8 will benefit from having different containers for their *Spending* money and for their *Saving* money. You and your kid can decide what type of container is desirable. A word of caution, make it accessi-

$mart-Money Tip

Avoid any "piggy bank" that can be broken, when you child wants to get money out.

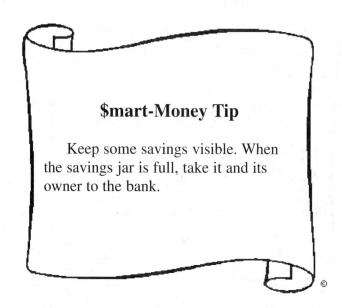

$mart-Money Tip

Keep some savings visible. When the savings jar is full, take it and its owner to the bank.

ble and preferably non-breakable. The emphasis should not be focused, however, on the container; but focused on the regularity of the deposits.

When Frank was 8, his savings were kept in three places. He had an account at the Young Americans Bank and in banks at his home and our home. He also had his own coin purse for spending money. When he got his weekly allowance, he portioned out his money to the home bank and to the coin purse. We (parents and grandparents) set a goal for Frank. When his home bank contained more than $10 he could go to the regular bank—Young Americans—and make a deposit in his savings account. This bank savings account gave him the real worldview of counting his money.

The 9 to 12-year-old is ready to move beyond the shoebox or piggybank phase of saving. One of the reasons for moving on is that their piles of money are now represented by bigger bills, not quarters and dimes. If a "real" savings account at a bank hasn't been opened—make haste. A new source of funds for savings, interest compounding, will most likely trigger a big "Wow" from your kid. Do some investigating of the kinds of accounts offered. Some banks charge maintenance or administration fees for their accounts and some require minimum opening balances. Some fee structures could discourage your child; fees can sometimes exceed the interest paid on the balance.

Most kids like the old fashioned passbook savings books (the kind I had when I deposited my 25 cents each week in school)—each deposit or withdrawal is noted in ink and date stamped. This book provides a very pleasing—

big people—alternative to the visual satisfaction the child experienced in look-ing at his money from his piggy bank. Many banks have eliminated the use of passbooks and have substituted a monthly or quarterly statement. If your bank doesn't offer a passbook you can create your own. Get a small notebook and a date stamp (small change items) at a discount office supply store near you.

Most parents will agree that too many people feel that they are "owed" for things. Entitlement has become an acceptable life style for millions of Americans. When you teach you kids about the merits of savings, the knowl-edge you will pass on will come back countless times over. The entitlement cloud won't be a factor in their adult houses.

The Importance of Goals

Some parents miss the boat when they don't provide their child with the tac-tile and visual reinforcements needed to keep the savings habit going. But worse yet, they deny their kids access to their money when they outlaw "touch-ing the money" in the savings account. I disagree.

There is a compromise (a magic word for growing the $mart-Money kid). If you are adamant that the savings account should be for a long-term goal—col-lege funds, be fair with your child. Give him reinforcement and access to his account by allowing him to have his own short-term savings goals.

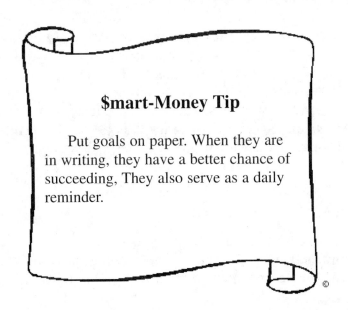

$mart-Money Tip

Put goals on paper. When they are in writing, they have a better chance of succeeding, They also serve as a daily reminder.

Frank just got a new bike. Frank and his Mom had set a goal and they met it. Half the money came from his diligent deposits to his savings account; the other half came from Mom. Frank's interest in attaining this goal was sustained by posting a picture of the bike on the refrigerator, mirror in his bathroom and by the side of his bed. A day didn't pass that he didn't look at the picture and focus on what he wanted to do with his hard-earned money. A definite goal.

A Month of Pennies

The first surge of hormones hits your child at approximately age 12. Do these hormones go directly to their brains and suddenly increase their wealth of experience and knowledge? Kids at this age are not shy about telling you that they know more than their parents do and all topics are included. Here's a great question you can throw at your kids when they hit the *I know it all* stage. Ask them: how many days will it take for you to become a millionaire if a penny doubles each day? The answer: 28 days. Beginning with 1¢ on the first day and doubling it, you would have 2¢ the second day, 4¢ the third day, etc. On the 28th day you would have $1,342,177.28!

The figure below denotes a 28-day month. You can explain leap year to your kid, if need be. Beginning on the first day with a deposit of 1¢, the penny is doubled for 28 days. Your kid will think that the end result is *Awesome* and it is. For the Month of Pennies exercise, have your child draw a matrix with 28 squares. Or, use the month of February from a wall calendar

Have them start at the upper left corner with 1¢ and double the amount in each square until they fill all the squares and get to the lower right corner. You can test their math skills and require that they do this using pencil and paper. However, the modern lad or lassie will probably prefer to use the calculator. Have fun! This can be a great wake up call that illustrates what can happen with a consistent savings plan. When Frank was off to California to visit his new step-grandparents, I gave him this as an airplane assignment during the two-hour flight.

It's of Interest to All

All of the previous probes and illustrations provide ways to introduce the "magic" of compounding (i.e. interest on their savings accounts) to your older kids (10 and up). The compounding elements are rate, dollars and time. Their

A Month of Pennies

1)	2)	3)	4)	5)	6)	7)
.01	.02	.04	.08	.16	.32	.64
8)	9)	10)	11)	12)	13)	14)
1.28	2.56	5.12	10.24	20.48	40.96	81.92
15)	16)	17)	18)	19)	20)	21)
163.84	327.68	655.36	1,310.72	2,621.44	5,242.88	10,85.76
22)	23)	24)	25)	26)	27)	28)
20,971.52	41,943.04	83,886.08	167,772.16	335,544.32	671,088.64	1,342,177.28

From 1¢ to $1,342,177.28 in 28 days!

money can grow in two ways: deposits and interest deposits from the bank. It's logical for your kids to ask why the bank pays this interest. Explain that the bank has their (the kids) money and uses it while it's there, and the bank has to pay for this privilege.

Here's a real life example of how the interest works to grow the savings account over a period of time. Let's say that your daughter is twelve-years-old. She has two burning interests now—music and clothes. She is very talented musician and hasn't met a musical instrument that she hasn't loved. She has confided in you that she wants to be the first female conductor for the symphony in your city. She is also a clothes hound and she hasn't met an outfit that she doesn't adore.

Being the astute parent that you are, you know the potential dollars needed to fund your daughter's goals in education and clothing has to come from some-

121

where. The unexpected source? Grandma has decided to gift each of her grand-children with $1000, come Christmas. Your goal as a parent is to convince your daughter to bank the money Grandma gives her and try to restrain her from blowing it all on clothes.

The table below shows specific savings balances and the growth rate for each using different rates of interest compounding. Here's how it works. Today your daughter is 12 and she will enter college when she's 19—7 years from now. You have checked with the local bank and found out that her $1000 can earn 6 percent interest over the next 7 years. First find the column labeled 6 percent and run your finger down to the number 7 (for the years) and you will see the figure 1.50. Multiply her $1000 dollars by 1.50, which yields an increase in value of $500. Your daughter's $1000 account will increase to $1500 in 7 years. All she has to do is put her money in the bank. Today, a certificate of deposit will pay approximately 6 percent. You can tell her that once she commits her money, the interest rate will not change on her—a commitment from the bank.

The Magic of Compounding

This compound-growth table tells you what any sum of money will rise to in any year in the future, if it compounds at a given rate. Look down the left-hand column, for the number of years into the future you want. Read across to the rate of increase you expect. Where those lines intersect, you will find a compounding factor. Multiply the factor by the sum you started with, to see what it would rise to in the years ahead.

Long Term Versus Short Term: Is it Worth it?

Your goal now is to convince your daughter that saving the $1000 and grow-ing it to $1500 for her future education is a better choice than spending it. This will introduce the concept of long-term goals versus short -term goals. The pay-off later instead of instant gratification now. You can point out that if she spends the money on clothes now, those clothes will most likely be: 1, out of style and 2, won't fit her in 7 years.

You can also teach your kids the Rule of 72. This rule states that if you divide the number 72 by a given interest rate, you will know how many years it will take for your money to double. For example: if you can earn 9 percent per annum, it will take 8 years to double her $1000 ($72 \div 9 = 8$).

				Sum accumulated at					
	5%	*6%*	*7%*	*8%*	*9%*	*10%*	*11%*	*12%*	
1	1.00	1.00	1.00	1.00	1.00	1.00	1.00	1.00	1.00
2	1.04	1.05	1.06	1.07	1.08	1.09	1.10	1.11	1.12
3	1.08	1.10	1.12	1.14	1.17	1.19	1.21	1.23	1.25
4	1.12	1.16	1.19	1.23	1.26	1.30	1.33	1.37	1.40
5	1.17	1.22	1.26	1.31	1.36	1.41	1.46	1.52	1.57
6	1.22	1.28	1.34	1.40	1.47	1.54	1.61	1.69	1.76
7	1.27	1.34	1.42	1.50	1.59	1.68	1.77	1.87	1.97
8	1.32	1.41	1.50	1.61	1.71	1.83	1.95	2.08	2.21
9	1.37	1.48	1.59	1.72	1.85	1.99	2.14	2.30	2.48
10	1.42	1.55	1.69	1.84	2.00	2.17	2.36	2.56	2.77
11	1.48	1.63	1.79	1.97	2.16	2.37	2.59	2.84	3.11
12	1.54	1.71	1.90	2.10	2.33	2.58	2.85	3.15	3.48
13	1.60	1.80	2.01	2.25	2.52	2.81	3.14	3.50	3.90
14	1.67	1.89	2.13	2.41	2.72	3.07	3.45	3.88	4.36
15	1.73	1.98	2.26	2.58	2.94	3.34	3.80	4.31	4.89
16	1.80	2.08	2.40	2.76	3.17	3.64	4.18	4.78	5.47
17	1.87	2.18	2.54	2.95	3.43	3.97	4.59	5.31	6.13
18	1.95	2.29	2.69	3.16	3.70	4.33	5.05	5.90	6.87
19	2.03	2.41	2.85	3.38	4.00	4.72	5.56	6.54	7.69
20	2.11	2.53	3.03	3.62	4.32	5.14	6.12	7.26	8.61

Getting Started

Getting your kids started on a savings plan or system is often an evolution. Usually it starts with the jar or the piggy bank talked about earlier in this book. If your child's school has an active PTA, your child can participate in the **Save for America** campaign. PTA volunteers collect your kids' money, once a week. It is quite similar to the bank day from my childhood.

Save for America volunteers record the deposits on a computer. After all the deposits for the week are recorded, the computer disk and the money collected are taken to the sponsoring bank. 50 percent of all states in the U.S. participate in the program. To get your child's school involved in The School

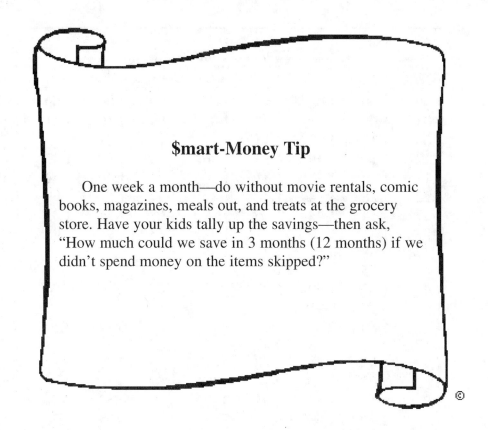

$mart-Money Tip

One week a month—do without movie rentals, comic books, magazines, meals out, and treats at the grocery store. Have your kids tally up the savings—then ask, "How much could we save in 3 months (12 months) if we didn't spend money on the items skipped?"

Savings Program, call 206-746-0331 or write to 4095 173rd Place SE, Bellevue, WA, 98008 for information. Talking to your local bank could also reveal some local school savings programs.

By now your kids should be very involved in their Saving, Sharing and Spending Plans. Hopefully, your kids have saved enough so that it makes sense to open an interest bearing savings account in their names. Emphasize that no additional effort is required on their part to earn interest on their growing deposits. You will soon find that your kids' druthers become growth. As their savings accounts grow, other options become available. One example is investing, which will be covered in a later chapter.

Thanks, But No Thanks . . . Dealing with the Reluctant Saver

What if one (or all) of your kids can't seem to hold on to a single dime. Not to worry, a saver is not born, he is made. We are dealing with learned behavior,

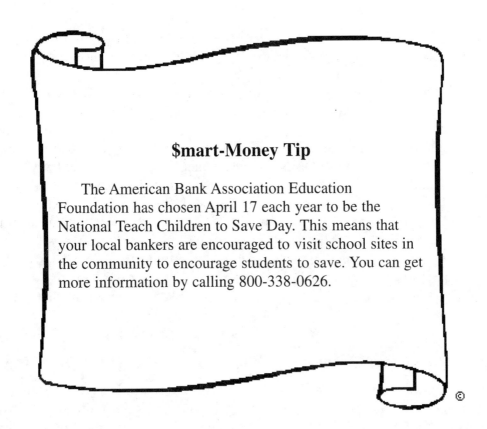

$mart-Money Tip

The American Bank Association Education Foundation has chosen April 17 each year to be the National Teach Children to Save Day. This means that your local bankers are encouraged to visit school sites in the community to encourage students to save. You can get more information by calling 800-338-0626.

not genetics. If money "burns" a hole in your kids pocket and if this kid is fast becoming your biggest accounts receivable (advances against future allowance), find out where the money is going.

There could be some legitimate cash drains such as: friends' or relative's birthday presents or an increase in the cost of school lunches (or his appetite). If your kid is dipping into his savings to meet "unexpected" expenses, investigate sooner, rather than later. He could be having trouble with his budget and some fine-tuning may be in order. Or, he may need to find some additional income sources. I never forget the time Frank came home with the story that bullies were extorting (my word) moneys from the smaller kids during lunch.

If your kid is still operating his savings out of jars, envelopes or piggy banks, temptation may be the real problem. Consider being his personal (in house) banker until the savings ethic is ingrained and money starts accumulating again. Then a less accessible bank account can be opened.

Your kid (and you too) may be very well aware of where all the money is going. All efforts to divert money to savings and out of this spendthrift's hand have failed. Force the issue with these two solution/incentive programs.

- *Payroll deduction* could be a solution that could work for all of you. On payday you withhold an agreed upon percentage from the allowance and bank it. Once the "pot" begins to grow, your son or daughter will hopefully see the merit of "out of sight, out of mind (and circulation)."
- *Your child's 401(k) plan* is a creative incentive plan for the truly reluctant saver. If you aren't familiar with 401(k) plans (or pension plans), here's what to do. You withhold or "deduct from the allowance (payroll)" an agreed upon amount of any income received and match it or a portion of it. This may help your child get on the savings bandwagon at long last. This is one of the things we did when Frank started to invest monthly in mutual funds. He put in so much—I matched it. Not a huge amount (a total of $25 each month), but it was a start.

Opening a Savings Account

You may not find a local bank that caters to children's savings account—fees, balance requirements, etc. may be prohibitive if your child hasn't saved substantial dollars. Your solution, pick up the phone and call The Young Americans Bank 303-321-2265 or write to 311 Steele St., Denver, CO, 80206. Ask them to send information regarding their accounts for kids (Your older kid may also be interested in checking accounts—ask for their full product line).

No matter what bank you select, be sure you understand the bank's rules.

- *Minimum Balance Requirements:* A certain amount is required to open the account, and the future balance may not fall below this amount without severe penalty.
- *Bank Fees:* A monthly or annual service fee deducted from the child's account could exceed the earnings on a small balance account. This is not a good bank for your kids' deposits.
- *Bank Policy:* State banking policies for kids accounts vary from state to state. Signatory regulations can be a problem. As long as your son or daughter can sign their name, deposits and withdrawals should be allowed. You will probably be required to be a co-signer for the

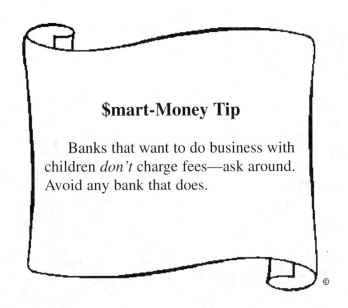

$mart-Money Tip

Banks that want to do business with children *don't* charge fees—ask around. Avoid any bank that does.

account (The Young American Bank I'm a great advocate for is no exception). Additionally, withdrawals could require both signatures (this prevents parents from withdrawing their kids' money without permission) but in some cases, kids can withdraw without their parents' signature.

♦ *Forms and Statements:* Make sure you and your kids sit down together to go over the deposit and withdrawal forms so they know what do with each one. Review carefully the statements and the copies of all the monthly transactions when they are mailed. If either of you don't quite understand them, immediately ask the bank for clarification.

Savings Bonds and You

Savings bonds have been around forever. The two bonds you will use, or consider will be either *EE* or *I bonds*. Both bonds have several items in common—they pay interest for up to 30 years; the interest earned is taxable only on federal tax returns; they are guaranteed; and when you buy them, you don't have to pay a commission or a fee.

EE bonds are sold at discount, meaning that a $100 bond will cost half when first available—$50. As time progresses, it costs a little more because interest has accrued. Savings bonds begin in denominations of $50 up to $10,000. With

$mart-Money Tip

To get the latest information and rates, call the Federal Reserve at 800-234-2931. You can also check out the website *www.savings-bonds.gov.*

today's interest rates, most bonds mature at full value in fifteen years. After that, they will continue to earn interest for another fifteen years. If the bond owner holds any bonds after thirty years, no additional interest will be added. In other words, if you buy series *EE bonds*, cash them in when they mature.

I bonds are fairly new. Created in 1998, they are sold at face, or full, value. These bonds range from $50 to $10,000 just like *EE bonds*. *I bonds* have two types of rates—a fixed rate which is determined when first sold; and an adjustable rate that can change every six months, depending on what inflation does. Because of the adjustment factor and purchasing the bond at a non-discount, *I bonds* will pay a higher rate of return than the *EE bond*.

If you cash your bonds in for educational purposes—college—any interest will be treated as tax-free.

Money Market Funds

At some point, especially when savings accounts hit the $500 mark, it's time to consider a money market fund. The money market fund is purchased through a mutual fund and will usually allow your kids to earn a higher rate of interest than what the bank pays. They are set up the same way you would a custodial account with the same access that you as an adult have. In later chapters, both investing and college planning are discussed. Money market funds are ideal companions to use with both.

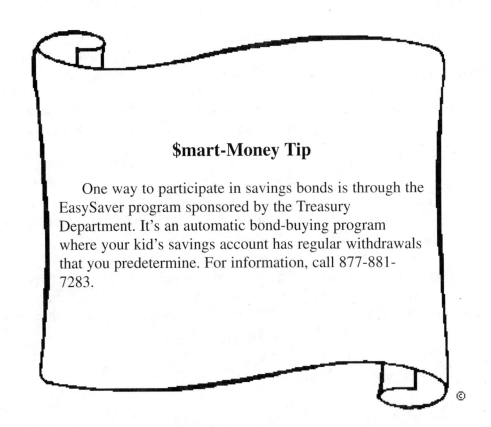

$mart-Money Tip

One way to participate in savings bonds is through the EasySaver program sponsored by the Treasury Department. It's an automatic bond-buying program where your kid's savings account has regular withdrawals that you predetermine. For information, call 877-881-7283.

The Kiddie Tax

Once your daughter or son is one-year-old, apply for a Social Security number. So says the IRS, and we parents comply. Any interest on savings or gains on investment accounts in your child's name will be reported to IRS and will be treated as income for tax purposes. The bitter truth is that kids under the age of 14 with investment income greater than $1500 get taxed at their parent's tax rate rather than their own. Future changes are subject to the whim of Congress.

This amount *doesn't* include the amount you originally deposited or invested. The only tax consideration is the interest earned, dividends or gain on sale from investments (stocks, bonds, mutual funds, etc.). An example: your daughter's savings account earns 4 percent interest annually. In order for her account to incur sufficient interest income that would be taxable, she would have to have a balance of close to $38,000 on deposit to exceed the $1500 investment interest income floor.

If your daughter is 14 or under and earned in excess of $1500, she would be taxed at the Kiddie Tax rate, which is her parents' tax rate rather than her own. If less, check the current tax rates for the appropriate tax. After the age of 14, all income a child earns is taxable at the 15% rate. The reason why the Kiddie Tax came into being was because some parents were hiding their own assets in custodial accounts with their kids' names on them to avoid taxation at their normal tax rate.

Here's the bottom line—no matter how young your kids are, if they exceed the filing threshold mandated by Uncle Sam, a federal tax return must be filed. Be aware that the threshold changes each year. As a rule, it increases each year. It's recommended that you check with your tax advisor for the current amount. The threshold in 2001 was $4,400 or more in wages.

You may be thinking—no big deal, my kids don't work for money . . . they just get interest and dividends. The threshold for non-working earners is $1500 in 2001. If your kids have a combination—earned and non-earned, a federal return must be filed if earned income is $4,200 and unearned (dividends and interest) is $250. (Use IRS Form 8615.)

To Withdraw or Not to Withdraw

Some parents set up accounts for their children and do not permit any withdrawals until the child reaches maturity or college age. Others are more flexible about withdrawals for planned expenditures. If you are a parent who refuses withdrawals, you might want to consider a second savings account that will allow your kids to save for something they want in the more immediate future—a bike, a computer, roller blades, even for Christmas presents. You may lose the kids' interest in saving their money if you make them keep their hands totally off their savings.

You can give yourself a major pat on the back when you succeed in getting your kids going with a regular savings program. You probably are a parent who has seen to it that saving is fun, exciting and rewarding for your child. Success calls for celebration. You can celebrate your success in instilling goals and demonstrating the "how tos" in meeting life's material needs. Your kids can celebrate their disciplined efforts to save more and spend less—they aren't sending so many dollars to "cash heaven" these days.

Chapter Nine

Money Talks Within the Family

When my kids were in the 11 to 15-year-old age range, I did something that made a significant impression on them. It all started when my son told me that his best friend's parents had said that I made a lot money. At the time I was a stockbroker with E.F. Hutton. And yes, there were months when I did make a lot of money. There were also months when I didn't make enough to pay the mortgage.

I tapped into the kids visual resources to make the impression I wanted. Every month that summer, I cashed my paychecks before depositing them. I told the cashier to give me nothing larger than a $100 dollar bill and that I wanted plenty of smaller bills too. When I got home with the cash, I gathered up all the bills that needed to be paid that month.

In June I called a family pow-wow. I told them that I had cashed my paycheck so they could see what "a lot of money" looked like. They were impressed with the size of the stack of currency that was my paycheck. "Wow"—was their reaction to the first $100 dollar bill they had ever seen. Then we got down to business. I laid out the mortgage and car payment coupon books. Bills were laid out for utilities, phone, auto & life insurance, department stores, gasoline—you get the idea.

Next, I dealt out the bills from my "cashed check" like a deck of cards. Each bill was covered with the requisite amount of cash—$1800 to the mortgage, $150 to gas and electricity, $200 for life insurance, $100 for auto insurance,

$300 for health insurance, $150 for gasoline, etc. My kid's eyes were wide with amazement when I finished. I said, "Well there's my paycheck. And, yes I do make a lot of money." They learned a valuable lesson. I had brought a lot of money *in* the door that day, but it would go *out* the door just as quickly.

Most kids have no idea how much it costs their parents each month for just the basics. And, my kids were no different. They couldn't believe that I had laid out several thousand dollars for the *needed* monthly expenses. And, we hadn't yet allocated anything for groceries and allowances, not to mention money for "fun" things.

As you know, paychecks are usually "after tax" dollars. I told the kids that my employer had deducted what I owed for some of my tax "bills" before I got my pay. Their mouths dropped open when I told them that state, federal and Social Security taxes had eaten up almost 40 percent of my gross pay—they had no idea that I had a tax bill to pay before I even got my check. And, I really had a challenge explaining that FICA and Social Security are the same thing—why does one tax have two names?

One of the kids quickly picked up on the fact that not all taxes were deducted from my pay. "What other taxes do you have to pay Mom?" I told them about real estate taxes, sales taxes and special city and county assessments. Some other items for the *Needs* list.

The month of July has always been an interesting month when it came to income. With few exceptions, it is our lowest income month. That July, there was not enough money to cover the basic *Needs*. My kids learned *why* a savings program was critical to us—we drew from savings that month so we could eat and keep our house. This was the first time that they really understood what I meant when I said, "We can't afford it this month"—and that this was, and always had been, a valid statement.

Remember that kids are very visual. Let them see where your money goes by piling it up on each bill you owe, or you can make a card for each bill (don't forget savings, charity and church). This exercise will put your kids light years ahead in their understanding of why spending plans and savings are critical to the successful $mart-Money family.

Frank's Spending Plan, in Chapter Four, is a model you could follow to set up your child's spending plan. When you set up the kids' plans, show them how they fit into the family spending plan—what they cost you for all the Needs, their allowance, family entertainment and so on.

Spending plans should not be set in concrete or etched in stone. They are

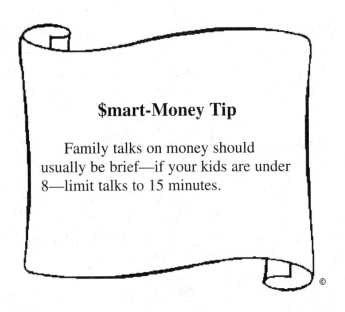

$mart-Money Tip

Family talks on money should usually be brief—if your kids are under 8—limit talks to 15 minutes.

simply guides for using your money. There will be times when you will over-step and others when you won't spend in certain areas at all.

Credit Cards: Friends and Foes

We Americans owe over a trillion dollars in consumer debt. 400 billion of this amount was owed on credit cards alone. The question always comes up—should you use credit cards? I believe that yes you should, but you need to learn how to use them responsibly.

An exercise to use for your kids (especially teens) is to review your credit rating. Get a copy of your credit report—make this an annual ritual. This report will show what you have been doing with your various credit accounts and it will let you know if your credit habits have been reported correctly. Mistakes are not uncommon.

When *Consumer's Report* did a test of the three major reporting agencies, mistakes were plentiful. Almost 40 percent of the files requested had some type of error. Any mistake can cause a potential creditor to turn you down. This isn't good news—it takes months and sometimes years to clean up a credit report.

The Big Three in crediting reporting are Experián (formerly TRW), TransUnion and Equifax. Because of the high error factor, many states have passed laws that state that you have to be informed if negative items or multiple inquiries have been made to your credit profile. If so, you get a copy for free. Otherwise, expect to pay approximately $8. You can request copies in writing, on the phone or online. They will, though, only be sent to you through the mail.

If you have been declined for an account or loan because of an item in your credit report (you must be notified in writing), you have the right to get a free copy up to 60 days from the rejection. If this is the case, immediately get a copy to find out what's been said about your credit payments.

Although this is a book about teaching kids about money, I encourage you to get a copy of your own most recent report. Why? For starters, there's the high probability of an error. It's also a good learning tool for your kids to know about. My kids starting being aware of credit reporting agencies when they were in their mid-teens. Around that time, car buying became a possibility.

For copies of your reports (get one from each), contact:

Experián	TransUnion	Equifax
800-687-7654	800-916-8800	800-685-1111
www.experián.com	*www.transunion.com*	*www.equifax.com*

Your credit report should show the following information for *each* merchant or financial institution that you do business with:

- The name of every credit account you have used and the date the account was opened.
- The type of account and its terms. Past accounts (paid in full and closed) are shown.
- The date of your last payment.
- The credit limit or highest credit balance established.
- The current balance owed.
- Status of your payments—current or past due (past due amounts will be shown as will the number of days overdue—i.e. 30 days, 60, days, etc.) and it will show how many times an account has been paid late.
- Special problems with your account—collection agency involvement, repossession of goods, etc.
- Public records: legal or court actions such as liens, judgments, bankruptcies or foreclosures.

- Your legal relationship to the account: are you individually or jointly responsible, or a cosigner.
- Any statements from you regarding your credit report, such as a disputed balance for faulty goods that have been returned but not taken off your record.

The First Denial

Years ago, my youngest daughter was denied a car loan based on her credit report. The bank told her that she couldn't afford to make the new car payment because she didn't have enough income to cover all the payments she already had plus a new one. In fact, they told her that she had not included all of her credit obligations on her credit application. The industry term for this analysis is called debt ratio—you won't get credit if the creditor concludes that your credit obligations are too high compared to your income.

Initially, Sheryl was puzzled, then she became angry. She knew she had filled out the application correctly and had listed all her credit obligations. Later she obtained of copy of her credit report and found that her older sister's credit file had been mixed up with (merged) with hers. Even some of my accounts showed on her report. The only similarity—we all had the same last name. The bank was right, of course she couldn't handle the credit of two other people beside herself. It took us 6 months to unravel the mess so she could get her car loan.

Kids and Credit

At the age of 16, we introduced our kids to credit. We selected a MasterCard account that wasn't used frequently. On their 16th birthday we notified the company that we wanted to add our child to the account as a valid signer on the account. I have to confess that we experienced mixed results. Shelley was our "clean credit" teenager. Her responsible attitudes about money, which were evident from childhood, continued. She never charged anything she couldn't pay for from her allowance or earnings within 30 days. My son Frank took a pass on using the credit card; he said he just didn't trust himself. My youngest daughter Sheryl could hardly wait to get her own card. And, when she did, she literally ran amok. Within a very few months, her card was confiscated and cut in half and thrown away.

The payment responsibility for the account always remained in my name so

I got the bills each month. This enabled me to monitor what the kids were spending and how they were paying.

If I were to go through this exercise today, here's what I would do:

1. Have my kids build up their savings accounts first.
2. Somewhere between the ages of 14 and 16 (maturity is the key factor here), I would get them a secured-debit card. This card would go against my daughter's account, not mine.
3. If she has her act together, uses the card wisely and grasps the concept of credit, I would assist her in getting an unsecured credit card when she is either 18 or goes to college, whichever comes first. Before you hand over the card, make sure you have set up rules and guidelines on when it is to be used.

The Debit Approach

Another way to introduce your kids to credit is to open a secured account—a debit account tied to a savings account. Here's how this works. You deposit money with the bank or credit card company and this amount is the maximum amount that can be spent by the child using it. The unused money earns interest for you. You have the option of having the charges deducted immediately from the account or a statement can be issued for payment and if payment is not made within the specified time limit, the money owed is deducted from the deposited funds.

Do's and Don'ts of Credit

Stress early and often, that credit card use is real money, as real as the money in their wallet or purse right now. This concept seems to pass over their heads and is not a lesson that is retained for long periods of time. Here are some Credit Card Rules you may want to institute for both you and your kids:

♦ Don't run the credit card to the limit—many kids think they are doing just fine financially, if they still have credit left on their card.
♦ Don't charge what you can't pay for in the next thirty days.
♦ Keep all your receipts in an envelope or box for use in reconciliation

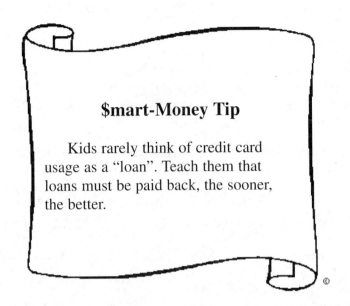

$mart-Money Tip

Kids rarely think of credit card usage as a "loan". Teach them that loans must be paid back, the sooner, the better.

with the monthly statement. Have your child verify that the receipt amount matches the statement—mistakes do happen (You may want to deduct any item not covered by a sales receipt from allowance).

♦ Discourage the habit of paying the minimum payment shown on the statement. If they don't understand why, when the card company has offered this privilege, explain about the interest charged on unpaid balances.

♦ Check your credit report once a year. Reporting errors need to be corrected promptly. In addition, some employers run a credit check on job applicants and do refuse to hire if credit problems are evident.

♦ **Never, Never** let anyone other than named cardholders use the card. Not even if it's the best friend. And, don't let anyone talk you into using the card for something you wouldn't ordinarily buy.

♦ Use the card sparingly for gasoline and food—emergencies only (unless you know for sure, that the balance for these items is paid when the bill arrives).

♦ Use the card for *Needs* not for *Wants* (parental permission or at least discussion required).

♦ Avoid using the card for cash advances. Reconciliation with the statement is hard to do because you rarely have clue where the money went.

Using the Credit Internet

Your teen-agers may be bombarded with offerings for credit cards. That's why the $mart-Money parent must forewarn before the advent happens. If you want to see what's being offered to kids—the high school and college markets, here's a few websites you can check out:

www.bankrate.com is an online publication. It rates the best card deals and will identify low interest rates on cardholders that carry a balance.

www.creditnet.com is the website for Credit Card Network, USA. Use it as a library to tap into for a variety of credit related information.

www.championmortgage.com has a Pay Down Your Debt® and Clean Slate® programs that assist you in controlling debt.

www.thecreditreportsite.com will tell you everything you would possibly want to know about credit, including questions about credit, credit scoring, credit reports and credit repair. Included is a test that determines how you handle credit.

www.firstusa.com is the home page for First USA Bank. It has a special section under Special Features that takes you to Practical Money Skills for Life. Within it are sections for consumers, students, parents and teachers.

A final point that must be emphasized with your card-carrying youngster is that your credit is on the line with them. Kids under 18 aren't issued credit cards without a guarantee from a credit-worthy adult. If your child isn't a "clean cred-it" kid, you won't be either.

Making Money As A Family

Adults make money and kids make money—why not do it as a joint effort? Think about the season. Winter brings Christmas and Hanukkah, which in turns creates gifts. In our house, receiving gifts was a privilege, not a right. We always encouraged our kids to plan on a major clean out of closets, toy boxes and anything that had not been used or played with for the last six months. The clean out also included us. My husband is a pack rat—it's painful for him to part with anything, even if it hasn't been worn in ten years!

With our clean out efforts, twice a year we had a family garage sale in the spring and late fall. Our kids were told that any new toys (and, as they got older, clothes, tapes, sports equipment) would not be added if we didn't see a need—or, for that matter, if items that were in use were either ignored, misused or abused.

Any moneys made from the sales went into the family pot. One year, we all decided that it was time to replace the family room TV. The current one was on its last legs and would most likely fail, beyond repair, within the next month. We checked out which TVs were the best in the latest edition of *Consumer's Report* and determined that the one that we all wanted was about $450.

As a family unit, we all decided that getting a new TV would be the ultimate prize if we were able to sell $450 worth of stuff, and believe me, it was stuff. Because we talked openly about the TV, and the kids knew that it was expensive for the time and that they would enjoy it as much as we would, they jumped in with grand energy in finding stuff to unload the following weekend.

Our outgrown games, toys, skates, old appliances, glasses, dishes—you name it, we tried to sell it. By the time it was over, we passed our goal, bought the new TV and still marvel that it still works seventeen years later. We had one other rule—anything that was put out for the garage sale was not allowed back in the house—it was taken down to the Goodwill the next day. You can also take all the proceeds from your garage sale and make a donation from your entire family—make sure you include your kids' names when the check is given to your favorite cause.

Other ways to make money include making and selling crafts if someone in your family is talented—I have a friend who makes the most amazing wreaths and sprays. Her reputation is so vast that she is considering quitting her day job and turning her talent and hobby into her vocation. Whether your family's skills are knitting, silk flower-making, painting, woodwork, cooking or making dolls, it may bring in money on the side. Someone out there will appreciate what you create.

Teaching kids that others cherish handmade items and are willing to pay for them could create a family project fund. Great places to gather ideas for future projects are charity and church bazaars as well as summer and holiday craft shows that are open to the public.

Another idea that fell into our laps revolved around a function I participated in every Christmas. It was an excellent way to model what we all preach—help others who are not as fortunate as you are. Every December, I participate in the Santa Claus Shop that is sponsored by the YWCA. Throughout the year, items from households and merchants are gathered up for kids who live in the projects to shop from. As a rule, the great majority of the items are new—from socks to soap.

Each child who lives in the designated housing project is invited to our "shop" where he or she could select any one gift for each adult who resides in the household. The chosen gifts are then wrapped and tagged and taken home. As a bonus, each left with a treat just for her or him.

One of my favorite times was when a little boy decided that the perfect gift for his mom was the earrings I was wearing. I took them off and we selected the perfect wrapping paper. He was thrilled, and so was I.

When Frank was six, he went with me to the Santa Claus Shop. I have to confess that he was a tad intimidated by some of the kids—they looked rough and were downright filthy. Soon he was into the swing of things, helping other kids find presents for their mom or dad. He learned an important lesson—not everyone has a clean bed of his own or gets pizza on Friday nights. Today, Frank saves duplicate toys that he receives for the kids who have less than he does.

Keeping Birthdays and Holidays in Perspective

The "gimmes" are a viral disease during the holidays and most kids catch them. This should be no surprise. The commercial barrage blitzes your kids for months prior to the event. The competition for your kids' attention is fierce and myriad and for the gifting dollar spent on them. Kids have a terrible time deciding what treasure(s) they really want.

The big day arrives and you hear something like this: "Why did Grandma get me this? I don't want it (or like it)." It's not always easy to return unwanted gifts. There can be hurt feelings (the givers). The supplying store may not be accessible. The gift may have been bought on sale or is otherwise not accepted as a return.

A few years ago, everyone in our family signed up on the family "Wish Lists." All could review the list for an affordable choice to give to each of the other family members. Did we get every item we wanted? Of course not, but at least a few wishes came true for each of us. Now, the lists are started up in the summer—those of us who are past 50 in our family find that we forget more. My daughter Shelley keeps the master list on her computer now and e-mails updates to family members when a change has been made.

JB's Wish List

Wooden spoons	Bowls	Pat Conway books
Black pants	Bette Midler CD	Purple napkins
Cell phone	Running outfit	Big steak knives

Catalogs presented another technique—they are abundant in the months prior to the holidays. Don't trash them, pile them up for a while and let each family member select one or two. Kids can circle the items they are interested in or they can cut them out and paste them on a poster board. Guaranteed, there will be a lot of circling or cutting. If your daughter can read the prices, have her select several items from different price ranges. The purpose is to give you (and Grandma too) some idea of what will really please them and also meets your spending plan requirements.

Gifts purchased via catalog order have two pluses going—they are generally returnable, no questions asked and if you are not satisfied, you can contact the credit card company you used and lodge a complaint for faulty merchandise, etc. The credit card folks must check anything out that you dispute.

As kids get a little older, they are more discriminate about gifts. Preschoolers want everything they see and they see something new nearly every day. Older

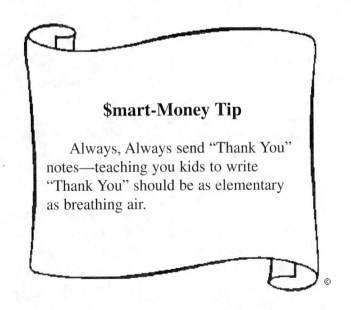

$mart-Money Tip

Always, Always send "Thank You" notes—teaching you kids to write "Thank You" should be as elementary as breathing air.

kids are blessedly more specific. That's the upside. The downside is that their taste is almost always more expensive.

We have all heard the saying that "It's better to give than to receive." Unfortunately, the focus for giving during the holidays is often on family and friends and not on those less fortunate. This recalls a time in my friend John's life. He would soon pass the big 50th birthday. He and his family were happily planning a big "to-do" to celebrate the event. Each year his family had adopted a less fortunate family, one that had experienced many setbacks and heartaches. They were truly happy in their giving to others.

Just before invitations were to be issued for the party, a local family with four young children was burned out of their home and everything was destroyed. The invitations included a copy of the newspaper story about this family that detailed the family's plight. A note was attached requesting that the attendees bring a gift for one of this family's members. No birthday gifts for John would be allowed.

What a party it was! Mounds of gifts arrived for every member of the needy family. Toys, clothing, housewares—many brought more than one gift. The biggest thrill for John, however, was his own children's enthusiastic response to a giving, rather than receiving, event. John believes that he reinforced the giving philosophy in his children, and that he introduced it to many at the party.

Kids Love Cash

Gifts of cash, checks and gift certificates are becoming more and more common. Once kids pass the 12-year-old mark, friends and relatives are not sure what CD is the right CD. Many wise parents set up a college fund savings account for their children and they encourage the primary cash givers, Grandma and Grandpa, to designate that at least a portion be put in this account. Your son may disagree and feel that he should get to use all of his gift money as he pleases. If he's over ten, here's you opportunity to talk to him about the cost of college.

What happens if your kids are blessed with two sets of grandparents, and one set gifts the kids beyond all common sense and the other does not? Granted, kids can be materialistic little animals at times. They may be confused by the apparent financial limitations of the one set of grandparents. You must step in to make sure they don't confuse love with money. Help them recall the quality time spent with each set of grandparents.

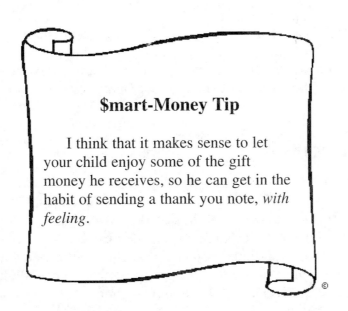

$mart-Money Tip

I think that it makes sense to let your child enjoy some of the gift money he receives, so he can get in the habit of sending a thank you note, *with feeling*.

The Wrong Gift

When your kids receive gifts that you don't approve of, silence doesn't work. You must speak up. Try to anticipate the possibility of this problem with family and close friends by offering suggestions, when asked of course. But should you be surprised by a gift that is on your "outlawed" list, let the giver know your feelings. Don't be afraid to have your son present when you speak up. It's wise to offer some alternatives to the giver and the receiver. You might say something like this: "We appreciate your generous gift, but we don't allow guns in our home. We can take it to the store and exchange it or your can. Billy, what would you like to exchange the gun for?"

Years ago, I was on an airplane returning from a business trip to New York. My daughter Sheryl was with me. We rented the earphones and settled in to watch the airline movie selection—*A Christmas Story*. The movie was based on a book called *In God We Trust, All Others Pay Cash*. It was about a little boy whose Christmas dream toy was a double action, sooper-dooper rifle he had heard about on his favorite radio show. We laughed for the next two hours. The hero of the movie, Ralphie (age 10) receives a big box from his Auntie for Christmas. The pink bunny outfit inside the box was definitely not a fit for Ralphie (may be for a 4-year- old?).

What do you do with the gifts that are the wrong fit for your child? This happens more and more often after the age of 10. The quickest and easiest answer to try to prompt the giver of such a gift. Encourage dialogue with friends and relatives on the subject. Sometimes, you simply don't have a clue what will satisfy an emerging teen. A gift certificate could fit to a tee. Last year, Frank got gift certificates to Old Navy, Blockbuster, and Barnes & Noble—he was a happy camper.

Down Sizing is Bad News

This past decade has dramatic changes in the workforce. During the first part of the nineties, millions of hard working men and women lost the jobs through downsizing. During the latter part of the decade, downsizing was downsized and expansion was abundant. Who knows what the next century will bring to the American economy? If you find that you are caught in one of the downturns (the news is full of companies who have cut their workforce when all the economic news is good), the family belt will have to be tightened up.

It's rare that a layoff or firing comes out of the blue. There is usually at least one warning bell that rings in your ear. The question is not, do you let your family know that financial problems will be coming to live with you. It is, rather, how do you let them know? Tell them the truth, and only to the degree that the child can understand at his respective age. And do it sooner, not later. Your kids will sense your tension and know that something is going on. Perhaps you can draw on the story recounted earlier in this book of my family's experience with bad news.

When cutbacks in spending are the inevitable choice, revisit the *Wants* and *Needs* lists. Kids need to know at this time that they won't be destitute, but the *Wants* list will definitely be a non-dietary item in family menu for a while. Reassure them that the *Needs will be addressed.* Your kids will be provided with food, shelter, warmth and clothing. The quantity and quality may downsize but you *will* weather the storm together.

Divorce: Putting the Gloves Down

Research shows that most parents don't go through divorce well. Some parents behave rather badly when they are involved the "divorce process" and sometimes continue these behaviors long after the final decree. The reasons: immaturity, mental illness, or a down right mean spirited nature. A divorce takes two to tango, and there are almost always two valid sides to the stories kids can't help but overhear.

144

$mart-Money Tip

Kids are almost psychic—they can "feel" when there is bad news in the air. It's Family Meeting Time.

Kids are often caught in the middle and witness hostile adult transactions that sometimes escalate into physical violence. In many cases the child is given a secret agent spy mission when visiting the "other" parent. And if this roughed-up child hasn't been through enough, he is used to carry messages (some not so subtle) that convey a thought the sending parent is too lazy or afraid to communicate on their own.

In the event of re-marriage, jealousy or angry reactions to the ex's new spouse may involve the child in an interrogation session when he arrives home from a visit. Interrogation leads to unhealthy secretiveness in the poor youngster. These kids are the middle of a battle, and they have no weapons to win the war.

For the Children of Divorce

In 1998, *The Dollars and Sense of Divorce* (Dearborn Financial Publishing) was released. This book looks at divorce strategies before, during and post divorce. It has several excellent sections in dealing with kids. My co-authors Carol Ann Wilson (the founder of the Institute of Certified Divorce Planners) and Edwin Schilling (an attorney specializing in pension distributions) feel strongly that this book will be a major guide through some of the treacherous divorce waters. *If you are going through, or contemplating a divorce, get a copy today.*

One of your goals as a parent is to pave the dialogue road for your kids, to get them really to talk about their needs. You must weed out all the personal issues that resulted in the divorce and focus on your kids. It's hard, I know—I've been there.

In custody battles, kids often become a commodity. They are used as bargaining chips in the battles that still are going on with their parents. Consider putting together a contract with your ex. All agreements, are drafted in behalf of the children, are signed by both parents. They can be filed with the court and later used as the basis for sorting out future disputes between the parents. Kids are rarely served well when you have a judge deciding their fate—too many horror stories surface that scream to parents to get their acts together. The marriage may be over, but the kids aren't.

Any agreement put together should identify these specifics: your kids' names, age and gender, their permanent place of residency and it's physical address (for joint custody, the times of residency are defined), and the individual parental responsibilities. These include:

- Decisions that are not covered in the agreement are covered by defining which parent has the ongoing decision making rights and responsibilities (sometimes this will be joint) for such areas as: communication between parents—when, where and how; who will pay for and choose lessons, vacations, health care, transpiration, and education; how undefined visitation periods will be handled.
- Who will care for the kids when the custodial parent has to be away and if, the "other" parent is to be advised of this temporary change in custodial care.
- Generally speaking, any illness and injury require that the other parent receive prompt notice.
- Information flow between parents regarding school: grades, special events, teacher's conferences.
- Arbitration of differences in opinions where the parents are either unwilling or unable to resolve on their own. Often times other professionals are identified that can be called upon for assistance in resolving such disagreements.

Telling Your Kids

One of the key sections in *The Dollars and Sense of Divorce* created a dialogue to use when telling your kids that the big "D" is upon them. Below is a segment that will be helpful to start it off:

You are still a family, one this is undergoing changes. There are several important things to get across at this critical first meeting when you first tell your kids. Ideally, both you and your spouse should be there when you have it. I know that this is not always possible, you and your spouse may find it impossible to be within 50 feet of each other, or your spouse has vacated the family residence suddenly. If either has occurred, you get the honors to set the stage. How you do it will impact your kids, and yourself, for years to come.

First, tell them that each of you still loves them and second, that they are not responsible *in any way* for the divorce. There will be lots of questions, usually starting with "Why?" They will wonder where they will live, with whom, what about their friends, even their toys. This first meeting can go something like this:

You   Your Dad (or Mom) and I have spent a lot of time talking about us. We have decided not to live together anymore. That doesn't mean that we don't love you, we do, very much. It doesn't mean that we don't want to be with you, and we will. It means that we will always be your Mom and Dad, no one else can take that from you. And that there will always be a room (space) for each of you in the homes we live in.

Your Spouse   Your Mom (or I) will be staying in this house until we decide what to do—either stay here (kids will vote for this) or sell it and both of us will get a different place to live. What ever we decide, we will include you so that you will not be uncertain of what is going on. There will be room for whatever things you want to keep at each place and you can decorate or put up posters and your stuff within your room.

Each of us wants to participate in school activities. We will be checking with the school. Please let us know what is going on so that we can both keep time free for any activities that you want us to attend. If you need help on homework, we both want to help. I'll call (or your Mom) each night to check in. You can always call me (or Mom) for help or with questions.

You   We know that this may surprise and hurt you. We aren't doing this to be mean. It just isn't working with us now. We tried to work out our differences. We are sorry. We will work out how time will be spent, when stay-overs occur and the details of where you will spend most of your time when not in school.

Note—if your kids are very young, input from them is probably not going to be solicited. If your kids are past 10, they are often cemented in their neighborhoods; if in teens, their activities focus around school—the last thing that they will want is to be uprooted and moved to another school.

Your Spouse   Mom (or Dad) and I are figuring out which special days and Holidays we split, and which ones we will share. There will be times when we will all be at the same event, like at school nights. We want you to still have your friends and to know that your grandparents and other relatives will always be there for you.

You   We know you have lots of questions. You can ask us together, or you can talk to either of us later. Please remember that we love you and will do what ever we need to do to help you through this.

The "talk" is a huge step. Believe me, your kids are not going to hear everything you have so carefully said. Expect them to have their own "rump" meeting after your talk. Make sure that you get across that they are not to blame, where they will live and with which parent, where their other parent will be living, when will this all happen, what changes should they expect and how will everyone communicate.

Here's the bottom line—you, dear Mom and Dad have just shattered their world. It doesn't matter that it's been a war zone (at least in your view), it was their zone too. You must talk with and to them.

Therapy: Help for the Pain

If divorce is a part of your life or in the offing, it can be difficult to look carefully at the next few days, let alone the next weeks and years. But, your kids will need lots of love and your respect in taking care of their near term needs and wants. If you are having trouble during the divorce process, being the good parent you used to be—get help for yourself and your kids through counseling now.

Excellent counseling can be free or low cost through your church and other agencies. Get all the information you can about organizations that are specifically for single parents, children of divorce and the like. Your involvement in such groups will help you and your child outgrow the pain and suffering caused by divorce.

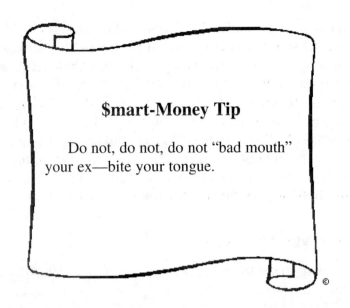

$mart-Money Tip

Do not, do not, do not "bad mouth"
your ex—bite your tongue.

Avoid Good Guy . . . Bad Guy

Your kids love *and* need both their parents, and have fierce loyalties to both. Kids will, and can, make their own decisions in time about who is the "good guy and who is the "bad guy". Most parents (this includes your ex) do the best they can with the resources they have available at the time. Avoid appointing yourself judge and jury. And, if you are caught in the middle of a "buying the child's love" scenario, don't join in. Granted, children's loyalties can be swayed at times by gifts and special outings. But remember—you are after long term results. The "Disneyland" parent is usually a short term situation. Grin and bear it and tell the child that he is lucky that his "other" parent is so generous.

Revisit Your Spending Plan

The financial demands on the divorced/custodial parent are tough. And, they are often made more difficult when support payments don't come on a regular basis. There are remedies for late payment of support through legal action that will not be covered here. What is covered, is the need for straightforward talks with your kids about this new financial environment that has resulted from the divorce.

Carefully go over the new spending plan with your kids. They need to know why things can't be like they used to be, and further, that you are really doing the best you can under the circumstances. Invite them to brainstorm with you.

Do they have ideas that can make the new spending plan more livable for all; can they be more helpful to you in making it a success? It's amazing how kids can pitch in—they have to be included, up front, for enhanced success.

Establish good communication with your ex—it's hard, but critical. Unfortunately, children master the art of manipulation quickly and divorce brings this talent out in a big way. They play on the guilt of both parents, and use it to get things that are definitely *Wants* and not *Needs*. Talking to the other parent will reveal their little plots and put an end to efforts to get you on the materialistic bandwagon. Quality time spent with the kids is the answer. Talk with your ex and establish routine allocations of this quality time that work for both of you.

Blended Families: Play No Favorites

Remarried parents have to guard against the "Cinderella " syndrome. Put simply, this is playing favorites with your children, to the detriment of newly acquired stepchildren. First your have to be sure that you are not afflicted with this child damaging illness. Then you have to deal with the relatives and friends on both sides. Let them know how important the new stepchildren are to both you and your new spouse. Make your "fairness" guidelines clear to them, and stick to your position when holidays and birthdays roll around.

Other Books to Help

There are a variety of books about divorce and the children of divorce. One of the classics is *Mom's House, Dad's House: Making Shared Custody Work* (Simon & Schuster) by Isolina Ricci. Add this one to your bookshelf. Another, *Surveying the Breakup: How Parents and Children Cope with the Divorce* (Ticknor & Fields) by Judith Wallerstein and Joan Berlin Kelly offers excellent advice. Two other books that can be helpful: one is *A Guide to Divorce Mediation* (Workman) by Gary Friedman, an excellent resource that will reduce the costs and get communication back on track; the other is mine, *The Dollars and Sense of Divorce* (Dearborn Financial Publishing) which looks at the reality of divorce and outlines what planning needs to occur before, during and after.

Cutting the Purse Strings

Nicole is one of my closest friends. I told you about her in the section on wills when she wanted a painting hanging in my kitchen. When her daughter was a junior at a west-coast university, she got a message at her office. "Mom can you fax me some food?" My friend's first reaction was amusement—this kid has a sense of humor. Then, the mother in her became alarmed. She called for the details behind the message. Her daughter said she had *no money for food*. This didn't make sense to Nicole. They had spent a lot of time on her college budget and there was more than enough in it to cover her basic needs. Truth will out, Jessica had been downtown shopping, and she just couldn't resist a sweater she found. The price tag—$100.

Like mother, like daughter—they both had expensive taste in clothes, so Nicole understood the enticement of a beautiful sweater. On the other hand, Nicole was angry. The sweater was not a budget item. Wise mother that she is, she offered two choices, "Take the sweater back for a refund, or eat it."

Jessica responded creatively. She took the sweater back and put it on layaway. She found another option. She got a partial refund, ate that month and got the sweater, two months later. A case of you can't have your sweater and eat it too!

Jessica was convinced that her mother would respond to her message with wired money to cover her need for food immediately. And, Nicole almost did. Nicole told her secretary that if Jessica called over the next two days, tell her that her mother was "out." She made a big step by saying "No" and cutting the purse strings. Kids often think that their parents have a bottomless pit of money and in some cases they are right. And, like Jessica, they have lapses of memory on the definition of *Needs* and *Wants*.

Save yourself some headaches and heartaches and make sure that you have equipped your teen with experience in: checking and savings accounts, record keeping and the balancing of same, credit cards, spending plans, all the things we have discussed in previous chapters. And, if you will soon have a college age youngster, take the time to go over new spending items: dorm or apartment rental, furnishings for the new residential situation, how phone calls to home will be handled (a calling card or an 800 number or special teen billing programs with one of the many phone companies are good solutions), how often you can afford the cost of travel to come home, etc. More on this in a later chapter.

When you begin to cut the purse strings, your child will be on the path to adulthood. Good for them and Bravo for you.

Chapter Ten

*Collecting 101—
Turning Junk
Into Money*

Besides being female, it tickles me to think that I actually have something in common with Elizabeth Taylor. Granted, Elizabeth Taylor's name is synonymous with multiple husbands and diamonds (no, that's not what I have in common with her!). There is another facet to this fascinating woman and her love interests—she just loves collectibles and she's into them in a big way. And so do I and the things that I love are many. But I am particularly interested in collecting things that have a history behind them.

My penchant for collecting first surfaced when I was just a kid. I admit, I was, and I still am a "pack rat." I don't know what started me off, but I passed this "pack rat" passion on to both of my daughters. The newest, A-1 pack rat, is my grandson. Frank has displayed exceptional potential, which makes me wonder, is it genetic or learned?

How about you and how about your kids? Is your daughter's room jammed with dolls, i.e. Barbie and your son's with comic books and baseball cards? Are they unable to part with the toys of their infancy and toddler years? Yes? Welcome then, like it or not, to the collectible club.

There's an old adage that if you keep something long enough, it will come back in style. Your childhood toys and some of your older kid's toys are "sought after" items because Americans are in love with nostalgia. When the nostalgia bug bites both adults and children, collecting begins with those loved and coveted things from childhood. What's hot today, will most likely be the hot collectible, 30 to 40 years from now.

When you absolutely can't stand the overpopulated condition of your kids' room and you tell them that *a lot has to go* (to the trash or Goodwill), think again. They may be hoarding the beginning of a collection that will appreciate in value over the years if they keep it. My parents did everything they could to discourage me from collecting. At the age of 6, I discovered comic books; you name it, I had it. Hundreds of comics filled every corner of my bedroom—Superman, Super Boy, Archie, Casper, Little LuLu and Nancy to name a few.

I had three brothers and was therefore more of a rough and tumble little girl; dolls were never a priority. But, an aunt gave me a Madame Alexander storybook doll, and I was enchanted. These dolls have a wonderful porcelain quality to them, perfectly coifed hair and exquisite period and ethnic clothing. They were not dolls to be played with, they didn't talk, cry or wet; they weren't meant for cuddling or taking to bed. They were meant to be looked at and collected. My aunt gave me more, one for each birthday and each Christmas. Over the years, my collection of these dolls became quite extensive.

When I married, my mother cleaned out my room. My collection of comic books and Madame Alexander dolls were discarded. Those comic books that originally cost 10¢ and the dolls that cost $10 would be worth thousands of dollars in today's collectible marketplace.

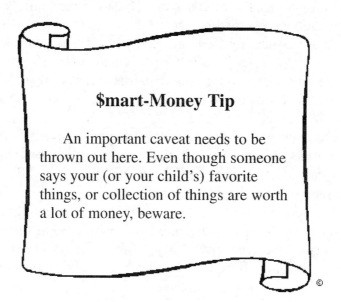

$mart-Money Tip

An important caveat needs to be thrown out here. Even though someone says your (or your child's) favorite things, or collection of things are worth a lot of money, beware.

Prices quoted on collectibles by a dealer are rarely the reality when you wish to sell your treasures. When selling collectibles, from comic books to fine antique furniture, it's a buyers market. It's like the spread in the price of a stock on the stock market, the bid and the ask. As a buyer, you usually pay on the high "ask" end; as a seller you receive the low "bid" end. To sell your beloved stuff, someone has to love/want it more than you do . . . it's that simple.

Be a Discriminating Collector

If you have a child that has shown signs of being a "pack rat" and seems to have potential as a collector, help him develop good collection skills. For example, if you have a sports enthusiast under your roof, one the many types of sports figure cards could be the choice. Is there money to made here? You Bet! The most famous baseball card is the 1910 Honus Wagner trading card from Sweet Caporal cigarette packages. Wagner demanded that his photo be removed from trading cards, because he was a non-smoker and didn't want to support the tobacco companies. A man truly ahead of his time!

In 1986, when I first looked at the value of the 1910 Pittsburgh Pirate Wagner card, it was worth a staggering $25,000. In the nineties, the price tag on this card rose to more than ten times that amount. If you can find a mint condition Honus Wagner card, expect to fork over $300,000 to buy it.

What about cards depicting some of the more contemporary sports figures like Michael Jordan, Joe Montana, Mickey Mantle or current slugger stars Mark McGwire, Barry Bonds and Sammy Sosa?—they all have value. In 1995, Mickey Mantle died. Before his death, a 1952 Topp Bubble Gum #311 card, in mint condition, was valued at $30,000! It will only continue to increase in value.

Marvel's Overkill

A few years ago, Marvel Comics decided that they were going to "kill" Superman. There was a lot of press concerning the impending death. Collectors/ investors lined up at comic book outlets to get the final issue that would recount the dastardly deed. The demand was so intense, that Marvel comics went back to press for this issue 7 times. As a result, the anticipated appreciation in value of this issue is not going to be great because too many copies were distributed. Collectible pricing, responds first to buyer interest and then to availability. Buyer interest in Superman's death declined and will remain depressed due to the great quantity printed. The first printing has some added value, but subse-

155

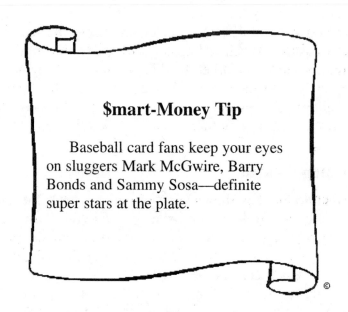

$mart-Money Tip

Baseball card fans keep your eyes on sluggers Mark McGwire, Barry Bonds and Sammy Sosa—definite super stars at the plate.

quent issues could be purchased today at the original newsstand price for the comic book.

Movies and Music Yield More than Entertainment

When the movie industry and fast food chains found each other it was love at first sight, and it's now a marriage made in heaven for them and their progeny—your child. Kids' meals at fast food operations come with a toy in the sack or box that is most usually oriented to a kid movie that was recently released. Those toys and the box, if applicable, are collector's items. Why?—most people toss them.

Do your kids love music? CD's and audio tapes they all know, but they won't recognize an LP or 33-1/3 or 78 record. Those old records in your (or your Mom's) attic are gathering dust. A kid who is a music buff, could embark on terrific collection. Truly a groovy way to make a buck. A Beatles recording sold originally in 1960 for $1, now is worth several hundred dollars—worth even more with the sleeve or jacket it came in.

In 1956, country and western singer, Jim Reeves, made his first album under the Abbott label and it sold for $3. It's value today is over $1000, if you can find copy of it. Then there are those records that were never released to the stores. They have more value than those that were released do.

Have your music buff collector keep his eagle eye out for special release or promotional CD's, audio tapes and records that are usually distributed only to

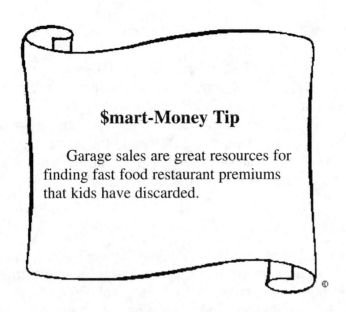

$mart-Money Tip

Garage sales are great resources for finding fast food restaurant premiums that kids have discarded.

DJ's. These are worth far more than the subsequent public releases. Movie sound tracks are also popular choices: i.e. *The Caine Mutiny,* the Humphrey Bogart movie track is worth over $10,000.

Action Figures are Where the Action Is

The first action figures for boys were the GI Joe series. These figures are so popular that there is a GI Joe guide to the value for each figure that has come out over the many years they have been around. Tomart Publications produces a series of guides for many action figure collectibles. Their version for GI Joe is called *Tomart's Guide to GI Joe Collectibles.*

Other action figures, primarily made to interest boys, have taken the throne from old Joe—Batman, The X-Men, Power Rangers, Ninja Turtles, Aliens, Star Wars and Star Trek and the like. Figures from Star Trek, The Next Generation disappeared overnight from store shelves, when they were first introduced. Each figure is imprinted with it's own serial number denoting the date of manufacture. The most popular Ninja Turtle figure was not one of the four Turtles, but is the lone female of the series, reporter April O'Neil—very few were made of her.

The most famous female collectible is, of course, Barbie. Barbie is 50 years old now. Collectors prefer that these toys remain in their original packaging—to your kids this means hands off. Barbie dolls sell for $6 to $30 each, today.

Remember the brouhaha about Barbie and math a few years ago? Mattel created the Teen Talk Barbie series—Barbie speaks. And, what she spoke about upset a lot of parents. The "Math-is-hard" line of dolls was immediately yanked from toy store shelves, when parents (and the media) complained. That small boo-boo in a popular line became a collectible overnight.

Encourage your collector kids to look for toy lines that are popular and for a line that has figures that are slightly different. In the Barbie line, you are more likely to find more dolls that are blondes. The Barbie with hair, other than blond, will be worth more as a collectible.

Beanie Mania

In 1997, Teresa Cheung started collecting Beanie Babies, a plush-toy phenomenon that took the country by storm. She went a step further than most parents and created a computer program for collectors of Beanie Babies, Teenie Babies, Beanie Buddies and other plush-toy collectibles. Her website *www.bejeanie.com* earned the Best of 98 award from Computer Journal magazine and received a five-star rating by ZDNet. Some Beanie Babies sell for $6, others for thousands. If your kids are caught up in the Beanie Babies craze (or you), the *www.bejeanie.com* site is the site to go to. It's bright and colorful, loaded with information (history, books, magazines, other Web links, where to buy and sell and pricing).

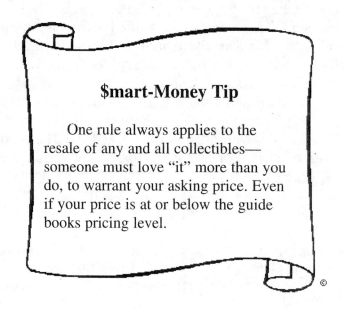

$mart-Money Tip

One rule always applies to the resale of any and all collectibles—someone must love "it" more than you do, to warrant your asking price. Even if your price is at or below the guide books pricing level.

Identifying Trends for the Future

- *Nostalgia Counts.* Adult collectors of toys focus, because of the nostalgic value to them, on toys from their childhood years and target ages 7 to 10. Collectors say that a bench mark for a collectible is that it must be at least 20 years old. So pay sharp attention to what your 7 to 10-year- old likes the most and help him or her focus on that toy line. And then, get the boxes and attic space ready for the 20-year wait.

- *Collect with Your Kids.* I almost fell over laughing when my brother told me he had just built a shelf for his Beanie Baby collection. He had the last laugh. His daughter had started the collection and he joined in. Some Beanies are worth thousands of dollars. They both laughed last.

- *Your Collector Kids Will Have to Treat Their Toys Carefully.* If they want to realize the best value from them later, as collectibles. And do keep the boxes these toys come in. Grandson Frank sold his six Power Ranger figures, even though he had played with them. He had kept the boxes. A year later, he garnered a lot more for them than they originally cost. For Frank, Power Rangers were passé, but the new bills in his pocket weren't.

- *Movies and TV Count.* Consider Walt Disney for a partner to your collector kid. Mega millions are put into commercial tie-ins. Collectors refer to it as Disneyana (any items that relate to one of Disney's theme parks or characters). And yes, millions of these toys and figurines are produced. They seem to just disappear. So have your kid pick up one, or two of each promotional series that comes out. Let him play with one of each and you put the others away as a nest egg for him. He can, of course, review his collection at any time, but back in the box they go when he's through.

- *Collect What They Love.* Collecting should be fun and not laborious for your daughter. Have her tell you what she really would like to collect and then help her to get a complete set if what she loves is a series, or has different models and types. Once the collecting bug bites, you will have a struggle at times convincing her that all toys are not collectibles.

Some definitely should make a trip to the flea market or the trash when she outgrows the desire to play with them or continue the collection.

Getting Info

Once the collecting bug hits, it's $mart-Money to increase your learning curve. Here are a few places to probe:

Let the TV Be Your Friend and Guide. When you tune into collecting, you will find that there are TV shows dedicated to it. A good one is the *Antiques Roadshow* on PBS. Where ever the show is airing, locals bring in their treasures and have the experts appraise them on air. Some times, a real jewel is uncovered; other times, it's just junk. A spin-off is the *Antiques Roadshow Jr.* for kids. Same thing—the local kids bring in their loot—some of it valuable, some of it just a cherished toy or just junk.

Hit the Antique Stores. This is a great time to check out prices. Most dealers negotiate some. The real purpose is to see what's being displayed and how much is the going rate. It's also a great place to ask dealers what's hot, and not so hot.

The Internet. Who would have thought just a few years ago that the thing called the Internet would be the source of millions of little businesses? Some of those businesses sell antiques and collectibles. One of the things that I collect is first edition books. Just a few weeks ago, I found an edition that I have hunted for a long time. I made a bid and won. Even the Goodwill has discovered the Internet. Their website *www.Shopgoodwill.com* has enabled the organization to raise more money for items sold on the Internet than in their stores. This all started when some of their items were sold through the *www.eBay.com* site and fetched ten to thirty times what the store would yield. The Goodwill website could open the door to some great buys.

Another website that will be quite helpful is *www.kovels.com*, the Internet home base for collector gurus Ralph and Terry Kovel. They can give you online advice, price check and a variety of other information . . . all available at your fingertips.

You will find that there are collector clubs dedicated to specific toys (like Barbie) and there are sites that handle just about everything (*www.eBay.com* is

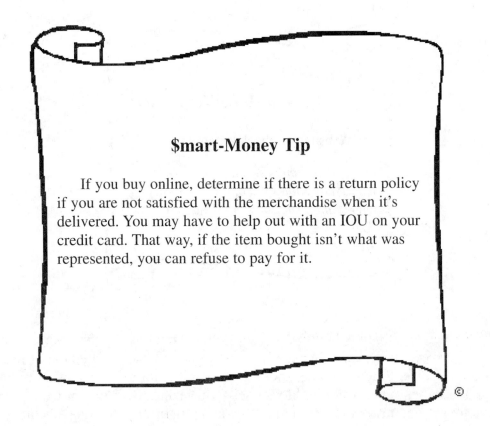

$mart-Money Tip

If you buy online, determine if there is a return policy if you are not satisfied with the merchandise when it's delivered. You may have to help out with an IOU on your credit card. That way, if the item bought isn't what was represented, you can refuse to pay for it.

one). The best way to start your search is either have the site address or just starting typing in words (i.e. Barbie, Beanie Babies, Furbys, etc.).

Hobby and comic book stores often carry published guides that serve as a starting point for you and your kids to determine the value of your collectibles. Book stores, both independents and the biggies—Barnes & Noble, Borders and Amazon.com all have collector guides that are revised on an ongoing basis. Another source, of course, is the public library.

Where to Start

Encourage your kids to have fun with their collections and buy what they can afford. If your kids could care less, then let them be, collecting may not be their cup of tea (but, perhaps yours?). Collectibles can be just about anything. As your kids become teens, the stuff they have an interest may be quite similar to what you would—don't be surprised if Gramma's Blue Willow dish set seeds a long term affair with dishes!

$mart-Money Tip

Websites to check out are:

www.eBay.com (eBay),
www.Shopgoodwill.com, (Goodwill)
www.YahooAuction.com (Yahoo!)

So, here goes. Think buttons, badges, political buttons, toy cars, comics, anything Disney, puzzles, Pez dispensers (Jerry Seinfeld had a collection of these), Beanie Babies, Barbie, GI Joe, sports memorabilia, trains, magazines (my husband has a set of the Amazing Stories sci-fi magazines from the thirties), premium toys from fast food restaurants, ceramic figurines, holiday decorations, miniatures, movie tracks, movie posters, records (I have lots of the 45s of the sixties) etc., etc. Your (and your kids) range of possibilities is almost endless!

$mart-Money Resource Center

- *Tomart Publications* put out a series of guides, and the range of collectible types referenced is vast. Some of their published titles include:

  Tomart's Price Guide to Action Figure Collectibles by Carol Markowski, Bill Sikora and T.N. Tumbusch. Covers most action figures. In addition, there are separate guides dedicated to specific figures, such as GI Joe.

  Tomart's Price Guide to Golden Book Collectibles by Rebecca Greason. Did you know that those little books from your childhood are worth money now? They certainly are. Learn more by reading.

  Tomart's Price Guide to Hot Wheels Collectibles by Michael Strauss. Hot Wheels are still hot—this guide let you know just how hot they are.

  Tomart's Price Guide to Character and Promotional Glasses by Carol and Gene Markowski. Tells you all you need to know about all the glasses from the fast food/movie tie-in promotions that are multiplying in your cupboard.

- *The Collector's Guide to Baseball Cards* by Troy Kirk (Wallace-Homestead Book Company) tells baseball collectors everything they need to know.

- *The Collector's Guide to Autographs* by George Sanders, Helen Sanders and Ralph Roberts (Wallace-Homestead Book Company) is the perfect guide for autograph seeker of the famous and not so famous.

- *The World of Barbie Dolls: An Illustrated Value Guide* by Ferris and Susan Manos (Collectors Books) belongs on the bookshelf of the Barbie devotee.

- *Comics Values Monthly* (Attic Books, Ltd.) is the perfect partner for the comic book aficionado.

Internet

www.kovels.com One of two all purpose websites. This one is hosted by Terry and Ralph Kovel and gives online advice and information on a vast array of antiques and collectibles.

www.tomart.com The other website that carries just about everything that you need to know about the toys filling your kids (and maybe your) rooms.

Part Three

The Teen Years

Chapter Eleven

Caution . . .
Teens at Work

Unless you are a rarity, the years of parenting a teenage are likely to be played out in the survival of the fittest mode. Teens have youth, and the resultant boundless energy in their corner. Often it seems that they are certainly more fit for the match than their parents. If the foundations laid in the previous years have been effective you can, with faith and a humorous outlook, survive the teen years and win at least a Pyrrhic victory or two.

A major concern as a parent is to rear your children in a way that assures you that they will be self-reliant adults one day. Strange as is may seem, teens have the same goal. So, in the teen years their efforts to break the ties that bind them to the big "P's" (that's you) are seen every day. Ah, but here's the rub. The other recurring theme of the teen years is MONEY. Teens truly believe they need, rather than simply want money. Your pockets may not be deep enough to meet their needs, but what parent's are?

Teenage Research Unlimited annually surveys teens and their parents regarding data on the employment of teens. In the last decade, one third of teens (the 12 to 19-year-old group) worked at jobs outside the home on a year round basis, not just summer vacation employment. The amount of money earned by the teenage work force is staggering. During the decade of the nineties, teens made 90 billion dollars a year. Who knows what this enterprising and expanding group will bring in as the century turns?

Teens earn billions of dollars, so do they also save billions? Nope. They out-

167

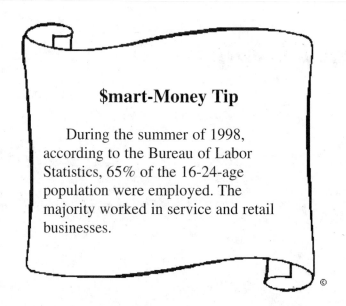

$mart-Money Tip

During the summer of 1998, according to the Bureau of Labor Statistics, 65% of the 16-24-age population were employed. The majority worked in service and retail businesses.

spend what they earn by approximately 5 billion a year. Where does the excess come from—you get three guesses, only the first one counts—you, the P's!

You can't help but wonder if a monster hasn't been created. What correlation can be expected between these teens' spending and saving behaviors and those the display in adulthood, if they are now outspending what they make by more than 5 1/2 percent? The potential for indebtedness could be a financial back breaker. It is, therefore, critical that your teen has broadly based financial management skills.

To find out what your teens know about money management, duplicate the test below and have them take it. But first, take the test yourself, giving the responses you think they are likely to give. You will have some idea about the degree of penetration your money counseling has had in their minds. Or, you will have a goal that they know what's below by the time they get ready to leave the nest.

$mart-Money Teens Quiz

1. Do you know how to open a checking account?   Yes ___ No ___
2. Do you know how to balance a checkbook?   Yes ___ No ___
3. Do you know how to open a savings account?   Yes ___ No ___
4. Can you name 3 types of savings vehicles, other
   than a passbook savings account?   Yes ___ No ___

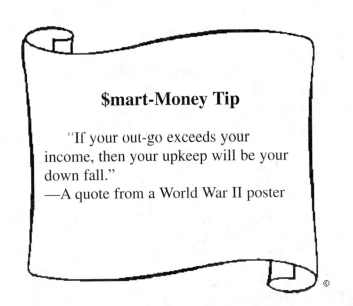

$mart-Money Tip

"If your out-go exceeds your income, then your upkeep will be your down fall."
—A quote from a World War II poster

5. Would you know how to stop payment on a check if you needed to? Yes ___ No ___

6. Do your outside earnings account for more than 15 percent of the total balance in your savings account? Yes ___ No ___

7. When you run out of checks, do you know how to order more of them? Yes ___ No ___

8. Do you understand all the entries on monthly bank statements for both checking and savings accounts? Yes ___ No ___

9. Do you know the difference between a bank, a savings and loan institution, and a credit union? Yes ___ No ___

10. Do you know what interest rate is charged on the unpaid balance of your credit card or on one of your parents credit cards? Yes ___ No ___

11. Have you been saving 10 to 25 percent of all money that you receive from parents, gifts and outside jobs? Yes ___ No ___

12. Do you have money left over at the end of your pay period, either weekly or monthly, after all your expenses have been paid? Yes ___ No ___

13. Do you know who to call if you lose a checkbook or a credit card? Yes ___ No ___

14. Do you know how to use an ATM card? Yes ___ No ___

15. Do you know how to get cash in an emergency—
day, night or out of town? Yes ___ No ___

16. Could you make up a livable spending plan for
yourself without your parents' assistance? Yes ___ No ___

17. Do you understand how to read a simple contract,
such as the one found on the back of a credit card
application? Yes ___ No ___

18. Do you know how to get car insurance? Yes ___ No ___

19. Do you know what penalty or penalties are assessed
when you make a late payment on a credit card? Yes ___ No ___

20. Do you know what a credit report is and how to
get a copy of yours? Yes ___ No ___

21. Savings accounts earn interest, do checking
accounts? Yes ___ No ___

22. Do you buy on impulse? Yes ___ No ___

23. Do you know how and when to file federal and
state tax returns? Yes ___ No ___

24. Do you know what an IRA is? Yes ___ No ___

25. Do you know what travelers checks are and how
to get them? Yes ___ No ___

26. Do you know what a lease is and what a lease
contract should contain? Yes ___ No ___

How To Score: Give every *Yes* answer 2 points. Give *No* answers 0 points

If you teen scores:

40 to 52 points— Help him pack his bag, he's ready to leave home or perhaps even support you.

25 to 39 points— He's on his way, but still needs input from you. He can
read this book, so get him his own copy.

24 and below— You both need to wake up fast, otherwise he will never be
ready to leave home. You may have to support him the
rest of your life.

The Pros and Cons of After School Jobs

High school seniors who have jobs (after school and on weekends) average
more than 20 hours of work in a week. These kids are really holding down two

jobs: school work and paid work. Four negative factors can bear on you child's success in these two endeavors.

The Pros: An after school job will help kids mature and prepare themselves for the real adult world. They become more self-reliant. The income from their job gives them the opportunity to learn and put into practice, a viable spending plan. As the newest member of the tax paying population, they come to appreciate how much of your money goes to areas that you can't directly control. With specific goals, they can sock away money for—preferably college, most likely—a car.

There is data that shows that both girls and boys enhance their self-esteem and gain confidence through outside work. Confidence comes from successful interaction in the real world of business, and self esteem comes from the realization of earning power—they are (at least in part) taking care of themselves.

The Cons include:

Grades often decline: Every once in a while you hear or read about a wonderful story telling of a student who excels at school, at home and at work. The reason that this is news on TV or in the newspaper, is this is the exception and not the rule. When kids begin to work, usually late in their high school careers, grades decline. Many teachers accommodate these kids by reducing their load of homework and the number of long-term assignments, which includes outside reading. It might be said that teachers take the attitude, if you can't lick them, join them. What a mistake!

Materialistic teens are made: America has evolved into a society of instant gratification. Too many Americans want it all and they want it now. Microwave cooking presents a good analogy—you've got a meal with a few zaps compared to hours of simmering to savory goodness in the oven.

Teens *work and spend*, get up the next day and do it again. And, it is a rare day when they *work and save*. They see the "gadget" they want to buy and, as soon as possible, they buy it. Then, the cycle repeats itself until they reach the pinnacle of teen materialistic endeavor—their own car.

Did they sit back and enjoy the fruits of their labors?—Probably not. Do they experience the savory taste of success?—They don't have time. What is alarming is that many American teens have become addicted to money.

This addiction results in an artificial standard of living that teens are loath to sacrifice to the altar of long term goals. Their educational aspirations become more oriented to the income the education will produce, instead of to that which

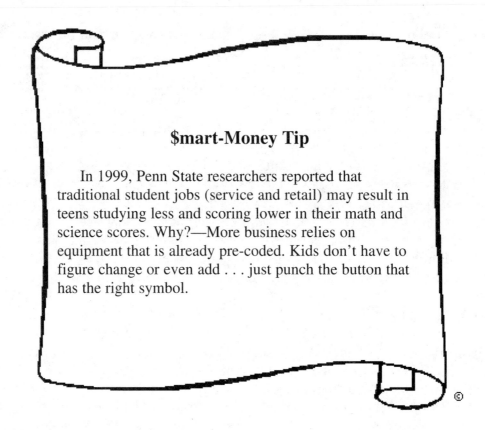

$mart-Money Tip

In 1999, Penn State researchers reported that traditional student jobs (service and retail) may result in teens studying less and scoring lower in their math and science scores. Why?—More business relies on equipment that is already pre-coded. Kids don't have to figure change or even add . . . just punch the button that has the right symbol.

will satisfy the heart and soul in the adult employment world. You see, they have watched many adults. They begin to feel that they too must have a new car, at least every 2 to 3 years, if not sooner.

Alcohol and drug use increases: Researchers have compared teens, whose primary income source is allowance from their parents, to teens whose income is from outside the home. The results show that teens with outside jobs use more alcohol and drugs. Sadly, the reasons for this are not totally clear; thus the remedy is not. The first possibility is that these kids have more money to spend. And perhaps, accountability for the dollars they spend is not a part of their family lexicon.

Additionally, these kids are exposed to older teens and they may take part in drug and alcohol use to appear "cool" and/or to enhance their ability to move up in the ranks of "fitting in." Another possibility is that, they may have seen their parents or others use alcohol and drugs to relieve stress and they follow suit. After all, it's hard to hold down two jobs and cover the home front too.

Your parental authority declines: According to recent studies, one-on-one interaction between parent and child total only 15 minutes per day. Teens have to leave early for their school job, and only sometimes have a minute or two to bolt down food that hopefully resembles a balanced breakfast. Then they hit rush hour to commute to school by bus, car or foot power. School is usually over for them by 2 to 3 PM and they can opt to socialize with friends, study or go directly to their second job.

Dinner at home with the family is a thing of the past for these teens. Fast food after school or during a work hour break is the usual fare, though penurious teens come home to eat a "delicious and nutritious" bowl of cereal or piece of cold pizza scrounged from the fridge. Study? Hopefully, they will if they didn't study earlier.

Lights out and an identical but new day begin in just a very few hours. When do you, the parent, get your 15 minutes with your teen whose existence is frenetic? Rarely.

What to do:

♦ *Place a limit on outside employment.* Make sure that you haven't portrayed that you think that working outside the home is neither the greatest thing they do, nor the worst. Your parenting efforts to create a sense of independence in your child should be positive for both of you. If your kids are going to work for pay, infuse in them a sense of moderation.

♦ *Help them dispel the philosophy of "more is better" and substitute a philosophy of balance.* Work together for this balanced philosophy through efficient allocation of their time spent with school (studying and activities), outside work, family activities, recreation with friends, church, etc. Emphasize the pitfall of over-commitment—poor performance will result in one or several areas. Teens need to learn to budget time as well as money. Very soon in their future, time will be money.

To give you a little support in asking your teen to cut back his work hours, here is what federal law says about child labor limitations. For 14 to 15-year-olds, the law says they can work a maximum of 3 hours on a school day or 18 hours within a school week. And, 40 hours of work are permitted during non-school weeks, with no more than 8 hours per day.

Summer time is not treated in the same manner with regard to the hours they can work. Between June 1st and Labor Day, these 14 and 15-year-olds can work from 7 AM until 9 PM. For teens over age 16, there are no restrictions on the number of hours they can work and none on the time of day they can work.

I believe that the biggest job you have in helping your child fine tune his time budget is in the area of homework. If grades slip, a family pow-wow is in order, *immediately*. Something has got to go, cut it now and make the cut as painless as possible for all.

♦ *Monitor Automobile Usage:* The automobile is the *really big* news at age 16. Before you hand them the keys for the first time, lay out the ground rules—yours not theirs. Responsibility for additional insurance and gasoline costs has to be, at least in part, the teen's obligation. What hours, days, destinations, passengers, etc. are allowable. In my opinion, teens should pay for all gasoline they use and they should pay for the better part of the insurance premium that resulted from adding them to your policy.

Some parents have found that the new teenage driver develops a case of grade dropsy. No errand is rejected, when you have a new teenage driver in the house—they're having a good time. Driving is fun! I strongly advise that you nip this attention to RPMs, mag wheels, etc. and quickly. It would be wise to suspend at least a portion of the teen's driving privileges if grades are suffering. Moderation of the suspension can be considered if grades improve or return to normal. Remember, driving is a privilege not a right—some drivers license test papers give teens this message for you. Perhaps you could get a copy and post it.

Finding the Perfect Job

Some people never find the perfect job. Teens don't have the range of choices and pay that adults do for some very obvious reasons. Teens first of all rarely put in a 40-hour workweek year round nor do they stay on a job for a long enough period of time to make extensive training cost effective for an employer. Plus, they don't usually have the qualifications, skills and experience that adults have. Like adults, teens prefer work that is interesting and not stressful. Where do kids usually start out?

◆ **Flipping Burgers** The affair with hamburger heaven lasts for relatively short periods with the teen. The learning curve for new employees is not at all steep. In a few months, they have mastered: being on time, working within the team, pressurized order filling at noon and dinnertime, and being pleasant to customers.

Most hamburger joints pay minimum wage. Don't expect bonuses or benefits. A plus is that drive time to work is usually minimal—just about everyone can get to a fast food stand within 5 to 10 minutes, from home or school. Many stores, such as McDonald's, actually applaud kids who maintain good grades while in their employ by paying an extra 10 to 20 cents per hour. Burger King runs the Burger King Academy. This is a private high school where at risk kids can work and study.

Some pizza parlors offer incentives for good grades. And if your teen gets on the delivery route, he can pick up tips. He needs to check with management to find out how tips are reported for taxes. Many restaurants assume a percentage and add it to the base pay when year-end income is reported to the IRS.

◆ **Web Design** Believe it or not, if your kids are computer and Internet savvy, they can farm out their skills to individuals and companies for $25-$70 an hour. Consulting and designing websites are hot!

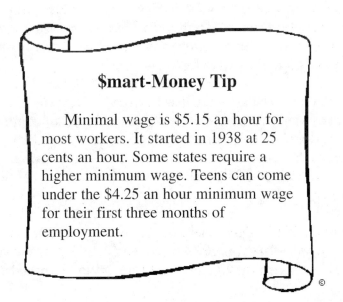

$mart-Money Tip

Minimal wage is $5.15 an hour for most workers. It started in 1938 at 25 cents an hour. Some states require a higher minimum wage. Teens can come under the $4.25 an hour minimum wage for their first three months of employment.

- **The Mall and Other Stores** My first job, in 1961, was as a sales clerk for the May Company department stores. The big pay was $1 an hour. Many teens start their real world job experience in department stores, working at minimum wage. Kids can learn about merchandising and hands on customer service. Working for a small retail operation does have additional advantages. In some cases the teen can work directly with the owner. Duties can include cashiering, setting and discounting prices, merchandise order and display and taking inventory. A fringe benefit is that merchandise can be purchased at a discount.

- **Pet Sitting** Pets are everywhere. Many families have both parents working (or in the case of the single household, one person working) and their beloved pets are left at home. Kids who get home early from school can take dogs for walks, water and feed and play with animals until their owners get home.

- **Babysitting** Most girls and some boys take their first, for pay, job baby-sitting. This job has a lot of responsibility because the care of young children requires a lot of decision-making skills, and some decisions require great maturity. Baby sitters don't usually make the money that teens make in retail and fast food. They do though, have the flexibility to set the hours that they work, the days they work and who they will work for. Pay will vary depending on location, number of kids to care for, even the time of day or night. Most likely they will receive $2 to $5 dollars an hour.

- **Paper Delivery** My kids started with papers—they made good money, but the early, early hours got rough. Except for small communities, the afternoon paper has pretty much gone the way of the dinosaur. If your kid heads in this direction, be very clear about responsibility and commitment (i.e., he gets up at the crack of dawn . . . not you to drive him around).

- **Yard Work** I live in Colorado. We get snow, sometimes lots of it. We also have wonderful summers where weeds and lawns thrive. In communities that enjoy the seasons, there are lots of weeds, leaves and snow to seed a handy kid business. For those that have fairly consistent weather, there's still plenty that can be done. Think of what you do around your house and make suggestions to your kids on the moneymaking side of it. Suggestion—you might want to put a "string attached" on their enterprising skills, as in, your yard duties get done first. Whether payment is included in allowances or is extra is up to you.

♦ **Community Volunteer** There are advantages to working and not getting paid. The pay comes in the form of experience in social work, medical careers, etc. Plus your teen may meet some prominent people that could be excellent contacts for the more permanent jobs of the future.

♦ **Small Businesses** Many small businesses are very willing to take on a teen as an intern. Pay ranges from zero, with the concept being that experience in invaluable, to minimum wage. This could be a "look see" way to find out if this business is interesting enough to pursue.

In the twenty-three years that I have had my own business, we have employed several teens through those years. Typically, they work 8 to 10 hours a week (after school), are paid minimum wage and get a few bonuses along the way (birthdays off and paid, tickets to events, etc.). Work included assembling press kits, inputting computer data, working on the newsletter, and preparing mailings. She or he can specify the days and hours worked. This kind of flexibility, especially for busy teens, is often the norm with small businesses.

Getting a job

One of the first things your teen can do, is to look for "Help Wanted" signs in the windows of shopette businesses nearby. The teen will fill out an application and will either interview on the spot or wait for a call. Encourage your teen to look for a job that is different from the usual jobs teens have—take the contrarian approach. Some interesting opportunities could come up.

If transportation is not a problem, have your teen check the classified ads. Many professionals now have evening and weekend hours for their businesses and practices.

Your Teen's Resume

Encourage your teen to put their accomplishments in writing. Include scholastics, extra curricular activities, and community activity and highlight the ones where bravos have been given. Your daughter, who is a master negotiator, might have a resume that looks like this:

1997 to 2001	Baby-sitting and child care. Skilled in negotiating with children from ages 2 to 10; skilled in creating new games to offset possible addiction to TV; expert in assisting children ages 4 to 10 in identifying their needs versus their wants. Baby-sitting started in 1995 with one family, increased to 10 families from referrals based on highly satisfactory performance of duties.

In addition, the resume will include name, address and phone number (day and evening if appropriate) and educational experience.

Where to Look

Looking for a job usually starts in the back yard. It could be yours, or your neighbors. Encourage your kids to be on the lookout for posted signs in the neighborhood, stores that they can get to easily, encourage them to read the "Help Wanted" section in the newspaper and don't forget to query friends and relatives. For older teens, there may be employment counselors at their high schools, or in some cases local government agencies.

Clothes Do Make the Teen Interviewer

No "grubbies" allowed, nor is formal dress appropriate, unless your teens have their eye on the Maitre d' position. Keep it conservative is the best choice—for girls a simple dress, blouse and skirt or stylish pants outfit; and for boys, dressy shirt and slacks, with or without a jacket, and possibly a suit. Tailor the clothing choice to the dress mode of other company employees where the interview is taking place. How do you find out? Check out the dress of employees by observing from the outside, visiting the reception area and observing "housekeeping" as well as the receptionist. Or, just ask.

$mart-Money Tip

Do not, do not, do not, wear clothes with holes in them.

If you wear any body jewelry, leave it at home (earrings are OK for girls), otherwise, get the job and gradually introduce the accessories.

Be Polite and Personable

Teach your kids how to shake hands. Boys are generally more skilled. Make eye contact. Repeat the person's name out loud and say "It's nice to meet you Mr. (or Mrs.) Smith." Practice does make perfect, and it's amazing how many people miss the boat by not knowing how to shake hands.

If your son or daughter is required to attend a function where nametags will be used, have them place the tag on the upper right shoulder. Why? Most people shake hands with their right hand and subsequent eye contact with the nametag.

The Tax Man Cometh

The real world of business really impacts your teen, when he gets his first paycheck. Federal, FICA, FUTA, state—all these withholding taxes are you kid's partners in work for pay every payday. Underage employees who earn less than $4400 annually (the current floor at this writing) are not liable for federal income tax.

Make sure that your child's employer is withholding the correct amount from each paycheck, if you feel that he or she will exceed the floor. Kid's are not tax wise and if their withholdings aren't correct and they owe tax to Uncle Sam, their tax bill could come out of your pocket if they haven't saved any money. An amount Uncle Sam doesn't credit you for!

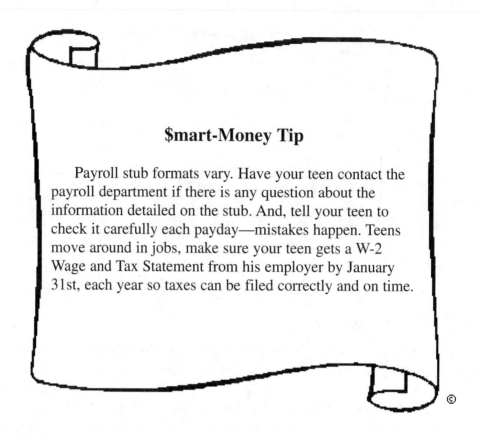

$mart-Money Tip

Payroll stub formats vary. Have your teen contact the payroll department if there is any question about the information detailed on the stub. And, tell your teen to check it carefully each payday—mistakes happen. Teens move around in jobs, make sure your teen gets a W-2 Wage and Tax Statement from his employer by January 31st, each year so taxes can be filed correctly and on time.

When your kids start working outside the home, one important form they will have to fill out is Form W-4, Employees Withholding Allowance Certificate. If you are very sure that your child will earn less than $4400 from all their jobs for the calendar year, she can claim an exemption from withholding. To be exempt they will have to meet one of the three following conditions:

♦ No tax liability is anticipated for the upcoming calendar year.
♦ If her income exceeds $1500 and parents plan to claim her as a dependent, she can't have any non-wage income.
♦ No taxes were owed in the preceding year.

In the 1990's, Take Your Daughter to Work Day was birthed. For the first time daughters were welcomed in the workplace by both fathers and mothers. Today, it has been expanded to take your son or daughter to work—a much wiser approach. After all, shouldn't all your kids know what you do, how much

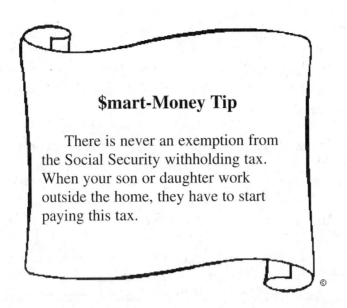

$mart-Money Tip

There is never an exemption from
the Social Security withholding tax.
When your son or daughter work
outside the home, they have to start
paying this tax.

effort it takes and what kind of obligations and situations you might encounter
in a typical day?

Many high schools have "Career Days" type of programs and these have
been going on for at least 25 years in some locations. They provide older teens
with an opportunity to check out job markets, ask questions about the pros and
cons of a specific job, the risks and rewards and the myths and realities.

They may see demonstrations of product development, manufacture and
marketing from wholesale to retail. And, they may see why some products
succeed and some products bomb. If your teen's school isn't hosting such a
program, see what can be done to get one going. Nothing teaches so well as
"Life 101."

Retiring Your Teens

Teens think they are invincible and immortal. They don't have a clue yet, as
to how very quickly the years do pass. For teens, retirement is not yet in the list
of events for their future.

Anyone who makes money is eligible to open an individual retirement
account—IRA. Tax deductible status will be a factor of the teen's gross pay during the calendar year. The primary reason for introducing teens to this investment opportunity is to get long range planning in their minds. Teens can, like
you, invest up to $2000 per year of their earnings in an IRA. With the Roth IRA,

they can salt money away that won't be taxable if it isn't touched until he's 59½, taps into the ability to withdraw $10,000 to buy a home or withdraws only the amount of the original moneys deposited. Otherwise, the traditional IRA will allow for an educational withdrawal, meaning no penalty but whatever is taken out will be fully taxed.

Let's say your daughter, age 19, has accumulated $2000 in an IRA account and you want to see what she can expect the account to be worth at age 39. The average rate of return for 20 years is 10 percent. At the end of 20 years, her $2000 has grown to $13,440. No taxes have had to be paid during the deferral period of time. Any subsequent deposits would, of course, up the ante of the gains in value. Add another 20 years at 10 percent, and the account would be worth $90,316.80. If this appeals to your daughter, show her what she would have at age 65—$145,410.48. All seeded with only $2000 at age 19, with an annual rate of growth at 10 percent. Not bad indeed.

By starting your kids thinking about retirement when it is a foreign word, you not only reinforce a savings habit but you introduce them to the concept of profit sharing, pensions, deferred compensation, and 401(k) programs. Life long habits, that will have pay backs, many times over.

$mart-Money Resource Center

There are some excellent books on jobs that are teen specific and there are others that require an "adult" minded teen for readability. Here are a few suggested titles.

Lifetime Employability: How to Become Indispensable by Carole Hyatt is a guide to the mysteries of the business universe and will help you evaluate your attitudes, skills and goals. One of the objectives of the book is to increase your staying power and to be alert to changing opportunities.

The Career Coach by Carol Kleiman. Kleiman has three columns that are nationally syndicated: *Women at Work, Jobs* and *Your Job*. This book will serve as a navigator for the ups and downs of the workplace. Available through Dearborn Financial Publishing, 155 Wacker Drive, Chicago, IL, 60606-1719.

Chapter Twelve

Entrepreneuring . . .
Your Kids ABCs

Quick. What do lemonade stands, garage cleaning, gift-wrapping, bike repairs and pet walking have in common? The answer: they are only five of over 150 project and business (hopefully for profit) ideas that kids of all ages can get involved in, that were culled from a few books on the subject. When kids express a desire to start their own business, the first ideas that come to their minds are the old standbys from your childhood and mine—lemonade stands, lawn mowing and baby sitting.

Encourage your young businessperson (and you too) to stretch beyond tradition for fresh opportunities to make some money and that fit their interests and abilities. That's what Daryl Bernstein did. In his book, *Better Than a Lemonade Stand* (Beyond Words Publishing) he describes 50 businesses. His book isn't just another idea book, he describes the "start up" parameters for each. Included are lists of needed supplies, the allotted time needed for set up and eventual operation. He even cites advertising ideas that are specific to the particular venture. Bernstein has "walked his talk," because he's tried, and been successful in, all the 50 businesses he describes. And, he did this all before he was 16.

He offered maid service for the homes of caged pets. His house sitting services included picking up mail, watering plants, feeding, watering and walking pets. And for real fun, he was a birthday party director for hire. He did what a lot of kids do; he started with a lemonade stand; success of this, his first venture, quickly led him to seek something more profitable. Bernstein succeeded, where so kids many don't, he observed a need and found a way to fill it. He found lots of innovative niche businesses this way.

The grand opening of a lemonade stand, during the winter months in my home state of Colorado would fail miserably—ice cold drinks on a snowy day—Not! Instead of taking the well-worn trails to entrepreneurship, open your eyes. Newspapers are delivered even on the worst of our winter days, and are left on driveways, sometimes thigh deep with snow.

A service a Colorado kid could provide would be to *re*deliver the newspapers to the front steps of his neighbors' homes. People flock to our state to enjoy the winter sports, but I suspect residents would pay to avoid skating or skiing down their driveways to get their paper. In fact, one way to initiate the service is to give it a free run. Have your kid redeliver the papers, and later in the day, he can call on the neighbors to see if they liked the convenience of getting their paper on the porch.

Most will respond quite positively. Then your kid can let them know what his terms are for continuing the service. Your kids could charge $1 per week or $3 a month, if paid in advance. Get 10 subscribers—an easy $30 per month that an 8-year-old would be glad to have.

Let's go back to the lemonade idea. In my state, it doesn't work in the winter. But, it does as spring rears its head, and in the summer, there's no question that sales will happen. This past summer, I was playing golf on a public course. The temperature was in the low 90s—hot. Two kids had pulled their wagon into the backyard of their condo, which fronted the fifth fairway. The wagon was filled with ice cold bottled water. How did they do? They told me that they sell several wagons a day—over 70 bottles each weekend day. Not bad for two eight-year-olds who make $1 per bottle over their cost!

Having the Right Stuff

Before your kids jump into a prospective moneymaking project, a critical question needs to be asked—do they have the right stuff to make it as an entrepreneur? Are they . . .

♦ *Responsible* Do your kids do things when they are told (or within reasonable period of time)? Do they follow through on things when they said they would? In other words, can you rely on them?

- *Talented or Skilled* Businesses require talent from the workforce—the kids. If your daughter wants to tutor younger kids, is she patient; does she listen; is she a good communicator?

- *Available* A budding business requires a commitment of time—does your daughter have time to do whatever she is planning on doing? Is she fairly organized so that she can keep track of what she's suppose to do for her customers, collect money, etc. If she doesn't complete tasks (including schoolwork), she's starting out with a bag of problems.

Business Skills 101

Most entrepreneurs will tell you that one of the reasons their business didn't work is that they didn't have a plan that should basically say what the business is and how it will work. A business plan or proforma includes the product or service; who will run the business; what is the overhead—supplies, equipment, etc. what income can be expected. And, most important to the bank: how much money is needed, how it is to be spent and the repayment terms possible from revenues of the business. The brochure The Young Americans Bank gives out shows kids how to define the issues they'll face in starting a business.

In advance of the preparation of a formal business plan (which few kids will do without help and encouragement), *$mart-Money* kids need to ask themselves a series of questions that are suggested from Young Americans Bank:

- What am I going to do?
- When will be my business be in operation (seasonal or year round)?
- Who will my customers be?
- Can I do this in my neighborhood, or will transportation be necessary?
- What will I call my business (will the name tell prospective customers what I do)?
- Is there competition for my product or service (if there is—are people satisfied with what they are getting—can I do it better or differently—how much are they paying)?
- What should I charge and how do I expect to be paid—at the time of service or delivery in advance?
- How much of my time will I have to devote the business and what time of the day and day of the week is appropriate?

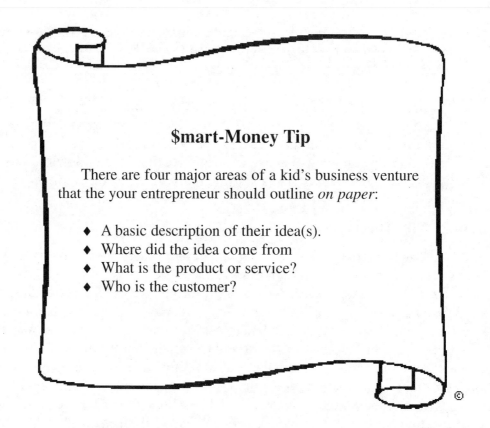

$mart-Money Tip

There are four major areas of a kid's business venture that the your entrepreneur should outline *on paper*:

♦ A basic description of their idea(s).
♦ Where did the idea come from
♦ What is the product or service?
♦ Who is the customer?

♦ Is any special equipment necessary—what supplies are needed to start and needed for continuing operation?
♦ How much money will I need to get the business started and where or how will I get it?
♦ How will I advertise to let potential customers know about my business?

And most important of all,

♦ Is there a **need** for my product or service?

The Drews, authors of *Fast Cash for Kids*, make some important points that even adults need to be reminded of. When kids are trying to pitch their ideas or services to an adult, they should:

- Never forget the WIIFM principle—what's in it for me. Potential customers want to know why the product is good for them.
- Tell them why it is important for them to purchase or subscribe right away.
- Don't give up, if told "No" (if they aren't interested, ask if they know of someone who might be).
- If they say "Yes," provide your product or service promptly, courteously and thoroughly, each time (Thank Yous are important too).
- Ask for referrals. This is the best way for their business to grow.

Mistakes Happen: Parent Alert

What if your kid bites off more than he can chew? Kids, like adults, often over extend themselves when they are excited about something new. *Parent Alert*—step in and help them focus on what they really can do with their resources of time and ability. If you see they are heading the wrong way, don't just criticize; offer a solution or two for their dilemma. Praise them when they succeed and pick them up, with love, when they fall. Also, ask your child if he is having any fun being a businessperson. If he responds negatively, go back to the drawing board for a new venture. Adults have the discipline to keep working at a job that they don't like, but kids don't.

When starting up a business, kids will make some of the same mistakes that adults do. Under capitalization is the most common; they don't properly identify what they need to buy in supplies, equipment, etc. And, down the road, what the costs are to sustain the business—the cash flow concept. Cash flow means getting enough customers to pay for the goods or services your offer, so you can replenish your inventory or supplies.

With the first blush of success, the young entrepreneur may be blinded by dollar signs in his mind's eye. It is very likely, that he will oversell his product or service, and thus be unable to supply his customers on a timely basis.

Kids, Inc.: Board Meeting in Session

You might want to encourage regular board meetings (parents attend these) to review your youngster's business progress. A review of the pricing for your

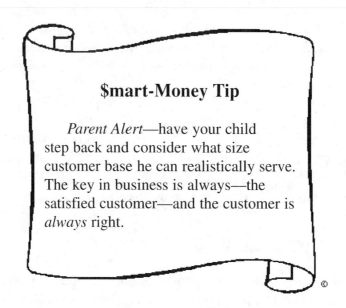

$mart-Money Tip

Parent Alert—have your child step back and consider what size customer base he can realistically serve. The key in business is always—the satisfied customer—and the customer is *always* right.

kid's product or service is important. He may be losing customers to the competition if the price is too high—regular review of the competition's services and pricing is a must. Or, he may not be charging enough.

Let's say your son has a lawn mowing and general yard maintenance service. His customer contracted to have the front yard moved and the front flowerbeds weeded, once a week for a price of $20. This customer now wants him to weed that backyard at no extra cost—time for review—ask for more money and don't do the extra work if the answer is *No*. Point out, that if he takes too long on one job doing "extras" he may not get another customer's yard done on time and correctly.

The second regular item to be reviewed at your board meetings is the income/profit picture of the child's business. Is the business making a profit, after expenses are paid? If not, identify the reasons and find ways to get the business in the "black." Or, encourage him to revisit other new ventures that can be profitable.

If the business is humming right along and your kid is making a bundle, what is he doing with the money he makes? Is he reinvesting his profits and/or spending every dime on himself? If so, encourage a savings plan that puts away close to 50 percent of his net profits (income less expenses). Encourage him as best you can to salt away as much as possible.

Here come the Feds: Forms and Taxes

Whenever there is money to be made, there is usually some red tape attached—taxes. If your kid's business has one employee—the young entrepreneur—and doesn't have any other paid "gofers," there are no restrictions on the number of hours he works or when, during the day, he chooses to work. Under federal law, age 14 is the minimum age for most non-farm work. The federal law applies only to employer/employee relationships.

So, to avoid this issue, both you and your kid need to think twice about hiring other kids to man the expanding business. It might make more sense to take in another kid for a partner, rather than to hire work done. But, if they do hire other kids to help with the work cleaning garages or repairing bicycles, say hello to the world of government forms. There is a free publication, entitled "The Handy Reference Guide to the Fair Labor Standards Act" which can be obtained by calling the U.S. Dept. of Labor at 202-209-4907. This booklet will, hopefully, clarify the dos and don'ts of the issue of employees.

If kids decide to operate their business under any name other than their own, they are required to register the business name with the county clerk's office in the county of their business operation. Most kid ventures start as a sole proprietorship. If your child's endeavors pan out to be a major gold strike, see tax and

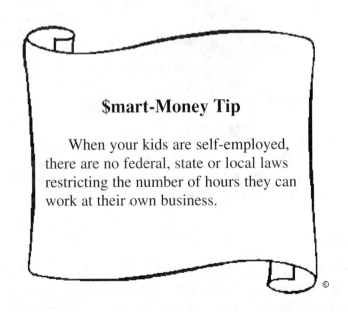

$mart-Money Tip

When your kids are self-employed, there are no federal, state or local laws restricting the number of hours they can work at their own business.

legal advice. It's amazing how businesses that were headquartered in garages and backyards have spawned young millionaires!

They may also need to get a business license. Check with your local authorities for their requirements on new businesses in your locale, and do this before your kid gets under way. There are penalties, and some are severe, for non-compliance. Also, before your kid starts plying his trade in your or nearby neighborhoods, have him check the targeted business areas for street signs that prohibit solicitation in any way. Some subdivisions or complexes have these signs only at the main entrances.

Check out the local tax situation. Your kid's goods or services may be subject to taxation, by one or all of the local tax authorities. Find out now. Unpaid taxes, and the penalties and interest assessed on them could come out of your pocket.

Take advantage of all the information that is out there for kids who want to get started in business. Your local bookstore has dozens of books on the topic. Don't forget tapping into the Internet as an ongoing resource. One of its advantages is that it changes almost on a daily basis with new information. Use it.

$mart-Money Resource Center

There are a few resources a supportive parent can obtain, to help their budding entrepreneurs get up and running. They include:

Books and Kits

The Busine$ Kit—a kit for ages 10 to 18.The cost is $49.95 plus shipping. The kit includes manuals, tapes, stationery and other tools. It shows kids how to start and run a business, with support via 800-hotline phone number kids (or you) can call for advice as the business progresses. This kit is expensive, but use of a toll free number could save you dollars and time down the road. To purchase or get further information call 800-282-5437.

A Lemonade Stand: A Guide to Encouraging the Entrepreneur in Your Child
This book written by Emmanuel Modu (Bob Adams, Inc.) includes information on tax considerations for the kid business, legal issues and various concepts your child should know. For example: if your kid's business will earn more than $400, self-employment tax is assessed.

The next two books work well for you and your kids, when used together:

Fast Cash for Kids—for kids under age 16
Written by Bonnie and Noel Drew (Career Press), this book identifies over 100 money making projects. Projects are grouped according to the applicable season of the year. Bonnie Drew is quite creative and has written several books designed exclusively for kids to spark their imagination. All are highly recommended.

The Teenage Entrepreneur's Guide—for kids 16 and up.
Written by Sarah L. Riehm (Surrey Books), this book includes information on business plans, bookkeeping and paying taxes.

Internet

There are a few websites (and more popping up everyday) that can offer a variety of information for kids interested in business.

www.kidsway.com	The Kids Way site is loaded with resources that will teaching elementary business skills.
www.4h-usa.org	4-H Clubs have been around forever to assist kids in agriculture related entrepreneuring activities.
www.deca.org	DECA (Distributive Education Clubs of America) offers prizes and scholarships annually to kids interested in starting their own business, management, marketing, etc.

www.ja.org Junior Achievement works with millions of kids each year teaching them about our free enterprise system.

For further assistance in helping your entrepreneur learn about the responsibilities of having his own business, there are several organizations that offer ongoing assistance and resources. They are:

Junior Achievement coordinates interaction between schools and businesses. They offer hands on experience to students with business organizations, management and marketing techniques and production procedures. For information, write to Junior Achievement, 45 E. Clubhouse Drive, Colorado Springs, CO, 80906 or call 719-540-8000. The website is *www.ja.org*.

The Center for Entrepreneurship is an organization that offers comprehensive (one stop) resources in educational opportunities for your young businessperson. Adults and students are welcomed. For information write to The Center for Entrepreneurship, Wichita State University, 1845 N. Fairmount, Wichita, KS, 67260 or call 316-689-3000 and ask for the center.

Your local *Chamber of Commerce* or a *Women's Chamber of Commerce* can be a good source for programs for aspiring entrepreneurs. In addition, NAWBO— The *National Association of Business Owners, Girls, Inc.* and the *Girl Scouts of America* all have programs designed to reach out to young people.

Don't forget your local library as another fine source for resources on entrepreneurship. Cassettes, videos and books, galore are available upon presentation of your library card. And, the price is right—free.

Chapter Thirteen

Look Out . . . My Kid Wants Wheels

A s teens march through their 15th year, they remind their parents that they will be driving soon. Some expect to have unlimited access to the family car, some expect to have some access to the family car, and some expect to have a car of their own. Do yourself and your kids a favor and give them the lowdown on buying cars, both used and new, before the magic 16th birthday.

As soon as you hear rumblings, it's time to feed information in. Kids rarely grasp the concept of what it means financially to own their own set of wheels. Before yours begin to salivate over the classified listings for cars, send them to the local library. *Consumer's Reports* puts together guides on both new and used cars. These cannot be checked out but copies of articles can be made on site. Or go to their website *www.consumersreport.com*. They need to start their research early if they intend to own a car of their own.

The Stockpile Builds

One of the most important things that you can do while you strategize what car is appropriate and how it will be paid for is to encourage your kid to stockpile every penny they can. If owing that car is the goal, then the majority, if not all, of gifts, after school and weekend jobs and any other monies that come their way should be placed in a savings account. Being prepared should become your teen's motto.

Until he or she has saved up enough money to either augment what you're going to contribute (if anything) or pay all of it themselves, be prepared to lend out your car and to chauffeur him or her around. Remind them they can hitch rides with their cronies.

A critical factor is to remind them what the bottom line of car ownership is. It's not just putting $5 in the gas tank. It's all the other goodies that are attached. From the cost of insurance, maintenance and "their time." Just about every parent will tell you that when their kids get wheels, time dedicated to schoolwork declines.

The Planning Begins

When it comes to buying a car, you and your teen's bottom line objective should be fairly simple: You want the best possible deal that you can get on the car that is selected.

Now saying that, keep in mind that the seller, whether it's a dealer or a private party, also has a bottom line objective. His is: To make the highest profit on the car you will buy.

In other words, you are on opposite ends of the pole. The commonality is that you both want a good deal. The way you and your teen will get the good

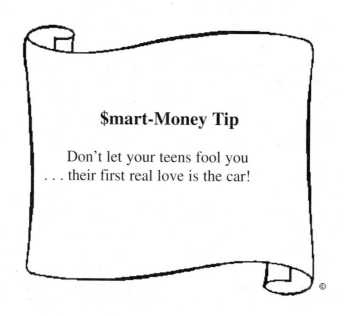

$mart-Money Tip

Don't let your teens fool you
. . . their first real love is the car!

deal is to plan. Planning means that there are steps involved. And there are several in buying a car. Your teen (and you) need to consider:

♦ What the car budget is
♦ What needs need to be met
♦ Understanding the seller's objectives
♦ Shopping for the car
♦ Determine the real value of the car
♦ Test driving the car
♦ Negotiating the best deal for you and your teen
♦ Completing the paper work
♦ Finally, taking delivery

When my oldest daughter Shelley graduated from college, my husband and I rewarded her with a Ford Maverick, the car of her choice at the time. She had worked hard the past four years—good grades and living on her own. We paid tuition; she covered all other living expenses 100%. Prior to its delivery, she had owned two other vehicles. The first was an old jalopy – a truck that she had fallen in love with. It only cost a few hundred dollars back in 1979 and it wasn't worth much more than a few hundred dollars. Within a few months, we knew that she had not bought wisely. She moved from the pickup truck to a more modest Subaru. Again, it was used, but far more practical.

For purposes of this chapter, I am going to assume that the car your teen will own will be a used car. Few teens have the thousands of dollars required for a new car. In reality, I think parents are nuts when a brand new shiny car is delivered to the brand new sixteen-year-old. Why? Let's start with statistics.

Teens have accidents. Boy teens have more accidents than girl teens. An insurance agent friend of mine confided that he has never represented an insured family where the newly licensed teenage boy has not had an accident within the first year. Granted there are times when it is not the teen's fault. But as you know, insurance companies don't pay a lot of attention to that. All they know is that money is going out and rates get raised to offset it.

When you sit down with your teen, the car budget needs to be probed and analyzed. Exactly how much money is expected to be paid for the purchase? In addition, how much will license fees and any taxes that may be required with the initial purchase be? How about car insurance and any emission and safety repairs that are often required with used cars? And finally, what about normal maintenance and any non-warranty repairs? It can add up to a hefty amount of money.

197

Separating the *Wants* from the *Needs*

What you ***need*** from a car is often different from what you ***want.*** Car wants can carry a potential car owner into la-la land. These are the dreams and fantasies with all the bells and whistles you'd like your car to have. The needs are more down to earth. Consider the tires; are they in good condition? Is the engine well-maintained? Is the car reliable in foul weather? All are necessary components for a safe automobile.

Unfortunately, a lot of people drive cars – and age is not a factor here – that they feel fulfills their self-image. Let's face it: if people buy cars for basic transportation needs, getting from point A to point B, the Porsches and Maseratis would probably disappear. When you sit down with your teen to evaluate what their needs are, not only is it time for you to roll up your sleeves, so do they.

There are a variety of factors you must consider. Ask, are they going to be driving on highways and freeways a lot? Or, are they going to be doing short stops and hauls? Will passengers be many or few? Are you going to need their assistance in taxiing siblings to events? What's the weather like? Do you have the four seasons or do you come from one of the sunshine states where driving conditions are usually a little bit more optimal? Is your teen a hard or an easy driver; i.e. do they make quick stops, do they ride the brakes? Keep in mind just because your teen drives conservatively when you are in the car does not mean their style is the same when you are out of it.

Stress upon your teen the seriousness of selecting, evaluating and purchasing a car. Below is a car condition checklist. It covers the exterior, interior, the driving conditions, engines and even the trunk of a proposed car. You have my permission to duplicate it because you will need several copies as you go through the car evaluation process.

Each item is rated 1, 2 or 3, with 1 being terrific or excellent condition, 2 being average and 3 poor—- avoid buying. After you and your teen have gone through each section for each car being considered, total the number of 1's, 2's and 3's. If you have mostly 1's you have a good car; mostly 2's average; and 3's, avoid it like the plague. Not one penny should be put in a car at this time that has less than an average rating.

Car Condition Checklist

Make _____ Model _____ Year _____

Vehicle ID number _____

Body Style:

2 Door _____ 4 Door _____ Convertible _____ Station Wagon _____

Van _____ Pickup _____ Hatch back _____

Drive Traction: 2 Wheel _____ 4 Wheel _____ None _____

Engine Size _____ Engine Type _____ Transmission Type _____

Interior Ratings: Excellent _____ Average _____ Poor _____

Air bags: Driver _____ Passenger _____ Air Cond. _____

Adj. Steering Wheel _____ Arm Rests _____ Cruise Control _____

Capering _____ DashBoard _____

Defrosters: Front _____ Rear _____ Dome lights _____ Door panels _____

Door locks _____ Emergency Flashers _____ Floor Mats _____

Glove Box _____ Headlights _____ Head Rest _____

Heater/Ventilators _____ Horn _____ Interior lights/other _____

Mirrors: Rear View _____ Side _____ Radio _____ Speakers _____

Seat adjusters: Manual _____ Power _____ Tape Player _____

Seat Belts/Front—functions & releases _____

Seat Belts/Back—functions & releases _____ Folding Seats _____

Sun Roof _____ Turn signals _____ Upholstery _____ Visors _____

All gauges on dashboard working _____

Wind Shield Washers _____ Windows: Glass _____ Cranks _____

Other _____ Other _____ Other _____ Other _____

Driving Condition:

Ease of Starting: Engine Cold _____ Engine Hot _____

Idle Speed: Engine Cold _____ Engine Hot _____

Steering Wheel Vibration: Idle _____ Low Speed _____

High Speed _____ Turns _____

Engine Revs up or down smoothly _____ Exhaust System _____
Manual Transmission—Clutch Release: From Stop _____ While Moving _____
Manual Transmission—Gear Shift 1st _____ 2nd _____ 3rd _____
4th _____ Revers _____ Park _____
Automatic Transmission: Shifting P to D _____ Acceleration _____
Underway _____ Reverse _____
Brakes: Squeal _____ Pull _____ Pedal Adjustment _____ Noise _____

Engine compartment:

Cleanliness _____ Fluid levels _____ Battery tie downs _____
Battery Cables _____ Air Filter _____ Radiator & hoses _____
Heater hoses _____ Vacuum belts _____ Fan belts _____
Smog equip. _____ Washer Reservoir _____ Oil Gauge _____
Spark plug wires _____

Trunk compartment:

Carpeting _____ Spare tire _____ Jack _____ Lug Wrench _____

Exterior Condition:

Dents in body _____ Paint _____ Signs of previous accidents _____
Top _____ Trim _____ Bumpers _____ Hubcaps _____ Antennae _____
Side mirrors _____ Brake light covers _____ Headlamps _____ Fog lights
Gas cap _____
Gaskets: Widow _____ Doors _____ Wiper blades _____
Door handles _____ Locks _____ Windshield & windows _____ Parking &
tail lights _____
Tires _____ Wheel Rims _____ Oil spots under the car _____
Front Suspension _____ Exhaust system _____
Rust: Rocker Panels _____ Undercarriage _____ Body _____ Overall Look _

Total #1 _____ #2 _____ #3 _____

If you have majority of #1's, the proposed care is in excellent condition.
If you have majority of #2's, it's average.
If you have majority of #3's, avoid this car like a plague.

Remember that this checklist will only work if you let your non-emotional side take a back seat to your keen eye.

To Market, To Market

There are several markets to look into for used cars. There are, of course, friends, yours or your teens, who may be replacing their present model with a new one. You do have a lot of possibilities. Consider:

◆ Independent used car lots
◆ Used car lots located at new car dealer locations
◆ Rental car company resale lots
◆ Bank and leasing company repossessed cars
◆ Public auctions
◆ IRS and government sales and auctions
◆ Company fleet sales
◆ Private parties

Let's look at each of these areas.

The Independent Used Car Lot

Prices are usually higher in independent-used car lots. The only way the owner makes money is by selling cars. They don't have new cars as "deal makers." What they have is what they've got . . . somebody's rejects. And what they've got is what they hope you buy. As a rule used car lot dealers should be avoided. These are places individuals often go when their credit is poor, they need wheels and they basically have no other alternative.

New Car Dealers Used Car Departments

The new car dealer's used car department is many steps higher than the independent used car lot. As a rule, a new car dealer will only maintain the better-used car in their inventory. And, because of their "reputation" in the community, they don't want to be known as a junk dealer. Expect to get some type of warranty from this dealer.

Rental Car Resale Lot

As a frequent traveler, I rent a lot of cars. My company maintains accounts with Hertz, Avis and National. In every city we travel, we are fairly confident that available cars will be in excellent condition. Rental car companies buy their fleet of cars directly from the manufacturer and they save big bucks. Believe it or not, they may pay less than a dealer would for a comparably equipped model. The rationale is really quite logical. Auto manufacturers are quite confident that if an individual rents their cars enough times it will influence their future buyer and buying attitude. A subtle marketing strategy!

Rental companies, such as Hertz, keep their cars in operation for 12,000-15,000 miles. After that, they go to the resale lot. During the "rental" life, they maintain their cars in top maintenance performance. When it is time to go to the resale lot, many agencies sell their vehicles for less than a dealer can. Why? Because they bought it for less.

It's not surprising that some dealers will attempt to discredit the rental car resale lots by telling people that renters usually abuse the cars during the rental period because they don't own them. The reality is that the opposite is true. Rental companies go out of their way and excel in better maintenance of their fleet than private parties maintain personal cars. In other words, their care of a rental vehicle is, as a rule, exceptional.

There are a few drawbacks. Not every make and model is available as most rental companies build their fleets with just a few models and brands. In the old days, a problem was lack of a warranty. New cars today carry such an extensive mileage or multi-year warranty that that doesn't seem to be a problem. It passes to the new owner.

If you are considering the rental resale market, know that there will not be any manufacturer rebates nor will they offer to service your car. But then, when you buy a used car, rarely is "service" a consideration. You go to the local mechanic or your teen rolls up his/her sleeves and changes the oil themselves. To track these folks down, look in the Yellow Pages under used automobiles or call Hertz, Avis or National or other rental agencies directly and ask where their cars are available for resale.

Repossessed Cars

We all know that people get into financial trouble. Whether it's of their own making or a series of catastrophes that have occurred in their economic and work place world, cars that are bought on time or put up as collateral get repossessed. Banks, finance companies and leasing companies have picked them up because the owner/buyers couldn't make the payments.

The graveyard for repossessed cars usually is a dealer auction. But there are times when a bank or a financial institution will advertise that they have cars available to the general public. A good place to call is a large bank in your community and ask if they have resales available for their repossessed cars. If they do, ask if you can view them before the auction.

As a rule, the financial institution is trying to cover their debt. Your objective is to pay the least amount possible—a deal. If the repossessed buyer only owned the car for less than 2 years, the "deal" that you are trying to make may be too rich; they don't want to take a loss. But if they owned it for more than 2 years, the "fat" of the loan/interest has been covered to a great deal. In other words, the remaining balance is the car value. Deal away!

Another way a lender can sell a repossessed car is on a "sealed-bid and quote" basis. This means that the public is allowed to look at the car and write an offer, place it in a sealed envelope and give it to the dealer. At a specified future date the envelopes are opened and the car goes to the highest bidder. In this case, don't be surprised if the lending institution sets a minimum bid.

If you are considering looking at financial repossessions, have the car thoroughly checked by a qualified mechanic. If the lender says no, then take a pass. You don't need someone else's headache/nightmare. When people are in financial trouble, they often redirect their energies and commitments away from the things they are going to lose. And, in fact, they could actually abuse it with the attitude, "who cares what I do or what it looks like. I'm going to lose it anyway."

Public Auto Auctions

There are two types of auctions, "dealer-only" and "public." Only licensed auto dealers are able to participate in the "dealer-only" auction. "Public" auctions are open to all comers. There is a myth that if you attend a public auction, you will get a great deal. Most cars that are at public auctions are usually ones that the dealer can't get rid of. In other words, they are passing their problems on to you. If you are considering going to an auto auction, make sure that you have a qualified mechanic/technician to give you input. It is going to cost you a few dollars, but in the end it could save thousands.

Company Fleet Sales

It's not unusual for large corporations and governmental offices to partici-pate in a fleet of cars for business use. As with the rental companies, they resell after so many miles and replace the sold vehicles with newer versions. These types of sales will be advertised in your local newspaper under the "legal notice" section and in used car ads.

As a rule, the cars are available for a look/see and sales are often conduct-ed either under the "open-auction" or a sealed bid with the highest bidder tak-ing home the new/used car. Use caution here too. If you can't determine the usage of the car and you don't have immediate access to a qualified mechanic or technician, take a pass. These cars are not as well maintained as a car rental agency vehicle.

IRS and Government Sales

When the IRS and the government decide to conduct a sale, they usually advertise quite heavily in the media, radio, print and TV. It's also not unusual for your local police department to hold an auction. The police will tell you if one is in the works. As a rule, none of these agencies conduct a sale more than twice a year. I wouldn't suggest this for the average buyer, because it is almost impossible to fully evaluate the cars, much less take a test run.

Private Parties

These sales usually occur from word of mouth, someone knows someone who's going to sell a car or the local classifieds. Most likely it's your best source for a used car purchase. Most private sellers have an incentive to sell their car fast. They have, or are on the verge of, replacing it with a newer model. Their belief, and it's true, is that one can get more money from a private resale than from their dealer in a trade-in option.

When looking at a private party purchase, it is important to clarify what the ad means. For example, if the car is advertised as recently tuned-up, does it mean that it has had a major overhaul that could cost many hundreds of dollars or just a minor tune-up? Find out exactly what they've done. As in any com-munication amongst parties, everyone has different jargon and different inter-pretations of meanings. Ask if they have copies of ongoing maintenance work.

If this is the route that you and your teen will most likely go, the best strategy is to look for a "one owner" seller and one who has kept track of their maintenance and service. I have a friend who is a strong believer in checking out the radio stations that have been programmed on the 4-6 automatic buttons most cars carry today. If they are programmed for rock and roll or heavy metal, the primary user has been a young person who has not been as kind and gentle as the person who is the classical FM music devotee.

Before you make a commitment to a car, make sure you have it checked out by a mechanic /technician. Visit either your local bank and/or public library and have a clear picture of what the automobile is worth with the help of The Kelly Blue Book. It may be your best friend. The normal number of miles a car racks up in an "average" year is considered to be 10,000-12,000. Anything over that means the car has had a lot of use; anything under gives you a bonus.

Buying through the dealer can be more expensive, but it is usually safest because of warranties, as well as the dealer's reputation. And the car will be discounted already. In addition, you are protected by the federal "lemon laws"; not so with a private sale. If you have a dud, dealers will eventually have to fix the problem. With a private party, they're out of the picture. No lemon law will help you.

In most cases when teens want a car, they will take just about anything they can get their hands on. Granted, their preferences may be for the sportier models. In many cases, you can get a better deal with cars that were family vehicles, such as a wagon or van, than that sporty red coupe.

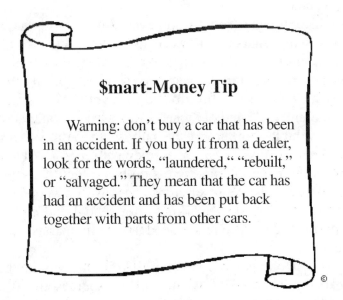

$mart-Money Tip

Warning: don't buy a car that has been in an accident. If you buy it from a dealer, look for the words, "laundered," "rebuilt," or "salvaged." They mean that the car has had an accident and has been put back together with parts from other cars.

Don't Forget The Internet

More and more buyers are avoiding car dealers. The newest port to seek is the Internet. In truth, the Internet sites actually compliment what a dealership can offer. Buyers become aware. Sites to check out include *www.cars.com, www.autoweb.com, www.carpoint.msn.com, www.carsdirect.com* and *www. priceline.com*. Also, don't forget the Kelly Blue Book site at *www.kellybluebook.com*.

Other Guides

There are several other resources that you can consider. One is a book *Don't Get Taken Every Time* (Penguin Books) by Remar Sutton. This is an excellent book for negotiating for a car. And, of course, *The Consumer Reports Used Car Buying Guide* which can be ordered by calling 800-272-0722. The cost is approximately $10 and worth every penny.

Putting It Together

Because of the track record of most teens and driving skills or lack of them as well as experience, I would avoid the temptation of getting anything brand new. As soon as a new car is driven off the lot, it depreciates 20 percent of the price that you just paid.

For money sense, it makes sense to do everything you can do to head your kids off from borrowing funds for the purchase of the car. After all, if they are under 18, which means they are underage, you get to be the co-signer. Most car loans are expensive. By the time the car is paid off, especially in the used car area, the car may have run its useful life and the cycle has to start over.

As a friend so bluntly pointed out when I was working on this section, "Few 16-year-olds *need* vehicles but, boys especially seem to think that they do." Sit down with your kids. Is this a *want* or do they truly *need* it? Do they live far enough away from their school and there's no bus to get them there? Do they not have transportation because of circumstances within your family that you can't be the taxi or are they now working after school and on weekends that they need transportation? Do you really need their help in assisting you as a taxi for siblings, etc.?

In summing up, encourage your kids to stockpile every dime they can, from gifts, from weekend jobs and from whatever their sources are. When it comes to buying a car, it costs a lot of money. It's just not the front-end price, it's the maintenance, repairs, paying for tickets (Have you decided who's going to handle that?), insurance and gasoline. It's even where it is going to be parked. As a parent, you must show them how to break out the real costs of operating a car.

Finally, I think it is important to lay out consequences. Consequences will happen if they don't pay their share of insurance, maintenance, gasoline—whatever you decide beforehand. Consequences come from when there are accidents and tickets. Most important, in my opinion, consequences should be directly tied in to grade point average. It is not uncommon for grades to drop when a car ownership is birthed. As parents of 3 former teenagers, both my husband and I felt strongly that maintaining decent grades, which in our household meant, nothing below a B was a critical element in car ownership. And, if a C cropped up, the car was grounded.

You may feel that that may be a hard line to take, but after all, my goal was to get them out of the house, independent and self-reliant. Having a decent education plays a major role. Owning a car is the first major visible step that adulthood is right around the corner. Your teen must be ready to accept all responsibilities and consequences that go with it.

The Ten Step Program to Buying a Car.

Taking all the information that has been given in this chapter, here is a step by step plan for both you and your teen.

1. *Know exactly what you teen wants.* Sit down and list his or her needs, the preferred model and what equipment is necessary. It's important to stick to the list except for a few small items that might have been initially overlooked. Don't make major changes.
2. *Know your budget.* Know exactly how much can be spent. Don't forget to include all the extra charges. The insurance, the maintenance, gasoline, etc.
3. *Be prepared to shop.* Even though your teen thinks they know it all (What teen doesn't?) it's important for you as a parent(s) to know what constitutes a good deal. Your teen needs your input here.
4. *Use the Car Condition checklist.* In other words, inspect the proposed merchandise, not one that is similar—only the exact one that you are considering. Be methodical and thorough, going over every inch both inside, outside and underneath the hood.

5. *Negotiate wisely.* It's a great time to teach your kids a lesson about negotiating. Eighty percent of successful negotiation is being prepared. In other words, they have done their research, they know what the values are, and they know what resale is. Let the classifieds as well as the Kelly Blue Book be your guide. One of the successes of the skilled negotiator is the ability to walk away. If the seller is not willing to meet what you feel is a fair and realistic price, be willing to walk away.

6. **Know exactly what the going price range is for the style and model you are considering**. Use the Kelly Blue Book and *Consumer's Report*. Check both websites—*www.consumersguide.com* and *www.kellybluebook.com.*

7. **Don't exceed your preset budget limits.** A valuable lesson can be taught here. After all, why set out what the maximum is beforehand in your research mode, what you can afford, and what it's worth and then go over it?

8. **Put everything in writing**. Don't leave any loose ends dangling. If the seller makes promises, have him or her put them in writing, especially if this is a private transaction. Remember that private transactions as in non-dealers are not covered by the "lemon laws."

9. **Have a qualified mechanic check the car out.** This is not an option. Unless you or your teen is a car mechanic genius, get input.

10. **Double-check everything.** Make sure all your figures, including taxes, vehicle registration are in line, and don't forget to have the car inspected by a skilled professional mechanic or technician.

Good luck!

Chapter Fourteen

College is Possible

Having kids adds a new dimension to your financial picture, not to mention what goes on in your personal life. Their impact on your financial game plan can't be ignored. Outside of a major health expense or buying a house, the biggest cash outlay for your kids will most likely be for college.

The costs of college tuition are high today and, according to experts in the field, will continue to rise at a rate of 7 percent per year. This means that one year's tuition at a private college could cost you as much as $55,000 in the academic year of 2010—a four-year degree program at Harvard University could cost more than $350,000. A huge commitment on your pocketbook's part and a tad disgusting when you think about it.

These are sobering figures for any parent to contemplate. With a little planning, you can reduce the future outlay for your kid's college education. As costs have continued to rise, college officials and parents have found ways to make college more affordable. And, without compromising the quality of the education your will daughter or son receive.

Most parents would love to be able to write a check and pay up front for all costs. Most parents don't. Through a variety of options, tuition gets paid, but rarely in cash. Most families take on some kind of debt at some time during the college years.

Throughout this chapter, I will assume that you will be footing a great deal of the costs. I'm a firm believer that kids should help pay the way. I've had

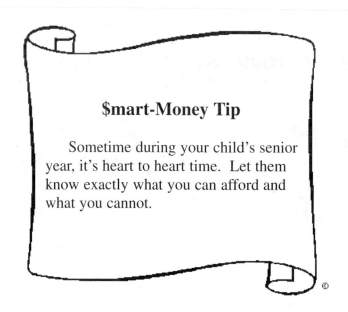

$mart-Money Tip

Sometime during your child's senior year, it's heart to heart time. Let them know exactly what you can afford and what you cannot.

friends say that they don't want their kids to emerge from college with any debt. "Well," I ask, "How about your debt? Are you going into hock when you should be stock piling for your retirement? Or, are you going to figure that one out at a later date?" No response is the usual answer.

If your kids are also on the line, whether it's their savings, investments, or student loans, I believe that there is a greater commitment on their part . . . and less goofing off. When kids set off for college, there is a high probability of partying, having a great time, and not as much time dedicated to studying. Yes, I know that lots of kids really do hit the books, but lots more don't. Being responsible for some of the money gets their attention fairly quickly—a good thing.

The bottom line—if your kids want to go to college, they can. Most can get some type of student aid if it's applied for—even if you have an income as much as $100,000! College takes work, as does planning for it. When your son or daughter becomes the "student," their primary commitment to you is to do well and not to be frivolous with time and money.

Should they pay 100% of the load? I don't think so—after all, with the cost, it's pretty unrealistic to think that they will be able to accumulate all the dollars from whatever sources to pull it off. Some do, but not a lot and not when they are 19 years old. When I grew up, my parents never intended that I go to school after high school. I did, on to masters and doctorate degrees. But that didn't happen when I was 19, or 29. It started in my thirties and I paid every nickel of it.

If dollars are really tight for you, or you don't think your son or daughter is quite ready, here are a few possibilities to consider:

- Consider forgoing the first year after high school and go to work full-time. Money can be saved and a vocation may be more clearly defined.
- If your son knows what he wants to do, encourage him to get a part-time job along with his high school "job" that will give him experience in his chosen field. It looks good on the resume and many kids end up working at their part-time job when they finally graduate from college.
- Skip summer vacation—it's work for pay time. Or, sign on as an intern in the field of interest—many pay a decent salary during this learning curve time. An added bonus is that it's not uncommon to get a job offer after graduation. That, of course, assumes that the work product was good. The workplace is more competitive than ever—having experience puts a student at the head of the pack.
- Consolidate a bachelor and masters degree program. Many schools are offering a combined degree program to save students money and time.
- Tell your kids that their under-graduate degree program is not a five-year one—they can do it the old fashioned way in four years.
- Cars cost lots of money—maintenance, gas and insurance. If a bicycle on campus will do, skip the car.
- Compare the costs of dorm living and off campus living. Many schools require that freshman live on campus in the dorms. If dorm living it is, then insist on dorm eating—you are already paying for it versus the off campus dining.
- Books cost money, big bucks. The college bookstore sells used books, but not at much of a discount. Messages boards should be sought out to see what's being offered.

The Big Day is Coming

As college admission time approaches, it is time to set up a planning session. Does your daughter want to live off campus in her own apartment? Will she live alone or have a roommate(s)? How is that going to be paid for? Is there a possibility of taking a year abroad within her study program? How would that be paid for? Will your daughter need a car on campus? Who pays for gas and insurance (and the car)? How about food and other incidentals? The list goes on. . . .

211

Have your kids work out their goals and how to pay for them. And, be realistic, they may not get them all. When making a financial plan for their college year, make sure that reasonable price tags, not guesstimations, are put on cost. If your child does not have a checking account by now, get one set up. If she is attending school away from your local area, a bank should be selected in the new location.

Once your kids enter college, get prepared. They'll be bombarded by credit card companies. Your kids may end up with more credit offered to them than has ever been offered to you. Does a credit card make sense? Yes. But, there are lots of cautions. Translation: restrictions to be set up by you. This is a good time to refer to Chapter 9 on *Money Talks Within the Family* and check out the websites on credit mentioned.

You must be very clear what the credit card is to be used for. If there's any violations, upon review, you may terminate it. It's not uncommon for kids to run up charges without a clue as to what they total. Some, unfortunately, expect the bank of Mom and Dad to bail them out.

Reducing the Costs

Most money books forewarn you about the enormous costs of college education, currently and in the future. Don't put up a mental block—that saving enough to cover college costs is an absolute impossibility. There are a number of growing ways that you can use to reduce your total education bill. Among them consider:

◆ *Start your child's further education at a community college.* An excellent $mart-Money strategy would be to select a local community college or a state college for the first two years of your child's college program, and plan for the junior and senior years at a "big name" university for the elite degree. Many of the college counselors are recommending this route to save big bucks in the beginning— especially when it is fairly well documented that kids don't know what they really want to do/be. Let them do the major switching at a less expensive dollar rate.

◆ *Send your kids to a public university.* Many states offer an excellent public university system. Residency status qualifies you for significantly lower tuition costs, which could lower your total outlay by 50 percent. The added bonus: travel cost for your kid to come home for holidays and extended weekends are very low—a lot less than an airline ticket from New York to California. Another bonus is that many schools participate in a shared region approach—for example, if you live in Colorado, you can attend the University of Las Vegas Nevada at the resident rate. Thousands can be saved with this kind of approach. Make sure you ask your college aid counselors if their school participates in such a program.

♦ *Finish college in less than 4 years.* Passing advanced placement exams when taking college courses in high school can quick start your child's progress toward a college degree. Well known universities, such as Stanford University in California, are proponents for completing college in their system in less than 4 years. Why? According to their president, advanced education has just gotten too expensive. Amen to that logic.

♦ *Enroll more than one of your kids in the same college.* Many colleges and universities give reduced rates for tuition to families with more than one sibling in attendance.

♦ *Send your kids to your Alma Mater.* Most schools offer tuition breaks to the children of alumni.

♦ *Work for the school your child attends.* One of the perks offered to teaching staff members is reduction in the amount of tuition paid for their kids. Some schools offer a free ride (but not for room and board). Non-teaching employees can sometimes tap into this as well. The key is to ask and determine if there are any strings attached.

♦ *Excel with brains or brawn.* Let's face it, being fantastic at scholarship or at sports can create some great scholarships for your student.

♦ *Get a job.* Many employers will pay (reimburse) employees for their tuition and book costs. The catch is usually the reimbursement is paid *after* grades are turned in and a specified average is maintained (i.e. a B average). Still, not a bad way to go and earn at the same time.

♦ *Prepay tuition.* Many private and public schools now offer prepaid plans—you write a check today for future costs. The tuition rate is locked in and if it raises (which you can assume it will), you won't have to pay extra. The negative here is that your kids may not want to go to the school you selected. Determine if there are any "out" clauses. As of this writing, 36 states offer tuition plans. They allow parents (any any willing donor) to contribute $10,000 each (for a total of $100,000) to a child's college account in a single year.

The bottom line here is that, in spite of the high cost of a college education, there are ways to get assistance using your own creative strategies, from the current offerings from State and Federal assistance programs, as well as from the programs available at the school of choice. The majority of students now get some form of aid—it comes in the form of student loans, work/study programs and grants. This doesn't include any checks from grandparents and other relatives.

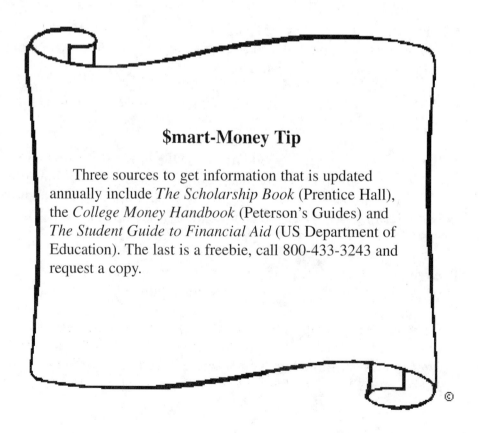

$mart-Money Tip

Three sources to get information that is updated annually include *The Scholarship Book* (Prentice Hall), the *College Money Handbook* (Peterson's Guides) and *The Student Guide to Financial Aid* (US Department of Education). The last is a freebie, call 800-433-3243 and request a copy.

$mart-Money College Investments

Many academic advisors say that, if you can save up 50 to 60 percent of the cost of your kids college education, you will be in pretty good shape. And what if you can't save that much? The answer is just common sense; any amount will help. The key is to start early and save regularly. If you do this, you will accumulate an investment nest egg. That nest egg can be used for investment opportunities in both mutual funds and stocks, that over a period of time, have increased in value more than the traditional savings accounts and bonds have increased.

Keep in mind that a higher rate of return on your investment usually means that a higher degree of risk is involved. So, no matter what degree of risk you are willing to accept, a variety of saving alternatives are available.

Uncle Sam and You: EE an I Savings Bonds

One of the most conservative options is the Series EE savings bond. Earnings from these bonds are tax exempt of state or local taxes. For certain income level families, any EE bonds purchased after 1989 that are cashed in to meet educational expenses, are exempt from federal taxes. Check with your local bank to see if you qualify for the exception. Basically, EE bonds are a no-brainer, and they do work.

EE bonds are bought at a discount of their mature value, taking 15 years to reach maturity. They will earn interest for another 15 years. After 30 years, no additional interest is paid. That means you need to cash them in.

The other government savings bond to consider is the I bond. It's not purchased at a discount, rather, at full value. It earns interest at a higher rate than the EE bond, enjoys a non-tax status on your state tax return. Information on purchasing savings bonds will be at your bank, you can call the Federal Reserve at 800-234-2931 or go online at *www.savings-bonds.gov*.

Zero-coupon Bonds

Zero coupon bonds (zeros) are a popular vehicle for college investment funds, because they pay all interest and principal at maturity. Many parents like to know exactly how much money they will have on the day their child will start college. Having zeroes that mature when you child enters school can fill that need. To meet college costs, you can buy zeros that will mature during the years

215

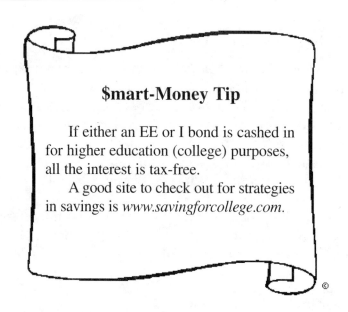

$mart-Money Tip

If either an EE or I bond is cashed in for higher education (college) purposes, all the interest is tax-free.

A good site to check out for strategies in savings is *www.savingforcollege.com*.

your child will attend college. There are two types: taxable and tax exempt. Taxable zeros might be appropriate for gifting opportunities, depending on the tax status of the recipient. Tax exempt zeros will generally produce a lower rate of return, but may be the choice for the higher income family.

Baccalaureate bonds are special municipal zero coupon bonds, that are issued by some states. The interest on these bonds is exempt from federal, and in some cases, state and local taxes. The zero coupon Treasury bond is issued by the U.S. Treasury. In these bonds the accumulated interest is federally taxable but exempt from state and local taxes. Because of the different way these bonds are handled tax wise, make sure you get tax advise before placing any moneys in the zero family.

CD's

The College Savings Bank 800 888-2723 sells certificates of deposit (CD's) that are federally insured. Known as the CollegeSure CD's, they have maturities of 1 to 25 years and usually require minimum investment of $1000. There is a significant penalty for early withdrawal prior to the maturity date. The rate of one CD is adjusted each July, and applies retroactively to all funds held for the year. In a rising interest market, this could be good news. If interest rates are declining, not so good.

Stocks and Mutual Funds

Most financial advisors believe that, if you have the time (more that 5 years to college age kids), your college kitty should be comprised mainly of stocks and mutual funds. The reason—earnings on stocks and mutual funds have consistently out performed bonds and other fixed income investments *since 1926.* Overall, the average return for stocks and mutual funds has been 10 percent per year. A portfolio of individual stocks and no load growth mutual funds will allow you to minimize your risk while accumulating college funds. When your kids reach college age, you can gradually shift assets out of this portfolio, to cash instruments. Specifically, money market savings accounts.

A word of caution. When you are in the process of identifying the right place to invest money for your college fund, don't go with the one that had the best rate of return during the previous year. Murphy's law usually comes into

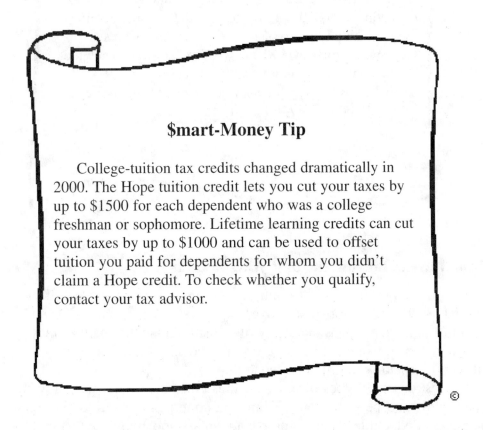

$mart-Money Tip

College-tuition tax credits changed dramatically in 2000. The Hope tuition credit lets you cut your taxes by up to $1500 for each dependent who was a college freshman or sophomore. Lifetime learning credits can cut your taxes by up to $1000 and can be used to offset tuition you paid for dependents for whom you didn't claim a Hope credit. To check whether you qualify, contact your tax advisor.

play. Today's star may be tomorrow's joke. Look at the track records of funds over a period of years—how do they compare for this period (3, 5, 10 years, etc.) compared to others. You want to choose from funds that show good performance over a period of time.

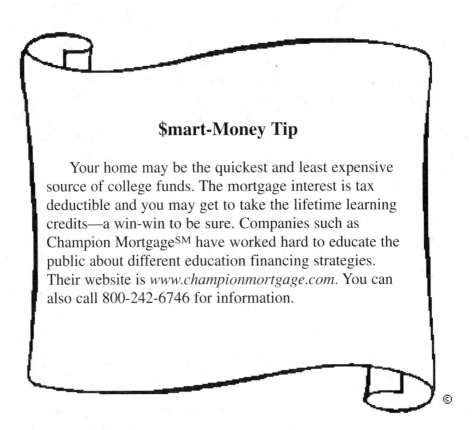

$mart-Money Tip

Your home may be the quickest and least expensive source of college funds. The mortgage interest is tax deductible and you may get to take the lifetime learning credits—a win-win to be sure. Companies such as Champion Mortgage[SM] have worked hard to educate the public about different education financing strategies. Their website is *www.championmortgage.com*. You can also call 800-242-6746 for information.

If You Have to Borrow, the Best Ways to Do It . . .

Even if you save or invest regularly during your child's' pre-college years, you may still need to borrow to cover expenses. If you are not eligible for any federally subsidized loans, a variety of attractive loan alternatives may still be at your fingertips. Interest expense on 2nd mortgage home equity loans, up to $100,000, generally is fully tax deductible.

Interest on other types of loans such as consumer loans, cash advances on credit cards and personal loans from non-commercial sources (i.e. relatives) are not tax deductible. There is no tax advantage to paying interest on this type of loan—that was the "old days." Some financial institutions offer credit lines that feature an interest only payment option, and defer repayment of the principal balance until graduation—afterward, your overall monthly cash outlays will be reduced significantly. Your 401(k) may be a source of moneys and offer a lower rate of interest. Check with your employer if it allows borrowing against your plan.

Educational IRAs

Beginning in 2002, you can place up to $2,000 a year in an Educational IRA, up from $500. Funds can be used for qualified elementary and secondary school expenses and withdrawals are tax-free when used to pay for certain room and board expenses, uniforms, computers and extended day program expenses. In order to qualify, you must meet stick income limits, so not everyone is eligible. Most likely, you would be better off with a 529 plan . . . read on.

529's—the New Kid on the Block

In a nutshell, 529s are state college savings plans that allow you to salt away a hefty amount of money in stock and bond funds (as much as $150,000). The money can be used at any school in the country and you get to keep control of the funds until your child goes to college. The earnings are tax-free if used to qualified education expenses and grow tax-deferred until withdrawn. There are proposals in Congress to make them completely tax-free. Many states offer extra tax breaks, so check with your tax advisor.

Perkins and Stafford/Ford Loans

Federal loans—the Perkins and the Stafford/Ford loans, are worth investigation. The financial aid officer at your child's chosen college can determine whether you will qualify for either of these loan programs—and can tell you how much money you will be eligible for.

Perkins loans carry the lowest interest rate and are at a fixed rate. The Perkins loan is designed for the low-income student. Interest owed is accrued and payments start nine months after enrollment ends.

Stafford/Ford loans vary with a cap at 9 percent. The good news is that no interest will be owed on either type of loan while your child is in school. When your child exits school or graduates, payment begins. You do not have to establish financial need to get a Stafford/Ford loan, but there is a twist if you don't. The rate and repayment parameters are the same, but interest accrual begins when the loan is taken out. These loans allow for loan limit increases each year—an allowance for increased tuition.

Presently (subject to change), the loan limit for the first year of undergraduate work is $2,625; for the second year, $3,500 and third and fourth years, $5,500. The government pays interest while your child is in school.

Another program that is available is the U.S. government's Government PLUS program. PLUS stands for parent loans for undergraduate students. PLUSes carry a variable interest rate. At this writing, they range between 6 and 7 percent, have 10 percent cap and charge a 5 percent origination fee. If you need to borrow a total of $20,000, this means that there will be a $1000 origination fee on top of it. In addition, you must begin to make monthly payments immediately. Payment is *not* deferred as it in other student related loans.

Money With No Strings Attached

What's better than getting money that you have to pay back? Not having to pay it back. The Federal Pell Grants and Federal Supplemental Educational Opportunity Grants (FSEOG) may be your cup of tea. A grant is a gift, meaning the moneys do not have to be paid back . . . ever! To find out if your son or daughter qualifies, contact the US Department of Education at 800-433-3243 or go to their website *www.ed.gov*.

Banks Loan Moneys Too

Don't be shy in approaching your local bank for funds. They usually charge a higher rate of interest on student-related loans than Uncle Sam does, but heck, probe every corner. Some banks are more aggressive than others—Wells Fargo, Norwest (soon to be Wells Fargo), First Bank, U.S. Bank and Union Bank & Trust are just a few of the biggies that are aggressively in this market. If yours is one that I mentioned, call where you bank and ask what programs they offer.

Financial Gifts for College

If you have excess money or you have a relative that wants to contribute to college for your child in the future, it's time to bring the topic to the table. Federal guidelines allow a $10,000 annual gift tax exclusion that is not taxable for the

$mart-Money Tip

There are a few websites to check out in your money search. Try The Financial Aid Information Page at *www.finaid.org,* the Ambitious Student's Guide to Financial Aid at *www.synet.com* and FastWEB at *www.fastweb.com.*

You don't need a zillion dollars to start your mutual fund participation. Many funds allow a minimum beginning investment ranging from $100 to $1000. Some are lower (In fact, a representative for Invesco funds told me that they would take any amount to get someone started!), but require a commitment to continue adding regularly to the fund, via automatic withdrawals from one of your bank accounts.

recipient. This applies to you and any relative and any gifts will be from "after tax dollars." Any amounts over $10,000 should be discussed with your tax advisor, prior to giving it.

How to Hold Title to Kid's Money for College

Every state has a Uniform Gifts to Minors Act (UGMA), that allows you to be the custodian for funds given to your child for any purpose. You have the legal authority to hold and manage them on your children's behalf. But don't forget the Kiddie Tax reviewed in an earlier chapter. If your kids are under 14, any gains, dividends or interest over $700 becomes taxable and your child will then have to file a tax return at a rate of 15 percent. Any earnings in excess of $1400 will be taxed at the parent's current taxation rate.

Any money held in a custodial account is still considered legally owned by your children. With UGMA, you must transfer the holdings to them when they reach the age of 18. This can be a "Catch 22" if your child is not very responsible. You may fear that money allocated for college will be spent possibly frivolous ways by the newly wealthy 18-year-old. Your dreams and plans literally go out the window or down the drain.

Some kids do not turn out to be college material but will be very capable of finding a good job with potential. Others, well some others, are problem kids. If you have assessed the situation and determine that you prefer not to have the college fund distributed at age 18, you have some legally correct options for UGMA funds. Place the funds in an investment, any alternative that restricts your child's access, with a maturity date later than your child's 18th birthday— zero coupon bonds, perhaps a CD. A small amount can be given to the youngster at the time you reinvest, with the promise that the funds will be turned over as they mature. Hopefully, your child will always want to reinvest the greater portion of this fund, but you have to let them grow and count on your previous good work in instilling the saving habit.

Another option for pushing out the disbursement date beyond the child's 18th birthday is to bypass UGMA provisions. You can use the UTMA, which stands for Uniform Transfers to Minors Act. The difference between the two is, that disbursements for UTMA occur on the 21st birthday versus the 18th for UGMA (In California, it stretches to 25). Unfortunately, not all states have passed UTMA, so check with your bank, financial planner, broker, lawyer or accountant to quickly find out what is available where you live.

There's No Free Lunch

The government does not require that you pay for your child's college education. There are a few states, though, that specifically require that the cost of college be included in calculations of support payments in divorce cases. Since the teenage population sits on a mega billion dollars a year income from all sources, it's not unreasonable to expect your teen to prepare herself for participation in the funding of her college education. After all, college education is the foundation of their future meal ticket.

In our household, we were willing to, and did pick up the tab for all undergraduate education for our kids (all post graduate degrees were to be their financial responsibility. And, so far none have gone on). We drew the line however, on paying for living expenses if they wanted to go to college and not live at home. How did my kids pay for these expenses? They had part-time jobs during school months and worked full time in the summer. They also took out student loans and their parents did not pay these loans back—they paid them back.

Getting College Aid

The amount of money your child can obtain for college assistance from the federal student aid programs will be based predominately on your income, not your assets. Current federal guidelines exclude your assets when determining student aid distributions, if your family's adjusted gross income is less than $50,000 and you file a 1040EZ or 1040A tax form.

When you file one of these tax forms, income becomes the test for qualifying for student aid. And, here's a clincher. Currently, parents are only required to use 5.6 percent of their assets to pay for college after various other allowances are taken into consideration. Kids are expected to pay for 35 percent of their accumulated assets. But then, if that's what they have been saving and investing for all these years, why not?

There are no standards for the student aid application forms used by col-

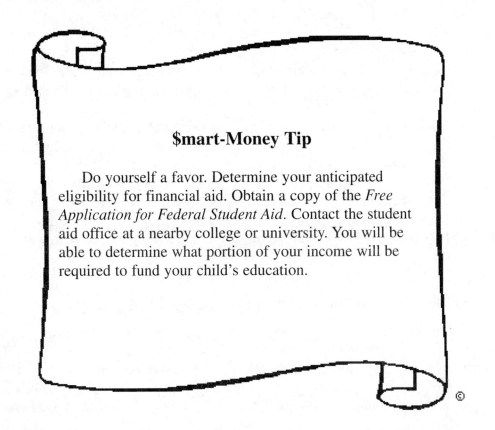

$mart-Money Tip

Do yourself a favor. Determine your anticipated eligibility for financial aid. Obtain a copy of the *Free Application for Federal Student Aid*. Contact the student aid office at a nearby college or university. You will be able to determine what portion of your income will be required to fund your child's education.

leges and universities. There are, however, some questions they all will ask. Included are:

- ◆ Do you have any cash value available on your life insurance policy(s)?
- ◆ Do you have access to retirement, pension, and 401(k) plans?

Federal student aid calculations don't include these amounts. Schools are looking for ways to reduce the amounts that they would have to supplement your child's educational costs. Some will meet as much as 100 percent of the difference that the "need" formula calculates based on your current income and assets if they come into play. That difference is made up of a mixture of work/study programs, student loans, scholarships, and grants.

Let's face it, the money pot is getting smaller in a lot of areas and that includes student aid. As your kids approach the time when they must make their choice of colleges, you as a parent must be prepared with the questions for the financial aid officers. Ask them how they treat outside scholarships. Some schools will take the value of the scholarship and reduce the amount that they would consider giving in the form of aid. Others exclude any scholarships, allowing you as the parent, to adjust your contribution via the scholarship funds.

There are many things included when the college figures the total student aid package you can get. The following are a few of the questions you can ask them:

- ◆ How do they determine whether a student and their family can qualify for student aid? If you know that you don't meet any of their criteria, don't waste your time.
- ◆ What are the requirements for students to meet the financial aid commitments? Do they have to participate in a work/study program?
- ◆ Do they include books and some spending money in their aid package?
- ◆ If your student does qualify for aid, will he qualify next year, assuming that your financial picture doesn't change?

Never Underestimate the Power of Bargaining

If your kids have a special talent such as golf, music or sheer brilliance, you now have a bargaining tool. Today's colleges are in a competitive marketplace and they want your college dollars. Don't be afraid to negotiate.

In the chapter on preschoolers, I told you about my niece Chrissy when she was age 3½. Since then her athletic talents, which include volleyball and basketball, have made her a star player. In 1996, she graduated from high school. Letters from coaches from all over the country marked the preceding year. Chrissy had something they wanted—her outstanding athletic abilities; her parents now had a bargaining chip.

The message here is that if your child has a special talent, make it known to the school of your choice (if they don't already know about it). And, check out what other schools might offer to have your talented youngster attend their college. What they offer might be a better offer. Bring it to the table at the chosen school, before you commit to the school. And perhaps you can get the school and the funds you want. It could be a great position to be in.

What About Scholarships?

When I was working on my doctorate, I subscribed to a service that proclaimed that they had the inside skinny on all the scholarships that were available. Did they? Not really, but I did part with $90 of my money. Too many times, the lists of moneys and awards are quite narrow in their eligibility. One of the most current services available today is the **College Aid Sources for Higher Education**. The service is available for $30 and can be obtained by calling 301-258-0717.

Don't be afraid to ask the financial aid officer, or the equivalent, at the high school that your kids attend. I have also found that your local community col-

$mart-Money Tip

A word of caution. Bargain before you commit or put any kind of deposit down on a college or university. Once the deal's made, it's unlikely they will give more when you go back to ask.

lege financial aid office can be of assistance. They are fully tuned to the fact that many students want to go on to earn a BA or BS and beyond, outside of the AA—the Associates Arts degree at the community college. These individuals often know of scholarships and other resources that may be within the mainstream, and could be a perfect fit for your child.

All in all—higher education—the entry fee for the ability to earn more money as an adult—is going to cost money. A lot of it. Start putting money aside. If you have relatives that are inclined to give gifts in excess of $25 for birthdays and special holidays, you've got a partner. Ask them to contribute to your child's college fund through gifts that would go toward investments in a mutual fund or savings account.

What Will They Be When They Grow Up?

Some kids don't have a clue what they want to do as an adult. On one hand, you want them to be open and study different areas. On the other, you don't want to produce a professional student that never graduates.

When your kids do show some interest, encourage them to seek an internship. One where they may not get paid one penny for the work they do with a company or a professional who is in the area of their interest. Recent studies show that companies are routinely hiring former student employees for full time positions, after they complete college.

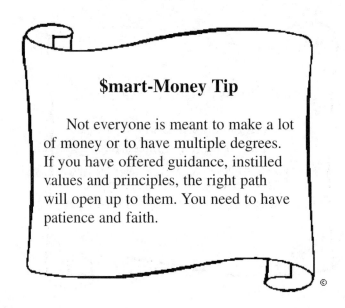

$mart-Money Tip

Not everyone is meant to make a lot of money or to have multiple degrees. If you have offered guidance, instilled values and principles, the right path will open up to them. You need to have patience and faith.

The professions that I have today include market research, speaking and writing. The only clue I had as a youngster that I would be a speaker and writer was the fact that I was a superb note passer in my middle school years. And, that I always got in trouble for talking too much. Other than that, nothing that I was interested in as a kid pointed me to the vocation I now pursue. If your kids aren't quite sure what they want to be, don't push too hard. I know some terrific doctors who started out majoring in PE.

You can lay out all the data about a college education yielding greater income earned—which is true—yet, there are many, many individuals who have never set foot in an ivory tower, and have succeeded handsomely. As a parent, one the most important things you can do is to help your child identify their talents and skills and nurture them.

What happens—gulp—if it looks like your kid is not headed toward college? They've expressed no interest and excelled at none of the academic pursuits that you feel are important. I believe that some parents need to back off. Just because someone doesn't go to college does not make him or her a reject. And, let's face it, there are lots of positions, especially in the blue-collar area, that don't require a college degree. What they require is mechanical, even sometimes technical, skills. Skills that can be taught through other trade and internship programs.

Chapter Fifteen

Creating a Wall Street Wizard

Picking stocks can be likened to playing a game of darts. Like the dart player, aim and fire at your targeted stock and you will have close to the same result—a complete miss, something in between or a bulls-eye. Yes, there is some luck involved in picking stocks, and even the best of professional advisors will admit to this. However, a logical, rational and educated approach to selecting stocks for investment might miss a few of the "shooting star" stocks but the end result—a portfolio of solid stocks with consistent earnings and growth.

Over the years, I have become convinced that there are ways that any novice investor (adult or child) can "play" the stock market. And with some homework, the novice can out perform the vast majority of the professionals. And, they don't need the dartboard.

In the 80's I taught a weekend seminar for 40 women at a local university. On the first day, I presented the basics of the stock market, highlighting a few of the simple rules for evaluating the available information to the investor who is considering a stock purchase. That kind of information is readily available in publications such as *Business Week, Bloomberg Financial, Money, Worth, $mart-Money,* etc.

I showed the group how to determine book values, percentage increases, price/earnings ratios, ratios of profits and dividend distributions to growth sales and earnings, etc. Of the companies that were presented, the corresponding *Value*

Line Investment Survey was included. *Value Line* is one of the top rated stock advisories and is available at no cost to clients at their stock brokerage office. If you do not have a stockbroker, the local library is also a source, you could subscribe on your own or you could go online at *www.valuelinesurvey.com.*

The seminar participants were taught how to read the *Value Line.* Homework for the first evening, they were asked to evaluate some stocks based on historical information such as: annual percentage increases (or decreases) for gross sales, profits and dividend distribution. The challenge was to identify the company they would invest in, if the money was available to them.

The following morning the results were presented. The majority of the class had chosen a stock that few of them had ever heard about. Ironically, one week before the class began, *Business Week* published an article covering the fast food industry, and one of the companies they reviewed was Wendy's. That unknown stock of the 80's, is today, a stock whose shares are held by major institutions all over the world as well as parents like you and me.

The following year this stock appreciated significantly and the underlying company displayed an aggressive and forward-looking approach to business. Investors seemed to appreciate the vision of the company's management. This was no surprise, later on, to the stock market neophytes who had attended my seminar. The stock—Wendy's named after the daughter of owner and founder, Dave Thomas. You are thinking, you were teaching adults, what could you teach to children? Plenty.

What Do You Do Mom?

When my daughter was in the 8th grade, she told me that she and her friends were discussing what their parents did for a living. Her question then to me was, "What do you do, Mom?" In 1972, I became a stockbroker. Four years later, I was in front of my daughter's 8th grade, to present what I knew about the stock market. We all had a great time and I learned that kids are basically capitalists at heart.

Together, we developed a typewriter company and named it after their teacher. As we took the company through production and sales of typewriters, they learned about profit and loss statements and balance sheets. They also learned about the different kinds of stock, common and preferred and also bond issues. We floated an issue called Grandma's Bond—7 percent maturing in 1977—to obtain operating capital to fund our projected growth. When we finished, each kid could dissect an annual report and put together a business plan that would be acceptable and even admired by any banker.

Ten years later, my youngest daughter's school asked me if I would develop a stock market class for their seniors. I fine tuned what I had done with the 8th grade, and took on the senior class. These kids developed a soda company; learned the ways to capitalize their venture and dug into the elements of a balance sheet (Do we really need to inventory that many bottle caps?). The company we developed together was The Mid-Peninsula Beverage Company. On paper, we developed the company, took it into the production and marketing of products and we eventually sold the venture.

Then we went on to learn about trading on the stock market. They devoured the Apple Computer annual reports I had supplied to them for dissection. Each kid was given a theoretical $100,000 investment account, with the challenge to increase the account through trading on the real stock market. I was their broker and they had to call me at a prearranged time each day with any trades (buying or selling) for stocks in their portfolios.

The kids *were not* allowed to just sit on their portfolio, and they were told they would flunk the class if they didn't actively trade the portfolio. Like the real world, brokerage fees and commissions were charged against their accounts for each trade that they made. By the time the class ended, most students had more in depth knowledge of the stock market than their parents did.

"A" Is Not For Easy

Were these two groups flukes? Were these kids brilliant "Whiz Kids"? What if I had had foreign students—kids who weren't brought up with a capitalistic approach to life? I soon found out. A few years after I worked with the seniors, I was asked to develop another class. This time it was for small liberal arts college with a business school. This type of class was already in their curriculum and was known as the easy "A" course—all you had to do was show up for class and the "A' was yours.

That changed when I came on the scene. I am a believer in the concept that you should earn what you get, and further, that valuable lessons should not be that easy. On the very first day of class, I gave a test to my new students to complete. This was a look—alike of what I planned for their final exam—the entire class flunked the test. Then I told them that if they came to class and faithfully completed their homework, they would be able to answer every question on the test they had just failed.

A few students dropped out immediately—definitely not the easy "A" class they expected. These students were seniors who were just about to complete a degree in business, so I did not include teaching the formation of a new business in my class curriculum as I had done for the 8th and 12th grade students. We played the stock market game, went on field trips—one of my friends owned a seat on the Pacific Coast Stock Exchange—and I introduced a new element.

The students were challenged to find a real company that was in trouble. Why? Not every company that gets into trouble is destined to sink like the Titanic, taking most of the assets to the bottom. With a little fine-tuning and rearranging of the deck chairs, it just might float. They had to research the company and write a "turn-around" business plan that would return the company to profitability. A portion of the final grade for the class was the presentation of their "turn-around" business plan, in both written and oral form, complete with visual aids such as overhead slides. These plans were presented to me as well as to their classmates.

Each student had liquidated his portfolio of stocks. During the turn-around business presentations, they were instructed to evaluate each presentation with the goal being to invest in the company that was pitched the best. How did they do? Their grades tell the story. Two thirds of the originally enrolled students finished the class and no one received a grade below a "B." For many years, I have kept in touch with several of these graduates. They have used the lessons from our class and have recounted to me many profitable experiences that are directly attributable to our time together.

Historically, no single investment has out performed the consistency of the stock market. It is true that there are people who have become millionaires overnight, some from the invention of some gadget or widget, but they are in the minority. The majority of successful investors use segments of Wall Street. If you are a novice to stock investments, you will learn a lot from this chapter and so will your kids.

How to Select Stocks and Eat Them Too

One of the best ways to get your kids involved in the stocks is to step up and purchase some shares. When you buy one or two shares of stock, you will be a bit dismayed when you see the value of your investment immediately decrease, via the deduction of brokerage fees and commissions. However, the lessons you and your child will learn are priceless.

When Frank was in his Mighty Morphin Power Ranger period, his adoring grandmother (me) checked out the local Toys-R-Us to see what toys resulted from the love affair kids had with this series of programs. And, I learned a lot. The general manager of the store told me that the shelf life of a Power Ranger

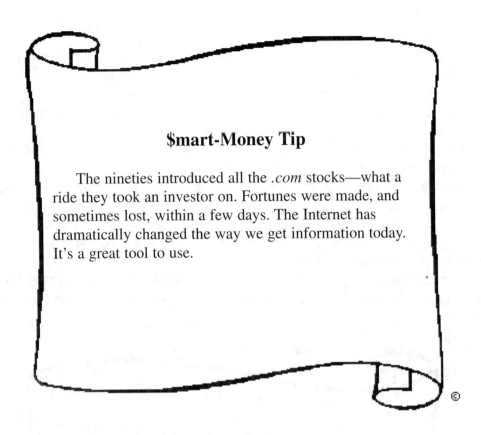

$mart-Money Tip

The nineties introduced all the *.com* stocks—what a ride they took an investor on. Fortunes were made, and sometimes lost, within a few days. The Internet has dramatically changed the way we get information today. It's a great tool to use.

related item was 7 hours—a merchant's dream—waiting lists for many items were routine. And here's one for you, the general manager of an auto parts store (an adoring parent?) offered to give a deep discount on prices of his merchandise to any store manager that would give him advance warning of the arrival of ANY shipment of Power Ranger toys. You didn't need a Ph.D. to know someone was making money—a lot of money and very quickly.

So, who is this someone?—The parent company. And, what about all the other someones out there? When considering stocks for your child's investment program, make your selection from a market segment he understands. You will have his interest immediately and you will keep it. Look at what kids are spending money on? There's Nintendo, Sony and Marvel comic books. And, don't forget what kids like to eat—why not a comparison of Pepsi and Coke for your first exercise in stock watching. Or compare the performance of Wendy's versus McDonald's.

Kids are into sports—consider companies that make sport shoes, clothing and equipment. Look at Nike. Golfer Tiger Woods is hot—what companies have signed him as the spokesperson? How about movies and music? Let your kids check out who the companies are that produce and/or distribute their favorites.

If parents and kids keep their eyes and ears open, the opportunities for interesting investments are limitless. And here is where the subject of supply and demand comes in. Once you have selected a few companies that interest you both, determine what the demand for the company's product(s) are/is and whether the supply is meeting the demand. Can you get all you want when you go shopping or is the supply always short?

Pay close attention to TV commercials as the holidays approach or take a walk in a big toy outlet to scan the huge array of toys and games, and both will beckon your pocketbook. One company, Hasbro, produces the old standby toy names, Tonka Toys and Playschool; Mattel produces both Hot Wheels and Barbie—the queen of all dolls.

At a garage sale, Frank and I came across something that was "hot" in the 80's. This item cost $5 new and could be purchased this day for 5¢. Do you

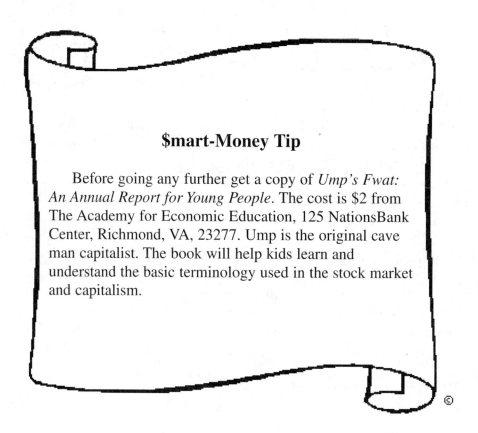

$mart-Money Tip

Before going any further get a copy of *Ump's Fwat: An Annual Report for Young People*. The cost is $2 from The Academy for Economic Education, 125 NationsBank Center, Richmond, VA, 23277. Ump is the original cave man capitalist. The book will help kids learn and understand the basic terminology used in the stock market and capitalism.

remember the Cabbage Patch Dolls? Parents spent many hours in lines to pay $100 or more for such a doll, but in a very few years the price of them plummeted and the producing company went into bankruptcy.

During Christmas of 1998, Furby's were hot—parents were paying over $100 for an item that sold retail for a fraction. In 1999, Furby's are everywhere for under $30. As I write this, Pokémon is hot among kids . . . for how long, who knows? Items such as these are thus categorized as fads and not trends. The only time that fortunes or empires are made as a result of a fad, is when an investor gets his money in the pot early when the stock price is low and out before the fad dies and the stock price and/or the company dies.

A Little Brainstorming Helps

First, set aside time for a family investment meeting at least once a month. Since the stock market can "move" a lot in a month you may want to meet more

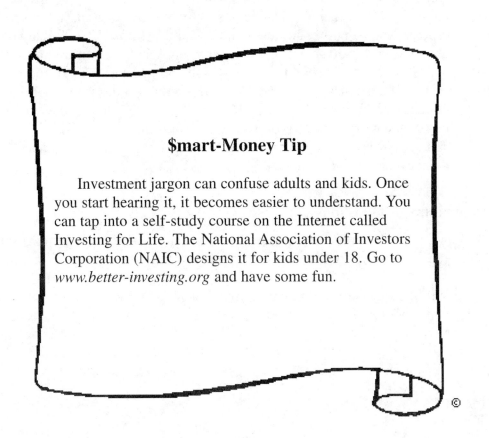

$mart-Money Tip

Investment jargon can confuse adults and kids. Once you start hearing it, it becomes easier to understand. You can tap into a self-study course on the Internet called Investing for Life. The National Association of Investors Corporation (NAIC) designs it for kids under 18. Go to *www.better-investing.org* and have some fun.

often. Let your kids know that this will be a time for brainstorming investment ideas and strategies. With your copy of *Ump's Fwat* in hand (you and your kids can each afford to have one at the low price of $2), roll up your investment sleeves.

- ♦ Whenever I taught a stock market class, to young people, the classics of Disney and McDonald's were on most kid's investment wish list. Their choices expanded after they were more familiar with the methodology of investing.
- ♦ A lot of information is free, so start with your library. Most have a terrific investment section, they also carry the *Value Line Investment Survey*. In *Value Line*, you will find on one page all you want to know about a targeted company—it's past, present and analysts' projections for the future. A sample from *Value Line* for Microsoft and how to read it is included later in this chapter.
- ♦ When your kids have narrowed down their investment opportunity target list down to a few companies, write or call for their annual reports. Their mailing address can be found in *Value Line*. Review the annual reports and select one company that you are comfortable with *and* excited about. Then take the plunge and purchase one or more shares. If a mutual fund is your selection, a minimum investment will be required. Review the *$mart-Money Resource Center* at the end of this chapter for a list of groups that can minimize commission costs.
- ♦ Teach your kids how to read stock prices quoted in the newspaper for the various stock exchanges they publish daily.

Pre-investment Questions

Before you spend one dime on any stock or mutual fund (or any other investment), there is a series of questions you and your kids should learn to address.

1. Will the return on my potential investment keep me ahead of inflation *and* render enough of a return to offset any tax obligation that results from these gains?

 If you can't answer yes to this one, pass on the investment. Keep your money in the bank.

2. What are the opportunity costs of my potential investment? Could you use the same amount of money for an investment with a greater potential for return? How much time will you have to put into this investment? Would it be better to make a 7 percent annual return versus a 12 percent annual return that would require more time? How much will you lose in interest income by taking money out of a savings account?

 Few investors ask, much less answer, these questions. Take the time to honestly answer each one before you invest.

3. Does this investment provide enough liquidity? My definition is that you can get your money out within 7 days. Most parent's savings goals are to have approximately 3 to 6 months of after tax living expenses put back at all times. For your kids, the parents are usually the *liquidity fund.* They get to pass go and proceed in investing.

 Until you have a *liquidity fund* in place—a spot from which you can get cash within 7 days, skip investing in anything, except a money market type of fund.

4. Do you have financial obligations due within the next two years? How much of that obligation will be met by the funds you are considering investing? Most kids get to pass go on this one too. As your kids get older, college expenses loom. This question then becomes very important.

 Any moneys needed within 2 years should not be jeopardized in any way, even if the stock market is skyrocketing. Take a pass. Use your money market funds for short-term waits.

5. Do you know the break-even point of your potential investment? This means: 1. What percentage return must your investment provide to pay any taxes that could occur from a gain, and 2. What percentage return must your investment provide to compensate for the loss in purchasing power due to inflation? 3. How much does the investment have to increase in value to offset any costs to buy it?

Before you place any moneys in an investment, figure out your bottom line—how much it costs you to be an investor (commissions).

6. Do you or your kids understand what the targeted investment company does to make money?

There are no stupid questions when it comes to investing and especially when it's your money on line. If you are working with a broker, ask questions until you are satisfied you understand the answers.

7. Does the investment match your objectives? If you are close to retirement your investment objectives will necessarily require an emphasis on income from the investment and you will place your funds only in investments that create income with some growth but not aggressive growth. If you are under 50 you will be more interested in aggressive growth. Kids should focus on growth, not income.

Objectives will continually change throughout your life, as they will with your kids. If you have a financial advisor, don't let them talk you into anything that doesn't fit your objectives.

8. Can you afford the risk of the investment—the possibility of losing part or all of your money? If the answer is NO, to any loss, don't do it. If the answer is NO, to all, you should reevaluate your timing in the investment. When you invest in stock, it is rare that they become worthless over night. Regular check-ups on the underlying company(s) progress are important and if bad news starts to hit, it is very likely that the company's stock price will decline.

If you can't afford to lose $1 (mentally of financially) you have no business investing. Stay with a passbook savings account and money market funds and don't invest in anything else.

9. When you invest, determine your up side objective . . . and your down side. Most view investing with "the sky is the limit" approach and you shouldn't. When you invest, set percentage increase and decrease goals. If your upside or downside goals are reached, sell and take your profit

or your loss. And if the investment stays flat for a long period, consider moving the funds along to another investment.

 Do yourself a favor, always identify the downside in any investment you make—20 percent works for me. If a stock or fund declines that much, I cash out.

 Here's another way to determine your buys, holds and sells. If you had more money to invest, would you use it to buy more of this investment? If your answer is *Yes*, maintain your position, If your answer is *Maybe*, consider selling a portion. If your answer is *No*, sell (there's always something you can put your money in).

10. A salesperson (or your broker) is constantly calling you to buy this and buy that. You are told that it's the deal of the century and time is running out. Should you?

 If anyone pushes you to invest in a stock or investment and your "gut" reaction is negative? Don't invest. Trust your intuition. There's *always* another deal.

Creating a Family Investment Club

Investment clubs are regaining their past popularity. Start your own with your family and ask any and all members of your extended family to join in— aunts, uncles and grandparents, etc. And make sure everyone includes his or her kids too. Actual funding for the club will come primarily from the adults and working members of the club and range upwards from $25. The kids are the beneficiaries, they inherit their proportional shares and when they reach working status or adulthood, they too can become bonafide financial partners in the club. This doesn't mean they can vote on specific investments but their input can be very insightful. Remember that they are a big consumer group.

In an investment club, money is pooled and research and information on investments (both existing and future) is discussed. Some of the existing clubs are very small and some are quite large. The rationale is that two or more heads are better than one.

Investment clubs are terrific for brainstorming potential and existing investments with family members. All age ranges can bring their "hot" issue up for discussion. How do clubs handling getting the pool of money for investing? There is usually a monthly requirement each voting member pays into the pool. New clubs will either have to start with large initial investment ($100 to $500) or wait until the smaller monthly ($25 and up) requirements add up to enough to begin buying stocks or other investment vehicles.

The voting members bring copies of information on investments to the meeting. Investment choices to buy or hold are made by poplar vote. A lot of clubs also have local financial advisors and stockbrokers speak at their meetings.

Investment Clubs are an easy and fun way to put your toe in the stock market waters. There are some wonderful success stories and most of the members had little or no knowledge of the stock market when they started. Some of the most successful investors started small—$100 and a commitment of $25 per month can be a major building block for anyone's financial house.

Unless your kid is a child prodigy, he or she may not be very enthusiastic about receiving stock shares for a gifting occasion. There are some ways to get their attention. Many companies offer a goodie bag or perks to shareholders.

$mart-Money Tip

If you are interested in starting a club you can contact: The National Association of Investment (NAIC) Clubs, P.O. Box 220, Royal Oak, MI, 48068, or call 248-583-6242 for their information packet. Their $32 annual membership fee (for a club) includes a subscription to *Better Investing* Magazine. NAIC also charges $10 per individual member per year and this includes a copy for each of the magazine. The information packet is a club partnership agreement form and general information on how to set up accounting procedures. Their website is *www.better-investing.org*

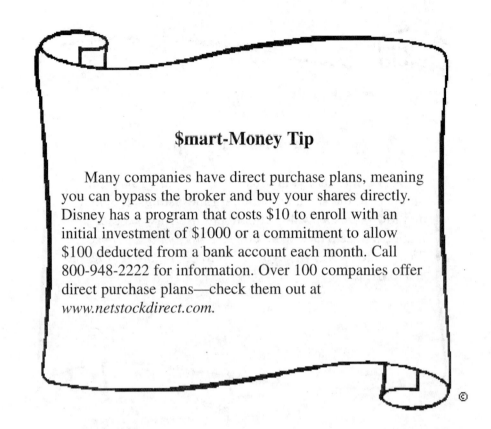

$mart-Money Tip

Many companies have direct purchase plans, meaning you can bypass the broker and buy your shares directly. Disney has a program that costs $10 to enroll with an initial investment of $1000 or a commitment to allow $100 deducted from a bank account each month. Call 800-948-2222 for information. Over 100 companies offer direct purchase plans—check them out at *www.netstockdirect.com.*

For example the *William Wrigley, Jr. Company* sends each stockholder a 100 stick box of gum at Christmas. *Tandy Corp.* routinely gives shareholders a 10 percent discount off a purchase at *Radio Shack.* This can add up quickly, and if fact *Tandy* allows the 10 percent discount on purchases of up to $10,000 as long as the purchases are all made at the same time.

If you like Disney, you may love its cruise ship. Disney's *Magic Kingdom Club* offers its shareholders the opportunity to purchase the club Gold Card. For $39 shareholders get a variety of discounts, ranging from 10 to 30 percent at different theme parks and resorts. There are discounts for cruises and rental cars.

Mutual Funds

Mutual funds let someone else make the investment decisions for you. Shareholders, you and the kids, don't get as involved in evaluating individual companies because in a mutual fund there are hundreds of companies involved in the fund investment—and who has this kind of time? Perhaps you think then

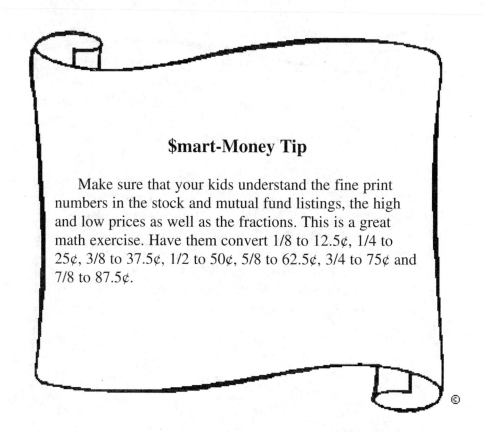

$mart-Money Tip

Make sure that your kids understand the fine print numbers in the stock and mutual fund listings, the high and low prices as well as the fractions. This is a great math exercise. Have them convert 1/8 to 12.5¢, 1/4 to 25¢, 3/8 to 37.5¢, 1/2 to 50¢, 5/8 to 62.5¢, 3/4 to 75¢ and 7/8 to 87.5¢.

that mutual funds don't have as much pizzazz (and no Christmas presents from William Wrigley Co.) but mutuals do have some advantages.

Mutual funds offer diversification (your risk is spread over many companies—all your eggs aren't in one basket) and hopefully a good professional management team (they watch the stocks in the fund and make daily decisions on them by watching the market carefully and probably more carefully than you ever would or could with your busy schedule).

When I first started in the stock market, in the 60's there were only a handful of mutual funds—a few hundred. Today, there are many thousands. Funds have a variety of objectives and most of the objectives hinge on growth and income. Most likely you will be interested in funds with objectives of growth or aggressive growth. In other words, you want your investment in mutuals to appreciated in value.

Income producing mutuals that pay periodic cash payments to the shareholder are not the usual investment for families with children. Any time you see growth as a descriptor for an investment or a fund, there is going to be some risk. But there always are levels of risks in any investment. Growth funds have a higher level of risk than income funds. Growth type mutual funds make the most sense for kids' investments. A few reasons make sense:

- When you have kids you have time to let the market "do it's thing" and make you some money as a result of the fund's good management team, who watch and react to the ups and downs that are inevitable in the stock market. Mutual fund performance, beginning in the 1920's, show that: funds that handle only large company's stock in their portfolio have had an average return of 10 percent annually, and for funds that concentrate on a portfolio of smaller companies have averaged 12 percent. And both have a better rate of return that a savings account.
- Mutual funds enable the small investor to get into the same pond where the big fish swim. Mutual funds can buy shares more cost efficiently than a small investor can because they buy volume. No they don't get a discount on the share price, but they do pay less for the attending commissions and brokerage fees. The small investor always pays a disproportionate amount in fees for his stock transactions.
- All funds have buy-ins (entry dollars). Some can be as low as $100 if you agree to a set monthly addition (as low as $25 per month) to the fund that is automatically withdrawn from your checking or savings account. You can consider this a tithe to your family's future financial security.

Money Market Mutual Funds

Once saving has become part of your life, money market mutual funds need to be explored. This type of mutual fund is comprised strictly of investments in money instruments—T Bills, bonds, notes, CD's, commercial paper, and banker's acceptances are the most common investment in a money market mutual fund. The value doesn't fluctuate, it holds at $1. The interest rate will change daily.

These funds are not covered by FDIC insurance which money market savings and CD's accounts are required to carry. But, and it's a big but, if the fund is investing primarily in U.S. Treasury obligations and CD's issued by major banks, the lack of FDIC insurance should not be a hindrance to your participation. Minimum balances will vary, you can get your money back by merely writing a check and as a rule, money market mutual funds will pay anywhere from 1 to 1½ percent higher than what a bank or savings and loan will pay on their money market funds.

Don't invest in a mutual fund unless it has a money market fund within it that you can step out of the market with a phone call and place your fund there until you are ready to continue re-investing on the stock side. The grandfather of money market funds is William Donoghue. His classic, the *Complete Money Market Guide* is available through Bantam Books and includes 800 numbers, mailing addresses, objectives and minimum requirements for each of the funds. It is available in paperback form and it belongs on your bookshelf.

Dividend Reinvestment Programs—DRIPs

Once you have bought shares in a company that pays dividends, you may be able to participate in a dividend reinvestment plan. These are also known as DRIPs. This means that when future dividends are paid, you can automatically take the money and roll into the purchase of additional shares instead of tak-

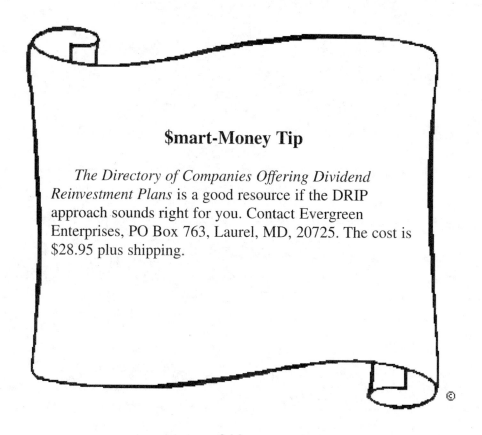

$mart-Money Tip

The Directory of Companies Offering Dividend Reinvestment Plans is a good resource if the DRIP approach sounds right for you. Contact Evergreen Enterprises, PO Box 763, Laurel, MD, 20725. The cost is $28.95 plus shipping.

ing cash.

The plus is that there is no commission cost for these purchases of new shares. Some companies will allow you to add additional cash from your pocket to the roll over without incurring commission costs. What you need to do is to ask if this is available to you when you purchase your original shares. Approximately 800 companies offer such plans, including companies like Coca-Cola and McDonald's.

Reducing the Costs of Investing

At some point discount brokerage houses and ways to save commissions will crop up. If you are investing with teenagers they will know all about discount shopping. Banks and many brokerage firms set up special fee schedules for custodial accounts. Here are four that enjoy excellent reputations.

Charles Schwab	Muriel Siebert	Discover Brokerage	E*Trade
800-648-5300	800-872-0711	800-688-6896	800-786-2575
www.schwab.com	*www.siebertnet.com*	*www.discoverbrokerage.com*	*www.etrade.com*

Value Line Investment Survey

It makes sense to compare a company, whose stock you are considering for

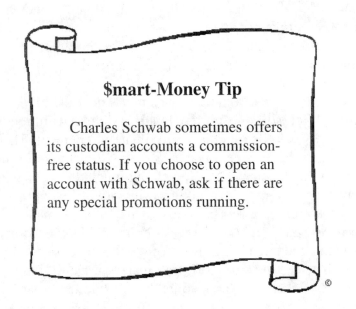

$mart-Money Tip

Charles Schwab sometimes offers its custodian accounts a commission-free status. If you choose to open an account with Schwab, ask if there are any special promotions running.

investment, to companies that are similar or in the same field. You want to determine what it's specific averages are, and it's increases and decreases in several areas, including net worth, dividends, earnings per share, revenues, etc.

I've enclosed a copy of a Value Line Investment Survey for the grand daddy of software companies—Microsoft. Note the key areas I have highlighted for you.

1. This chart illustrates the fluctuation in Microsoft's price beginning in 1988 where it sold for only a few dollars a share (it doesn't even register on the graph, it's so low) to a high of approximately $80 per share as of the date it was published (March 5, 1999

2. Note that Microsoft has had 7 stock splits—some were 2 for 1, others 3 for 2.

3. Be aware of the timeliness and safety ranking. Both of these are based on a 1 to 5 scale with one being the best and 5 being the worst. Microsoft is ranked 1 in timeliness. This means that it is above average and it's market value is increasing ahead of the overall Dow Jones Industrial average. Its safety is 2 and based on the financial condition of the company as well as the oscillation of the stock. In other words, you shouldn't lose much sleep if you own it.

4. Take projections with a grain of salt. They are not guarantees of stock movement, price increase or profit.

5. The actual financial reports are important. Note the increased sales per share, earnings per share, book value per share, capital spending (if a company is planning for growth, there should always be funds allocated for capital spending), average annual PE ratio and net profit margin.

6. If you desire income from you investment, note the kind of dividends per share. Microsoft doesn't pay much in dividends in relation to the price of the stock. Its yield is approximately 4 percent. Therefore if you need income, this is not a stock that will meet your criteria. The company's past history is not to pay out much of its cash earnings to shareholders. You may be thinking, why would I want this stock if I didn't get an ongoing return on my financial investment. The answer is that returns are not always measured in dividends. Companies that are growing and expanding like Microsoft need cash to grow. Growth usually enhances the stock's overall market price. Rapidly growing companies often create stock splits, which Microsoft has aggressively

done.

7. The center section is important. It tells who the company is; what their major products are; who the CEO (chief executive officer) is; the company address and phone number. It often indicates what major product lines contribute to the company's revenues. An interesting side note, when you address complaint letters to the CEO action usually results.

8. Major information is noted as well as changes in the directions of the company and how the investment community feels or projects. For those of you interested in career changes or job repositioning, this is an ideal section to read. Knowing about future products could put you or your kids, one up in an interview.

9. Current position represents the last two years as well the current year with a break out of assets and liabilities.

10. Represents the annual rates for the last 5 and 10 years on percentage increases for sales, cash flow, dividends, earnings and book value (means that if all the assets were liquidated and all the liabilities paid off, the remaining money would be divided by the number of outstanding shares.). Another term is net worth. These annual rates include estimates in increases and decreases for the next period of time.

11. Current financial data on dividends paid, quarterly sales and earnings for the preceding 4 years as well as estimates for the current year.

12. The company's financial strength is important. If you are conservative then it makes sense to go with an "A" or better rating. If you are willing to take a some risk and look at companies that may be growth oriented or turn around candidates, then a less than "A" may be perfectly all right.

Report on Microsoft *Value Line Investment Survey*

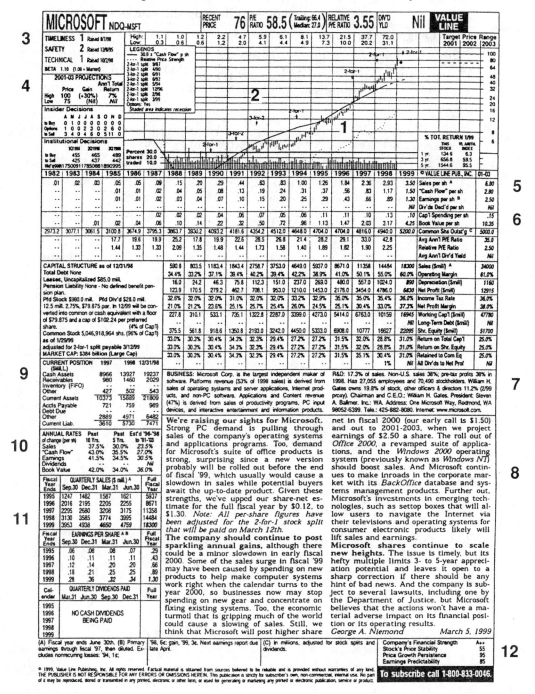

3
4

MICROSOFT NDQ-MSFT

| RECENT PRICE | 76 | P/E RATIO | 58.5 (Trailing: 66.4 / Median: 27.0) | RELATIVE P/E RATIO | 3.55 | DIV'D YLD | Nil | VALUE LINE |

TIMELINESS **1** Raised 8/7/98
SAFETY **2** Raised 12/8/95
TECHNICAL **1** Raised 10/2/98
BETA 1.10 (1.00 = Market)

2001-03 PROJECTIONS
	Price	Gain	Ann'l Total Return
High	100	(+30%)	7%
Low	75	(Nil)	Nil
Options: Yes

Insider Decisions
	A	M	J	J	A	S	O	N	D
to Buy	0	1	0	0	0	0	0	0	0
Options	1	0	0	2	3	0	2	6	0
to Sell	3	4	0	4	6	0	5	11	0

Institutional Decisions
	1Q1998	2Q1998	3Q1998
to Buy	455	465	489
to Sell	425	437	442
Hld'000	1750091	1785098	1890995

Percent shares traded: 30.0 / 20.0 / 10.0

LEGENDS
30.0 x "Cash Flow" p sh
.... Relative Price Strength
2-for-1 split 9/87
3-for-2 split 4/90
2-for-1 split 6/91
3-for-2 split 6/92
3-for-2 split 5/94
2-for-1 split 12/96
2-for-1 split 2/98
2-for-1 split 3/99
Shaded area indicates recession

% TOT. RETURN 1/99
	THIS STOCK	VL ARITH. INDEX
1 yr.	134.6	6.3
3 yr.	656.8	59.5
5 yr.	1544.6	95.5

Target Price Range 2001 | 2002 | 2003

	1982	1983	1984	1985	1986	1987	1988	1989	1990	1991	1992	1993	1994	1995	1996	1997	1998	1999	© VALUE LINE PUB., INC.	01-03
Sales per sh	.01	.02	.03	.05	.05	.09	.15	.20	.29	.44	.63	.83	1.00	1.26	1.84	2.36	2.93	3.50		6.80
"Cash Flow" per sh	--	--	--	.01	.01	.02	.04	.05	.08	.13	.19	.24	.31	.37	.56	.83	1.17	1.50		2.80
Earnings per sh B	--	--	--	.01	.01	.02	.03	.04	.07	.10	.15	.20	.25	.29	.43	.66	.89	1.30		2.50
Div'ds Decl'd per sh	--	--	--	--	--	--	--	--	--	--	--	--	--	--	--	--	--	Nil		Nil
Cap'l Spending per sh	--	--	--	--	.02	.02	.02	.04	.06	.07	.05	.06	.11	.11	.10	.13		.10		.15
Book Value per sh	--	--	.01	.02	.04	.06	.10	.14	.22	.32	.50	.72	.96	1.13	1.47	2.03	3.17	4.25		10.35
Common Shs Outst'g C	2973.2	3077.1	3061.5	3100.8	3674.9	3795.3	3863.7	3930.2	4093.2	4181.6	4354.2	4512.0	4648.0	4704.0	4704.0	4816.0	4940.0	5200.0		5000.0
Avg Ann'l P/E Ratio	--	--	--	17.7	19.6	19.9	25.2	17.8	19.9	22.6	28.5	26.8	21.4	28.2	29.1	33.0	42.8		Bold figures are	35.0
Relative P/E Ratio	--	--	--	1.44	1.30	1.33	2.09	1.35	1.48	1.44	1.73	1.58	1.40	1.89	1.82	1.90	2.25		Value Line	2.50
Avg Ann'l Div'd Yield	--	--	--	--	--	--	--	--	--	--	--	--	--	--	--	--	--		estimates	Nil

CAPITAL STRUCTURE as of 12/31/98
Total Debt None
Leases, Uncapitalized $85.0 mill.
Pension Liability None - No defined benefit pension plan.
Pfd Stock $980.0 mill.   Pfd Div'd $28.0 mill.
12.5 mill. 2.75%, $79.875 par. In 12/99 will be converted into common or cash equivalent with a floor of $79.875 and a cap of $102.24 per preferred share.   (4% of Cap'l)
Common Stock 5,046,918,964 shs. (96% of Cap'l) as of 1/29/99
adjusted for 2-for-1 split payable 3/12/99
MARKET CAP: $384 billion (Large Cap)

	1988	1989	1990	1991	1992	1993	1994	1995	1996	1997	1998	1999		
Sales ($mill) A	590.8	803.5	1183.4	1843.4	2758.7	3753.0	4649.0	5937.0	8671.0	11358	14484	18300		34000
Operating Margin	34.4%	33.2%	37.1%	39.4%	40.2%	39.4%	42.2%	38.9%	41.0%	50.1%	55.0%	60.0%		61.0%
Depreciation ($mill)	16.0	24.2	46.3	75.8	112.3	151.0	237.0	269.0	480.0	557.0	1024.0	890		1160
Net Profit ($mill)	123.9	170.5	279.2	462.7	708.1	953.0	1210.0	1453.0	2176.0	3454.0	4786.0	6430		12915
Income Tax Rate	32.6%	32.0%	32.0%	31.0%	32.0%	32.0%	33.2%	32.9%	35.0%	35.0%	35.4%	36.0%		36.0%
Net Profit Margin	21.0%	21.2%	23.6%	25.1%	25.7%	25.4%	26.0%	24.5%	25.1%	30.4%	33.0%	37.2%		38.0%
Working Cap'l ($mill)	227.8	310.1	533.1	735.1	1322.8	2287.0	3399.0	4273.0	5414.0	6763.0	10159	16945		47780
Long-Term Debt ($mill)	--	--	--	--	--	--	--	--	--	--	Nil	Nil		Nil
Shr. Equity ($mill)	375.5	561.8	918.6	1350.8	2193.0	3242.0	4450.0	5333.0	6908.0	10777	16627	22095		51700
Return on Total Cap'l	33.0%	30.3%	30.4%	34.3%	32.3%	29.4%	27.2%	27.2%	31.5%	32.0%	28.8%	31.0%		25.0%
Return on Shr. Equity	33.0%	30.3%	30.4%	34.3%	32.3%	29.4%	27.2%	27.2%	31.5%	32.0%	28.8%	31.0%		25.0%
Retained to Com Eq	33.0%	30.3%	30.4%	34.3%	32.3%	29.4%	27.2%	27.2%	31.5%	35.1%	30.4%	31.0%		25.0%
All Div'ds to Net Prof	--	--	--	--	--	--	--	--	--	--	1%	Nil		Nil

9

CURRENT POSITION 1997 1998 12/31/98 ($MILL.)
	1997	1998	12/31/98
Cash Assets	8966	13927	19237
Receivables	980	1460	2029
Inventory (FIFO)	--	--	--
Other	427	502	543
Current Assets	10373	15889	21809
Accts Payable	721	759	989
Debt Due	--	--	--
Other	2889	4971	6482
Current Liab.	3610	5730	7471

10

ANNUAL RATES
of change (per sh)	Past 10 Yrs.	Past 5 Yrs.	Est'd '96-'98 to '01-'03
Sales	37.5%	30.0%	23.5%
"Cash Flow"	43.0%	35.5%	27.0%
Earnings	41.5%	34.5%	30.5%
Dividends	--	--	Nil
Book Value	42.0%	34.0%	36.0%

11

Fiscal Year Ends	QUARTERLY SALES ($ mill.) A				Full Fiscal Year
	Sep.30	Dec.31	Mar.31	Jun.30	
1995	1247	1482	1587	1621	5937
1996	2016	2195	2205	2255	8671
1997	2295	2680	3208	3175	11358
1998	3130	3585	3774	3995	14484
1999	3953	4938	4650	4759	18300

Fiscal Year Ends	EARNINGS PER SHARE A B				Full Fiscal Year
	Sep.30	Dec.31	Mar.31	Jun.30	
1995	.06	.08	.08	.07	.29
1996	.10	.11	.11	.11	.43
1997	.12	.14	.20	.20	.66
1998	.18	.21	.25	.25	.89
1999	.28	.36	.32	.34	1.30

Cal- endar	QUARTERLY DIVIDENDS PAID				Full Year
	Mar.31	Jun.30	Sep.30	Dec.31	
1995					
1996	NO CASH DIVIDENDS				
1997	BEING PAID				
1998					
1999					

BUSINESS: Microsoft Corp. is the largest independent maker of software. Platforms revenue (53% of 1998 sales) is derived from sales of operating systems and server applications, Internet products, and non-PC software. Applications and Content revenue (47%) is derived from sales of productivity programs, PC input devices, and interactive entertainment and information products. R&D: 17.3% of sales. Non-U.S. sales 38%; pre-tax profits 38% in 1998. Has 27,055 employees and 70,490 stockholders. William H. Gates owns 19.8% of stock, other officers & directors 11.2% (2/99 proxy). Chairman and C.E.O.: William H. Gates. President: Steven A. Ballmer. Inc.: WA. Address: One Microsoft Way, Redmond, WA 98052-6399. Tele.: 425-882-8080. Internet: www.microsoft.com.

7

We're raising our sights for Microsoft. Strong PC demand is pulling through sales of the company's operating systems and applications programs. Too, demand for Microsoft's suite of office products is strong, surprising since a new version probably will be rolled out before the end of fiscal '99, which usually would cause a slowdown in sales while potential buyers await the up-to-date product. Given these strengths, we've upped our share-net estimate for the full fiscal year by $0.12, to $1.30. *Note: All per-share figures have been adjusted for the 2-for-1 stock split that will be paid on March 12th.*

The company should continue to post sparkling annual gains, although there could be a minor slowdown in early fiscal 2000. Some of the sales surge in fiscal '99 may have been caused by spending on new products to help make computer systems work right when the calendar turns to the year 2000, so businesses now may stop spending on new gear and concentrate on fixing existing systems. Too, the economic turmoil that is gripping much of the world could cause a slowing of sales. Still, we think that Microsoft will post higher share

net in fiscal 2000 (our early call is $1.50) and out to 2001-2003, when we project earnings of $2.50 a share. The roll out of *Office 2000*, a revamped suite of applications, and the *Windows 2000* operating system (previously known as *Windows NT*) should boost sales. And Microsoft continues to make inroads in the corporate market with its *BackOffice* database and systems management products. Further out, Microsoft's investments in emerging technologies, such as settop boxes that will allow users to navigate the Internet via their televisions and operating systems for consumer electronic products likely will lift sales and earnings.

Microsoft shares continue to scale new heights. The issue is timely, but its hefty multiple limits 3- to 5-year appreciation potential and leaves it open to a sharp correction if there should be any hint of bad news. And the company is subject to several lawsuits, including one by the Department of Justice, but Microsoft believes that the actions won't have a material adverse impact on its financial position or its operating results.
George A. Niemond   March 5, 1999

8

(A) Fiscal year ends June 30th. (B) Primary earnings through fiscal '97, then diluted. Excludes nonrecurring losses: '94, 1¢;
'98, 6¢; gain, '99, 3¢. Next earnings report due late April.
(C) In millions, adjusted for stock splits and dividends.

Company's Financial Strength	A++
Stock's Price Stability	55
Price Growth Persistence	95
Earnings Predictability	85

12

$mart-Money Tip

For a hands on stock market game, try The Reward Game. Players learn to buy and sell stock, bonds, real estate and gold. Inflation is a factor and it does fluctuate. Players are allowed to borrow to buy assets, but they have to pay it back. The player who accumulates 10 million dollars, free of debt, is the winner. The cost is $35 plus shipping. Contact the National Center for Financial Education, P.O. Box 34070, San Diego, CA, 92163.

$mart-Money Tip

10 per cent of kids age 11 and over put savings into stocks and mutual funds.

$mart-Money Resource Center:

The Stock Market Game is an excellent aid for teaching about the stock market. It covers research, analyzing portfolios, current events and their impact on the market. It also sharpens math skills. Contact the Securities Industry Foundation, 120 Broadway, New York, NY, 10271 for information on using it at your kid's schools.

Donoghue's Mutual Fund Almanac by William Donoghue ($40).
Call 800-343-5423 to check total cost for shipping and handling. One of the best overall books for you to read to sharpen up your knowledge of the mutual fund market.

The Handbook for No Load Fund Investors. To check costs (around $49) Call 800-252-2042 or write: P.O. Box 318, Irvington, NY, 10503. Follows over 1500 funds and includes all performance data.

The Investor's Guide to Low Cost Mutual Funds published by the Association of No Load Funds can be obtained by writing to the Mutual Fund Education Alliance, 1900 Erie Street, Suite 120, Kansas City, MO, 64116.

The Individual Investor's Guide to No Load Mutual Funds is published by The American Association of Individual Investors. It is updated annually. Current costs can be obtained by calling (312) 280-0190.

The Morningstar Mutual Funds is one of the recognized experts in mutual fund analysis. They are also quite expensive. It's expensive, so it makes sense to review this at your public library or a brokerage house before you buy it. Over 2500 funds are covered and rated each year. Morningstar's website is *www.morningstar.com*.

A few of the magazine and newspaper resources that you can go to: *Bloomberg Financial, Money, Business Week, Fortune, Worth, $mart-Money, Wall Street Journal,* and your local newspaper routinely contains articles about mutual funds, stocks and other investments.

Part Four

The Adult Rises

Chapter Sixteen

A Wedding to Remember

Throughout this book I have emphasized financial planning for the events in your kids' lives. A wedding is certainly an event that will require planning and money. Many of you will be asked to march into the wedding zone with your offspring, and you may get to be old hands, if you have more than one child. You and your soon-to-be-married son or daughter want and definitely deserve to have the perfect day you anticipate. You can start by learning about the traditions and new trends for weddings from the myriad of books and magazines published about this industry.

Yes, industry. Believe it or not, the average wedding is planned for 200 guests and costs approximately $15,000. Your first thought—*that's impossible*! But consider the elements: the wedding gown, the flowers, the cake, photos, invitations, music and then there's the reception and/or catering. A caterer is probably going to charge anywhere from $20 to $35 per person for just the food. Then, there's all the bubbly.

That sounds like a lot, but there's another important category called miscellaneous. Weddings are big bucks, and families have floundered financially when the wedding plan is allowed to grow to monstrous proportions—both in budget and size. A second mortgage on your home to pay for a wedding—is it necessary? I don't think so.

Thousands of dollars and countless hours of planning allocated for an event that lasts only a few short hours? Feel free to make this choice, but it wouldn't be mine. How may can *really* afford a $15,000 party? For many families, that amount can cripple whatever savings they may have.

Many brides and grooms pay for their own weddings today. These couples are usually educated and have their careers in order before marriage. Their attitude is often, "It's our bash, no matter what it costs." Anything goes! It's not unusual for the groom's family to share expenses or contribute substantially. Why should the entire burden fall on the bride of her family?

The days are over when the groom's mother simply hands her guest list to the bride's mother and expects not to pay for anything. The financial situation of each family should also be taken into consideration. If the groom's family is better able to afford to pay for a wedding, *wants* to do it, and does not have to go into debt to do so, then that's the way it should be. Let them open their pocketbooks. It's also not unusual for the couple to open theirs. With later marriages, many have funds they have set aside—the modern hope chest—for their big day.

One of the great myths, promulgated about weddings, is that most are perfect. That's almost impossible. Why? Because of the number of people that are necessarily involved in a wedding. And, each one is a variable in the complicated wedding formula. You won't be able to please everyone, and Aunt Matilda (you haven't seen her for 23 years) is bound to find something she can criticize. Most weddings are for the bride and groom but paid for by their parents. So these are really the only people that must be truly satisfied with the end result.

Another myth is that all wedding consultants and businesses are committed to helping you meet the goals of your well-planned wedding budget. Though many truly do help the wedding party get the most for their dollars, there are some whose primary game is to make money. Making a profit is the goal of all businesses. However, those who encourage the expensive and unrealistic decisions made by naive brides, grooms and family participants who are mesmerized by the romance of it all, are very wrong. All merchants and suppliers for your wedding should be checked out through your local Better Business Bureau. And definitely try to check out reputations by word-of-mouth.

Instead of aiming for the perfect wedding, when your time comes to be the parents of the bride or the groom, be smart and plan for a wonderful wedding. Heck, why not even a fun wedding. If your target is the latter, rather than the former, you'll not only survive but you could have some laughs along the way.

Our Weddings

In my immediate family, we've had two weddings—both with the same daughter. The first was in 1986 when my youngest daughter told me that a wedding was in the works. I had no idea what I was getting into. We actually started our wedding plans with a notebook. We listed out the essentials. Many of my friends had already experienced runaway wedding costs. So, I thanked heaven very early on—Sheryl didn't want a wedding that would compete with the national debt in total dollars spent. This also pleased my husband (her stepfather). We would be picking up the entire tab for Sheryl's big day.

The first thing that we had to secure was the site and the date. There was never any question about the site; it would be at the church we attended. Sheryl wanted an evening wedding. Since we were members, there was no cost for the church rental. However, additional costs included the organist, the wedding coordinator and the minister. Non-member families were generally charged $500 for the church alone. Since each church varied widely, check out your preferences before making a commitment.

With our name on the church calendar, the next on the agenda was the reception site. Sheryl wanted something different, but a fun approach that would help keep the costs to a doable level for the 100 people we estimated would attend the wedding and the reception. Both she and her soon to be husband loved Chinese food and thought it would be great to put together a meal of oriental hors d'oeuvres. They wanted a local and well-known Chinese restaurant to cater and host the reception. Our wedding was to be their first official wedding party. The menu sounded delicious and they assured us that their remodeling project would, without a doubt, be complete several weeks before the wedding. So, the dates would work.

Our next project was The Dress. She thrilled me with the good news that she did not want to spend a lot of money. She found the *perfect* dress in the J.C. Penney catalog. This sounded good to me and I loved the price—it was only $225. Score one for Sheryl.

We still had more to do. The invitations were ordered. A band that she had heard had been secured for the evening at reasonable cost. Several members of my church offered to help in the music area. And our favorite bakery would provide a beautiful cake. The vocalist had referred the photographer. Video taping then was not as big as it is today, when Sheryl got married. A videotape was

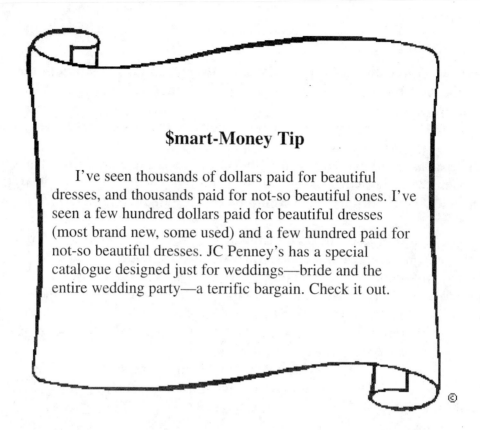

$mart-Money Tip

I've seen thousands of dollars paid for beautiful dresses, and thousands paid for not-so beautiful ones. I've seen a few hundred dollars paid for beautiful dresses (most brand new, some used) and a few hundred paid for not-so beautiful dresses. JC Penney's has a special catalogue designed just for weddings—bride and the entire wedding party—a terrific bargain. Check it out.

done of the wedding, but by friends who brought their camcorders. The only expense here was for making copies of the tape.

Our snags came in the areas of photography, the reception and the miscellaneous. The vocalist did a terrific job, her friend the photographer's efforts were mediocre at best. Our perfect wedding teetered on the brink of disaster less than 48 hours before the wedding day. The Chinese restaurant called and said the remodeling hadn't gone as scheduled. In other words, they wouldn't be open, they wouldn't be ready, and we couldn't have the reception there. The owner told me to go to my "back-up" plan. *What back-up plan?*

Our small evening wedding for 100 guests now numbered 250. I told those in my office not to tell Sheryl that we had a "snag". All normal work ceased in my office for the next 48 hours; everyone's full concentration centered on resolving *the problem*. In a short period the major hotels in our area knew about the Briles wedding. And several did have suggestions about possible places for us to consider. The day before one hotel actually had a cancellation of an event on the same evening that we needed.

We now had a place for our wedding reception, but our guests didn't know there was a last minute change of venue. As the guests left the wedding ceremony they were handed maps to the new reception site. The good news was we did have a place for our guests to go, but this party ended up doubling the overall costs for Sheryl's wedding.

One of the most important things I think you need to keep in mind as the underwriter or partial underwriter of a wedding is to be careful to stay with your plan. Be vigilant about the most common problem in all wedding plans—guest list inflation. And please don't forget the miscellaneous expense items. For instance, Sheryl made me very happy about her choice of a $225 wedding dress, but she also needed undergarments, shoes, a head piece, veil, a petticoat and the "going away" clothes. Then there are gifts for the bridesmaids and the groomsmen. What about a limo ride for the bride and groom from the wedding to the reception? And last but not least, what is the plan for the honeymoon?

A Cruise to Remember

Wedding #2 was quite a bit different. It all started when I called my daughter to ask if grandson Frank could again go with us on a three-day cruise over Labor Day Weekend. After saying yes, she added, "Wish we could go." For whatever reason, I responded, "Well, why don't you and Matthew get married on it?"

Within a few weeks, I was up to my eyeballs brainstorming with her about the possibility. My company regularly sponsors a cruise for professional development in the fall each year. This year's destination was Mexico. As a group, we had reserved several cabins and my cut-off date was within the next few weeks. The wedding was a go—so we all went into high gear, very high gear.

Friends and relatives were contacted. I was able to pass on cruise costs to all wedding participants at my cost. Think about this—where can you get three hotel nights, all the food you can eat and great entertainment for $369? Wedding guests loved it; it was a feast to their party souls to get together with friends and relatives that too little time was spent with. A total of 72 of us had a grand time over the three days.

Here's what we did:

- ◆ We brought the minister who did the ceremony with us (some cruise lines have wedding programs in place now—ask)—she

259

loved the holiday and I only had to pay her airfare and passenger costs.

♦ Reception music was supplied by the DJ setup in the disco lounge (we had had classes only a few hours earlier in the same room).

♦ Royal Caribbean sent a string quartet up to play Here Comes the Bride—live music was a nice touch, no cost.

♦ Sheryl brought along silk flowers for the wedding parting—made up all in advance, $150.

♦ Her dress was a tad different this time. We had already done the first wedding outfit—this time she went red. A gorgeous full-length sheath she found on sale for $70. She looked smashing.

♦ To relax them both (it was Sheryl's second wedding, Matthew's first) they made an appointment to have massages the morning of the wedding in the ship's spa. Sheryl also had her hair done. They paid for all spa expenses.

♦ I supplied the bubbly. When I originally negotiated the contract with the cruise line, I had scheduled a bottle of wine for each cabin the third night and a bottle of champagne in their cabin the first. I rearranged the deliveries and had a bottle of wine upon arrival and held back the champagne for our reception after the wedding. We had so much champagne, that after the reception, I had the remainder delivered to the dining room to share with wedding and guests who were attending the seminars. They loved it—they knew a wedding was in the progress.

♦ Last, the dinner. Royal Caribbean offered to give us a private room at $20 per head. My response was, "Why should I pay for food again when it's already included in our cruise cost? The bride and groom, and everyone else will dine at the regular time." And we did. Our section of the dining room had a great time sharing in the celebration.

♦ Photos were a snap. The ship's photographer had a great time and took lots of photos. We bought the ones that we wanted the next day at a special rate. We also had lots of the throwaway cameras and had guests aim and shoot. Sheryl and Matthew developed at their expense.

What was my cost? A grand total of $1500. Not bad.

Remember, something old, something new, something borrowed and something blue. The bottom line is that you can spend a lot of money. If a traditional wedding is on your calendar, here are some areas you need to consider:

The Bridal Gown

"The Dress" is for some daughters, the first and most important step in their wedding plans. And all agree that she should be the most beautiful bride ever. She will spend many dreamy hours with bridal magazines and catalogs. And, she will likely fill a folder with clippings of her "favs". When her feet touch the ground again and the budget for the gown and all of the accessories has been decided upon, the place to shop will hopefully be somewhat defined. Be sure to go for an initial tour of various types of stores to see what really is the most flattering style (in your price range, of course) for the bride-to-be. The best thing you or your daughter can do is take along a trusted friend who is willing to say that dress looks like a potato sack on her.

If you are considering using a bridal shop or the bridal section of a department store, query your friends and encourage your daughter to do the same. What places of business would they avoid like the plague? Where are the bargains and the most reliable service? Keep in mind that some shops add enormous markups to their cost for a gown and also may use false discounting. You may wonder what I mean by "false discounting". Let's say the recommended retail price from the manufacturer for the gown you like is $1000. The bridal shop tag says $1200—the clerk offers a discount of 10 percent. Your net price is $1080—not such a good deal. You pay $80 more than the suggested retail price.

Some shops will cut the designer/ manufacturer tags out of the dress, so you can't do any comparison-shopping. Beware of their sales pitch. *Never* buy a gown from which the labels have been removed! There are so many "copies" floating around that one would have no way of telling whether or not she got the "real" thing.

Small bridal shops will quite often make an excellent deal on a gown, especially if it's a discontinued sample. Bridal manufacturers have style changes *every six months*, but gowns do not "go out of style" for many years. Last year's gown can be an incredible bargain! Because of the tremendous competition, quite often a small bridal shop will give the bride wonderful personal and caring service that she wouldn't find in a department or larger store.

Word-of-mouth" will provide seamstresses who work from their homes and create fabulous gowns. One thing to remember is if you have a custom-made gown, you may save several hundred dollars in alteration costs. If a bride does choose a seamstress who works from her home, ask to see her "portfolio" and samples of her work, as well as references. You don't want a dress that looks "homemade"! Both bridal shops and reputable fabric shops can also recommend someone, but just make sure to check out her work first. If you are talented in sewing or you have a friend or relative who is talented in sewing, this might be a way to save several hundred dollars. Patterns and fabrics for bridal gowns are readily available at your local fabric shop.

The JC Penney Catalog worked well for us. Alfred Angelo, one of the largest and oldest bridal manufacturers, manufactures many of the gowns in their catalog. The catalog gowns are specially made for JC Penney, and are not the exact ones found in bridal magazines, although styles are similar. Because of the volume of gowns purchased by JC Penney, they get their own styles and lower prices from manufacturers. All gowns in their catalogs have the "JC Penney" label (but who is going to see the label when the bride walks down the aisle?) Their wedding catalog is excellent and also features attendant apparel and "mother of the bride" dresses.

There are stores in many big cities that rent wedding and bridesmaid gowns. Again, check the Yellow Pages under the "bridal", "rental" or "wedding" categories. Also check with tuxedo rental shops, as they may know of a source for rental gowns. Some places will even order in your "dream gown" for you, and you will be the first one to wear it. For a bride who doesn't attach a lot of sentiment to her gown and has no desire to "pass it down to her daughter," this is a great money-saver.

If a rental place is renting you a gown from their stock, ask to see the gown and examine it carefully before you sign a contract to rent a specific gown. Some gowns have been rented and cleaned so many times that they are in very poor condition. Bridal brokers also rent gowns. The best in the country is the Discount Bridal Service. They can be reached at 800-874-8794 or 800-441-0102. If you are in the buying market, this establishment has a network of representatives available in most major cities.

The Yellow Pages as well are an excellent source of discounted wedding gowns *only* if you know *exactly what you want and have previously tried on the dress*. With them, you can save anywhere from 20 to 40 percent when buying a gown. Tell them you are interested in a designer gown, but you just don't have the bank account to afford it.

Finally, be leery of sales women who make a huge fuss all over the bride. Make sure you ask who the manufacturer of the dress is; if the dress has to be ordered, how long will it take to get in; what kind of financial terms are needed—all cash now, a percentage as a deposit with the remainder when the dress is delivered (put deposits down on a credit card); if alterations are needed, what will the costs be. And don't forget to ask what services are available for free.

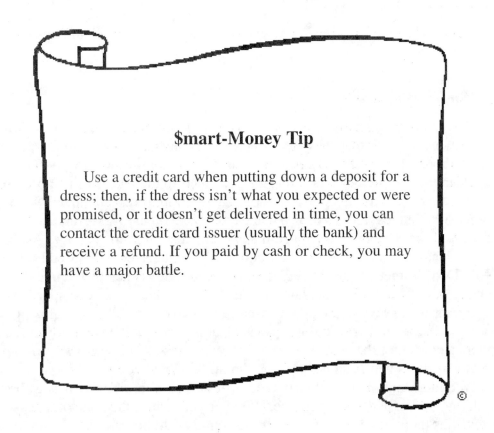

$mart-Money Tip

Use a credit card when putting down a deposit for a dress; then, if the dress isn't what you expected or were promised, or it doesn't get delivered in time, you can contact the credit card issuer (usually the bank) and receive a refund. If you paid by cash or check, you may have a major battle.

Two years ago, I attended a wedding of the daughter of one my close friends. Her gown was the gown her mother wore 30 years prior. We all thought it was a kick that Dad got to walk down the aisle twice with the same dress. This can save you lots of money and in some cases with little or no alterations are needed. It's very special for a bride to choose to wear her mother or grandmother's gown. However, these old gowns can be very fragile. Make sure that it is taken to a *reputable* cleaner that specializes in wedding gowns so the fabric doesn't fall apart! If the gown needs alterations, most of the time the aged color of the fabric can be matched by "dying" new fabric in tea to give it a slight color!

Don't forget shopping at bridal outlet stores (look in the yellow pages) or consignment stores or thrift stores. It's amazing what people give away or finally turn over to a consignment shop. They realized that they won't wear this gown again and they need the room in the closet. The previous owner gets some money for their clothing budget and you find a real treasure and save on yours. Mothers of the bride and groom can do well in consignment shops too. To select a gown in a consignment type shop (some cater only to brides) you need to be a patient and astute shopper—-but you may find a real "gem" among some of the "garbage".

The Supporting Cast

One of my favorite weddings was that of one of my employees. Her brides-maids wore dresses that they could actually wear again. Contrary to popular belief, another life for a bridesmaid dress is possible. Unfortunately, most brides-maids are asked to buy dresses that are relegated to the back of the closet after the wedding. Who designed the dresses that my employee's attendants wore?—Jessica McClintock, a well-known name in the fashion industry. Another design-er whose fashions can be worn again and don't cost a fortune is Laura Ashley.

Look around, there are plenty of good styles that can be purchased for under $100. Don't forget the bridal department store sections such as the one that JC Penney has, as well as their catalogue and discount malls. Also consider rentals. If you must have your attendants wear expensive apparel that will only be appropriate for another wedding or at a costume party, do them a favor and offer to pay a portion of the cost. Your daughter's friends usually can't afford to pop for $150+ dress that is unusable. Nor should they have to.

Weddings and men—either tuxedoes or suits are in order. If it is a formal wedding, the tux will be the choice. Whether you rent or buy is another case. If it looks as though the men in your life or family will be participating in sever-al weddings within a year, it probably makes sense to buy. Tuxedos range in price from a few hundred dollars to several thousand dollars. Consider what my husband did, we bought him a used tuxedo for $150 that has been worn many, many times since. Tuxedo rental establishments retire their suits after a given number of rentals. This was a great buy for us. If you don't see many weddings or formal occasions on your calendar in the near future, rent by all means.

The cost for a rental will be under $100. Many places rent tuxedos for about $50, plus shoes (about $10). Formal shoes are an important part of the outfit, as everyone should match. Also, many stores offer the groom's tuxedo free with rental of perhaps 5 or 6 other tuxedos. Shop around for the best deal! It's also important to make sure everyone in the bridal party tries on their tux *before* the wedding, so any necessary adjustments can be made. If the wedding is not for-mal or less formal than the tuxedo style, a dark suit is perfectly acceptable. The shirts and accessories for the men should be coordinated for continuity when suits are worn.

Wedding Sites

House of Worship

Seventy-five percent of all weddings are held within a house of worship. That leaves twenty-five percent in civil ceremonies, ranging anywhere from a local park to a judge's office. Churches usually offer their members a discount or even free use of their facilities for weddings. The requirements for religious ceremonies vary from one denomination to another. Most will require some type of pre-marital counseling. Some forbid the performance of inter-faith marriage ceremonies on their premises.

When you book your site, make sure you understand what is included in the fee. If the church supplies a wedding hostess—someone who acts as the coordinator with you and the church before and during the wedding—it will cost you several hundred dollars. She will attend the rehearsal and wedding. Rarely seen by guests, she is a tremendous help to the bride and the wedding party. The organist gets paid, and of course the minister. Know what you are getting, as well as the cost, so there are no big surprises.

If you are not a member of the church where that the wedding is held, expect to pay more. In fact, many churches expand their membership through their weddings. Young couples attend, like it and stay; or they actually join to reduce the cost of the site. Whatever is done, make sure you understand what the restrictions, set-up times and what the clean-up requirements will be for your wedding party. Determine who the contact person will be prior to and during the wedding.

What kind of financial expectations beyond the cost of the wedding site will be required? What additional equipment will be needed such as microphones or lights? If your church is already committed for the day you must have and there is more than one minister, he or she may be more than happy to perform the ceremony off-site.

Country Clubs

You may not be a member of a country club, but a friend or relative may be. Or, a club may open its facilities to the public for a fee. Many of these clubs barely make ends meet, so wedding reception moneys become an important part of their revenue stream. Consider business clubs and social clubs as well. Many will allow you to bring in an outside caterer and you may find them less programmed than the traditional sales and catering department in a hotel.

Civic Sites

One place you can save dollars is by using a civic site. They include gardens, parks, amphitheaters (for the really, really big wedding) recreational centers, museums, even colleges and universities. Outside of the lower cost, other advantages include the ability to bring in your own food and caterer and the simple fact that you may have a unique place to create the big event. Since you will not be alone in thinking about a civic site, there will be a demand and you may have to move your date if the site is already taken.

One of my friends selected a beautiful park and had a potluck picnic dinner—all the guests brought their favorite dishes. No menus were set, just bring what you loved. It was a wonderful evening that was perfect for her minimal budget and her enormous heart. No one cared that it wasn't an elegant sit-down dinner with seven courses and huge vases of flowers everywhere. What mattered was that it was a great afternoon and evening for over a hundred friends and family members.

One of the more unique settings we found ourselves at was a wedding held on the bridge connecting Concourse A and B at the soon to be opened Denver International Airport in Colorado. The groom was a principal in the design and engineering of the bridge between the two concourses. The wedding was scheduled a week before the official opening of the airport. One hundred-plus friends and family gathered to celebrate the grand late-afternoon event as the sun set in the west.

The bride was stunning. She wore sapphire blue—a dress she has worn to several dress-up occasions since. The reception was held across the bridge in the Continental Airlines Club for it's frequent travelers. Food was brought in by a Denver caterer.

We were treated to a great event—a sunset to die for; a facility that hadn't been open to the public, the wedding group was the only one on the bridge and club area; and the use of the facility didn't cost the groom or bride a dime. That wedding is still talked about years later.

Often, remodeled or new complexes can create an unusual background. I attended a wedding that was held in an enclosed shopping mall after hours. Imagine the unlimited dance floors—the bank loved it! Check around and see what is being built in your community. Merchants love the idea of publicity, especially when it is unusual and doesn't cost them anything. A rental cost (if any) will vary, so it's a good time to hone in on your negotiating skills.

Some civic sites have restrictions and requirements. For example, there may

266

be alcohol restrictions and the use of candles. You may have to buy event insurance, hire security guards, or donate a contribution (AKA—a fee). Many of these sites don't have tables and chairs—you will need to determine what the rental costs will be.

With the expansion of bed and breakfast inns across the country, many now cater to the wedding trade. A special suite for the bride and groom and rooms aplenty for guests to stay in.

If you have a home that is suited for a wedding and/or a reception, this could be the ticket. When my younger brother Terry married, the ceremony was at the church within a mile from my home. Our gift to him was the reception in a three-acre oak studded property that was perfect.

Other Sites

There are endless options open for the wedding ceremony, and your choice of a religious or civil ceremony doesn't limit the range of site choices. The home wedding is a popular choice. Home weddings can range from very thrifty to very posh. Some couples have a very private civil ceremony and a big bash reception at a later date.

Weddings have been performed in planes, hot air balloons, under the sea, on cruise boats at sea, on mountain tops and even in chapels with Elvis. Many sites that host receptions also offer you the option of holding the ceremony in their facilities. There are, of course, wedding chapels and civic sites that are designed specifically for weddings. The choices are limited only by one's imagination. For any site other than the church you attend, get all the details in writing and signed by someone in authority.

Wedding Flowers

Every bride needs a bouquet, right? Right! But, what can help break your wedding bank will be the components of the bouquet. Granted there are specialists in weddings out there who can help you, but you can do some of the work yourself and save a lot of money. For example, stay away from major holidays—Valentine's Day comes to mind. The winter months are also expensive for bringing in fresh flowers.

Avoid the exotic lilies and orchids. Consider eliminating the big traditional bouquet. A single, elegant orchid or lily could be picture perfect. Ditto for the bridesmaids. Some brides are using silk flowers versus fresh ones like my daughter did. Or, they substitute the more expensive center flowers with the artificial variety.

Don't forget corsages for the mothers and grandmothers and boutonnieres for the fathers and grandfathers or anyone else you deem special. Often the person who handles the wedding guest registry, the organist and vocalist (both male and female) are given flowers to wear. Depending on who attends, there may be other "important" guests who get flowers.

There are some low cost options for floral arrangements within the church or your chosen site. Ask if there's another wedding scheduled the same day as yours. If so, why not contact the party and ask if they'd like to share the cost of flowers, other than those that will be worn or carried. At some weddings the pews are decorated with greenery and even flowers. Many dollars can be saved if you have volunteer help set out your floral and greenery. If anyone within the wedding party has a flower-arranging thumb, they might be induced to help arrange and set up flowers at a much reduced price.

Consider renting green shrubbery (real or artificial), such a ferns as fillers for the sanctuary or for the home wedding. There are a number of companies whose business is to supply office buildings, restaurants and hotels with plants. These plants are rotated in and out to maintain their perfect appearance.

A bride who enjoys crafts and creativity might consider taking short class on silk flower arranging (offered by many large craft stores) so she can do her own flowers, which will save a considerable amount of money. One of the nicest things about using silk flowers as opposed to fresh is that they can be done far in advance of the wedding to avoid the last minute rush. My daughter packed all of her silk flower bouquets in one hard suitcase for the cruise wedding.

If you are considering a wedding around Easter or Christmas, most sanctuaries are already beautifully decorated for the season with either Easter lilies or poinsettias. Why not use them as a major backdrop and skip any other floral arrangements, except for what the bride and bridesmaids carry.

Last, but certainly not least, many weddings use candles today. Some, just three—candles that are lit by both Moms and the third by the couple; or one with the couple lighting it together; or some with huge candelabras in the evening. It's a miscellaneous cost in décor for the church and are provided by you. Good candles are costly.

Before deciding on a florist, ask to see photographs of weddings they have prepared for recently and ask the cost for the things they show. Make sure that you get good references and you are able to view, in person, some of the florist's

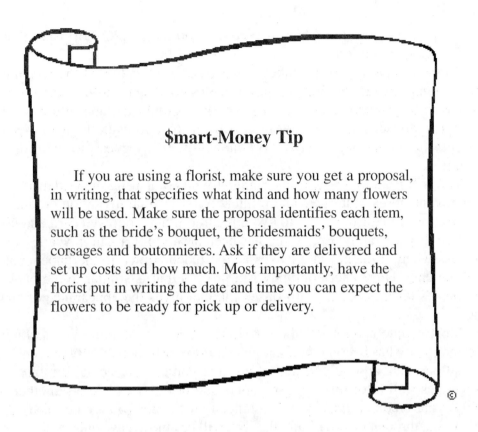

$mart-Money Tip

If you are using a florist, make sure you get a proposal, in writing, that specifies what kind and how many flowers will be used. Make sure the proposal identifies each item, such as the bride's bouquet, the bridesmaids' bouquets, corsages and boutonnieres. Ask if they are delivered and set up costs and how much. Most importantly, have the florist put in writing the date and time you can expect the flowers to be ready for pick up or delivery.

actual work. Many florists take the cookie cutter approach. Every bride gets the same kind of bouquet. That's probably not what you had in mind.

Many families have the floral work for the wedding party done by a florist and handle all the rest on their own. In the larger cities there are discount floral operations that can supply you with flowers and greenery in bulk. Again, get things in writing and locate a van that is air conditioned to pick up the flowers.

Invitations

The average couple pays anywhere from $200 to $300 for stationery needs. Expect to put down a minimum of a fifty-percent deposit. Besides the invitations, some brides choose to include a reception card which identifies location and time of the reception, a response card which asks the invitee to say yea or nay and how many or if any guests are coming. And some invitations include an inner envelope lining which is a color-coordinated piece of paper that pizzazz's up the invitation.

To save some money, it makes sense to put the location of the reception on the wedding invitations. I also think it makes good sense to include a response card with a stamped return envelope, which should include return to assure prompt response. You will want to have your invitations in the mail at least 6-8 weeks before the wedding so you know how many guests to plan for at the reception.

You will need to do some shopping around comparing the bridal stores, the department stores, stationers and printers for your final invitation product. One way to save a lot of money is to avoid the traditional engraved card and use the modern thermography. Engraving has been around for a zillion years. This is a process where a metal plate leaves actual indentations on the paper. You can feel the engraving. Thermography is a process that is similar to the ones used on today's business cards with raised ink that gives the appearance of engraving.

Most people cannot tell the difference. Because of improved technology, thermography has become popular and can save as much as fifty percent on the invitations. Ask around and make sure that you can get actual samples of the process as well as of the types of papers and print styles. Here's another place to use your credit card as extra insurance in the event you are not pleased.

Again, through "word of mouth," you will be able to save quite a bit of money working with someone who works from their home selling invitations—-about 20 to 25% off the "book" price. You will also receive terrific personal service from a home business. Check your order carefully and ask for a copy to take with you. Always order at least 25 more invitations than you think you may need. While the cost will be minimal with your original order for the extras, a re-order of only a few invitations can cost almost as much as your original order!

Photography

One of the best ways to find a good photographer is from a recently married couple. They'll tell you in a nano-second if they had a good experience and if it was reasonable in the money area. Another resource is to go to the church or site and talk to the person who coordinates the events, such as the wedding hostess. They're going to know who works well and who doesn't. This is not the time to let your fingers do the walking through the Yellow Pages of the phone book. You need good references for the person who is going to record your memorable event.

Don't forget to tap into friends and family members. Some the best photos I've seen of weddings are those candid ones. Some ways to save money include avoiding peak wedding times—Saturday evening is one of the most preferred dates of the week. Many photographers charge a premium price for a Saturday booking.

Another way to save money is to avoid some of the photo frills—having pre-engagement photos made can be very costly. Do yourself a financial favor and have all photos made at the time of the wedding and reception. Another way to save money is to have a professional photographer present only for the wedding, and turn your family and friends loose at the reception with the candid cameras. Finally, when it comes time to encase your treasured photos, shop around for the photo album. Prices can range from $75 to several hundred dollars for the wedding style album.

A fun idea for the wedding is to provide guests (for example, one on each table) with a disposable camera. Ask the guests to take photographs and then leave the cameras for you to develop. One suggestion—tell them not to go for distance shots—close-ups within six feet work the best with the disposables. You can get some fantastic candids this way!

At my daughter's wedding we made mistakes with the photographer. He turned out to be a personal friend of the vocalist and she was trying to do him a favor. Granted, he did take some good pictures but he also took several bad ones. We paid too much money for what was produced.

To help you avoid the pitfall we fell into, ask to review a complete album from a wedding that he or she has done in the recent past (at least within the last year). Ask if there is a limit to the number of rolls or exposures they will take before, during and after the wedding. If the photographer is sick, who does he or she use as a backup? Finally, make sure that you are sure what the costs are.

Many photographers offer packages. Be realistic. Is the package—i.e. 60 to 80 pictures—the right fit for the size of your wedding? If you have a lot of guests, over 100, it's not going to be enough shots. That is, if you intend for the photographer to do the wedding plus the reception. If you have friends and family handling the candid shots to a reception, it may be enough.

Wedding Cakes

At every wedding there is a cake and sometimes two if a groom's cake is desired. Make sure you know what you are buying. Cakes come in all kinds of shapes, sizes and tastes. Bakeries who specialize in cakes are usually pretty good about showing you extensive photographs of the real thing. Rarely are there any hidden expenses within the quoted price. Make sure you understand what the total cost will be including any delivery or set up charges. Expect to pay anywhere from $2 to $7 per serving, depending on what type of cake is selected.

How do you find a really good cake? Draw on friends' or your own recent experience at weddings you have attended. New trends in the cake area include different flavors and even types of cakes within the layers. Some weddings have the cakes decorated with flowers, either fresh or artificial, besides the traditional icings. If this is something that appeals, make sure the cake is available in time to get this done by you or someone else. Some bakers are glad to provide this service for free or at least a nominal amount.

Make sure you ask how long the cake is prepared in advance. The last thing you need is a dry cake. What about the tradition of saving the top layer of the cake for the first year anniversary? My response is—when's the last time you ate and enjoyed something that had been frozen for a year? I suggest you trash this tradition and eat the entire cake at the reception. When anniversary time arrives, order a small cake for your celebration.

After the bride and groom have cut the cake, the cake will have to be readied for your guests. Some additional icing to your cake costs is the potential of a cake-cutting fee. Be sure to cover this when planning the reception (coming up soon).

Here's a money-saving tip for cakes. For example, if you are expecting 250 guests, have your fancy display cake prepared to serve perhaps 100; have your baker prepare a sheet cake in the same flavors to serve 150. The cost is much less for a sheet cake, and after it's cut up in serving pieces, no one is the wiser!

Music

Weddings mean music is in the air—from harpists to dance bands to recorded DJs. There is something for everybody. Most weddings call for different music for the ceremony and for the reception. Most churches have an organist or a music coordinator who can help with the selections before and during the ceremony. Costs will vary anywhere from $50 to $150 per musician per hour. If the wedding is at home or at another site, taped music is often the choice. A string quartet is also a nice choice, but more costly.

For the reception, you usually have a choice of a live or canned performance.

The live being a singer/pianist, a quartet or a band. Your live option might be listening music or get up and knock 'em down with dancing music. Prices can range from a few hundred dollars to several thousand dollars. Many couples, especially young couples, are contracting with a DJ who carries a type of jukebox with them filled with tapes, albums and CDs. As a rule a DJ will be much less expensive than a live band will and the cost is generally only a few hundred dollars.

The best place to find your entertainment is through word of mouth and personal experience. Ask people you know and trust and whose tastes are similar to yours. Try to recall weddings or events that you have personally attended that were enjoyable. You will need to contract with your music provider(s)– and do it in writing. If you go "live," make sure that the musicians that you saw and heard will be the musicians that show up for your wedding. Live music requires that you clearly understand how long that they will play, how much the charges are, how music will be selected and how many breaks they take and for how long.

Your best saving money option for the music—entertainment area is a live DJ. They have several advantages. One, they cost a lot less. And two, they rarely take a break. Your music continues throughout the reception. And, assuming they are playing what you love and the crowd enjoys, you get much more entertainment for your wedding dollar.

Limousine

All brides have to get to the church and from the church on time. In most cases, family members arrange to arrive on their own. It is post wedding where a limo usually comes into view. If you decide to hire a limo, a driver comes with it. The average cost will range anywhere from $60 to $100 an hour, with a minimum of a 3-hour rental time. And remember, there's usually a gratuity on top. The best place to look for limos, outside of personal experience and referrals, is in the Yellow Pages under limousines and wedding services.

Ways for you to save money include using a company that has a short minimum time requirement such as less than 3 hours. Ask if the company has a pick up—drop off service. Definition: you hire them only for driving the wedding party to the reception. Why pay for time when the car is idle? An interesting option for a summer wedding would be horse drawn carriages.

The Reception

Prepare yourself, you will spend money on the reception. You can have any-

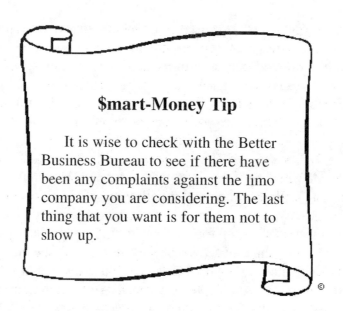

$mart-Money Tip

It is wise to check with the Better Business Bureau to see if there have been any complaints against the limo company you are considering. The last thing that you want is for them not to show up.

thing you want from snacks—hors d'oeuvres—to a sit down meal—but this is where the checkbook comes out. Understand what you are buying. Are you paying a flat fee for the entire afternoon or evening, or are you charged per hour with only a limited number of hours available? Reception sites vary in what you will be allowed to do. Some allow you to bring in the food and in some cases your beverage selections. Or they will require you to exclusively use their product. As a rule, if you are using their food services, there's not a charge for the use of the facilities.

Ways that you can save money include having the reception in the early part of the day, such as a brunch or lunch versus dinner. Dinner receptions will probably cost you twice as much as brunch or luncheon. If the site that you choose for your ceremony has facilities for the reception, you can use a caterer and usually reduce the per person as charged by the traditional hotel site. In fact, most places that allow you to use your own caterer will be less expensive than using a site that requires you to use their in-house services.

Many wonderful receptions have been held at a home, possibly yours. Wedding tables and chairs and often utensils and china are usually a requirement and these can be rented. If you have a big enough group and depending on the time of year, a tent can be pitched. Do yourself a favor, make sure you have someone come in and do the clean up. When considering a site, make sure you probe the following questions.

- How many guests will the space accommodate?
- If your reception will be at a site other than where the ceremony is performed, what does the rental fee cover and for how many hours?
- Will there be any overtime charges?
- What are the clean-up requirements, if any?
- If you can bring in an in-house caterer, are there restrictions, including cooking?
- If you are planning on dancing and having music, are there appropriate facilities available including the dance floor?
- What else is happening at the site of your wedding? The last thing you need is a competing wedding or event that is using a band that could conflict with the program or music that you plan on having.

Hotels

There are certainly advantages and disadvantages at reception sites. Looking at hotels, the advantages include the fact that when you book your reception at a hotel, you don't have to worry about tables, chairs, serving pieces, dance floors, etc. When Sheryl's reception site bailed out on us, we were fortunate to find a hotel that did hundreds of weddings a year. Their efficiency saved us hours of agony, although in the end, we paid for it.

The choice of a hotel usually means that everything is included within the price quoted to you. If you are planning a large wedding, hotels are the efficient choice for taking care of parties that involve many hundreds of individuals. Many hotels aggressively go after the wedding business and offer special wedding packages. Ask for details. Some hotels have turned the wedding ceremony into an art form.

This all sounds good but there are disadvantages. The decor in many hotels is boring. Most are also expensive. The catering representatives in a hotel are on commission. The more money you spend, the more money they make. Their druthers would be for you to select foods that are more expensive. This means that they may try to steer you away from the less costly chicken dishes and suggest prime beef or a shellfish.

If you plan on serving liquor, hotels grossly overcharge. This is one of the areas where they make big profit. Finally, never assume that anything is free. Hotels can charge extra for ice carvings, corkage fees, cake cutting, and extra

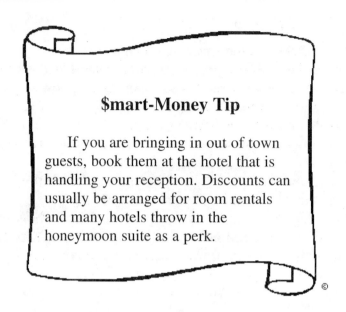

$mart-Money Tip

If you are bringing in out of town guests, book them at the hotel that is handling your reception. Discounts can usually be arranged for room rentals and many hotels throw in the honeymoon suite as a perk.

food attendants. When in doubt, ask and get your answers in writing.

Let's Eat

Several times throughout this chapter I have mentioned a caterer. What are some of the things that you look for in a caterer? First of all, get references. Draw from your own experience or that of people that you know well. If you select a reception site that doesn't have an in-house caterer they often have lists of caterers that they recommend. Don't bother to look in the Yellow Pages. This is definitely a time to count heavily on personal references.

Ask if you can talk to the contact person for several of the weddings that they have done in last six months, and specify weddings that are similar in size to yours. A good question for these contacts is, "If they had their druthers, what would they change about their wedding?"

When it comes to deciding on the menu, eat your way through it. Most caterers and hotels will allow you to sample items that you are considering. Take several friends so that you get feed back from multiple sources. Keep in mind that you will save money if you avoid items that are labor intensive. Fancy dishes and unique hors d'oeuvres may be labor intensive in their preparation and thus very costly.

Once again, I suggest that you time the reception for a brunch or luncheon and save money by avoiding the dinner. And do yourself a favor, avoid expensive food items such as shrimp, prosciutto and the like. If you have the option to provide the beverages, shop at the discount outlets for them and provide for the bar service by enlisting friends or relatives. Most likely, you will be save a lot on labor costs.

Caterers have fixed expenses and you are going to pay them if you have 50 people or 100. So never assume that if you have fewer guests that your catering costs will necessarily be less. Other questions to ask your caterer:

1. Where will the food be prepared—on site or will they bring it in?
2. What flexibility do you have to change times and dates, if any?
3. What are the options on their menus?
4. Do they write a contract? (They should)
5. Do they have a license to be in the catering business? (They should)
6. How will the staff be attired during your reception?
7. Who will be the supervisor in charge during the reception? I think it is a good idea if there is a representative from the catering firm who at least stops in for the reception to make sure that everything is running smoothly.

One of the plusses of catered wedding receptions today, is the advent of the food station. Instead of a long winding line at the buffet table, your guests can sample at one of several food stations that offer them a variety of foods. Food usually stays hotter and the long lines are a thing of the past. Consider this idea for wherever you decide to have the reception.

There are two other items that you could be hit with either from the reception site, the hotel or the caterer. And that includes a cake cutting fee and a corkage fee. Corkage fees usually involve liquor, although I have seen corkage fees charged for sparkling waters or any liquid that is not supplied directly by the reception site. Some places charge several dollars per bottle. When you have several hundred people, this could add up.

The other exorbitant fee is the cake-cutting fee. Some facilities charge anywhere from $.50 to several dollars per guest to have their staff cut and serve your cake. If you have staff involved in serving, you are already paying a mandatory gratuity, so you should be able to avoid this extra charge by simply saying no. Or, you can put some family members or friends in charge and tell the hotel you will not pay extra for a cake-cutting venture.

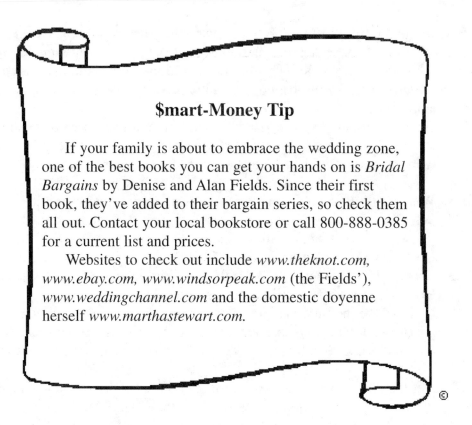

$mart-Money Tip

If your family is about to embrace the wedding zone, one of the best books you can get your hands on is *Bridal Bargains* by Denise and Alan Fields. Since their first book, they've added to their bargain series, so check them all out. Contact your local bookstore or call 800-888-0385 for a current list and prices.

Websites to check out include *www.theknot.com, www.ebay.com, www.windsorpeak.com* (the Fields'), *www.weddingchannel.com* and the domestic doyenne herself *www.marthastewart.com.*

Summing Up

Too often weddings get played out of proportion. Everyone involved gets frustrated, and a little angry when they can't understand why they couldn't have the simple small wedding they originally planned for. The answer is, they can. But to maintain that, a plan—strategy needs to be set out which identifies possible pitfalls as the process moves along and realistic budget and expectations. I have attended small weddings, including my own with 16 participants, that were lovely with minimal dollars spent, and I've attended huge affairs with hundreds and costing many thousands of dollars and it seemed like World War III was about to erupt. The choice will be yours.

In the end, weddings are a celebration of a love a couple has for each other. There is no reason why the bride, groom and parents shouldn't have a great

Chapter Seventeen

Leaving the Nest

When your kid leaves the nest, it is a momentous event. An element of surprise may be a factor when she or you as the parent, decide/announce that it is time for her to set up housekeeping on her own. Surprise may be unavoidable, but in this chapter I will give you some ideas to help you and your teen accomplish a successful take-off. Flaps up?—here we go.

Our oldest daughter Shelley was in her third year of college when she broached the subject. She had never wanted to live in one of the dorms on campus. But now, an apartment of her own began to look quite inviting. Shelley was a responsible young adult and had always been the most responsible of our kids. She balanced her checkbook, saved, worked after school and on weekends, maintained good grades, pitched in around home, earned her allowance and paid all her debts. Both my husband and I said "Bravo" when she announced she was ready to start out on her own.

The previous year had been a bumpy one for our family; my son Frank had died in an accident. Shelley's dedication to her schoolwork and other activities never faltered, even though she was grieving for her cherished brother. Her ability to handle adversity and maintain her previous level of performance indicated to both to John and I that she was indeed ready to try her wings and live on her own. And, we felt sure that we had little to worry about. At 22, she had a year to go to complete her degree. She was ready to jump ship.

Ah, but a complication surfaced. Sheryl said, "Me too." Where Shelley was always responsible and conservative, her younger sister was the exact opposite. Sheryl didn't lack intelligence; her problem was that she was reckless and head strong– definitely an impulse person. If she saw it and wanted it, she was going to get it. Sheryl, who was then attending her first year of college, pricked up her ears when her older sister started making noises about going out on her own. Sheryl thought hooking her independence declaration onto Shelley's was the perfect way to go.

Sheryl started her campaign– she came, she saw and she would conquer. Did she make her wishes known to John and I? No way. She astutely discerned that Shelley would be her ally. She used one of the typical kid ploys—gang up on the parents. She convinced her older sister that living alone could be lonely and she wouldn't have as much spending money. Wouldn't it be a "lark" if the two of them lived together in an apartment? They could split all the costs fifty-fifty and spend more time with each other. Sheryl hooked Shelley's conservative and responsible side and her emotional side too. She convinced her sister that this would be the perfect and right thing to do. And fun, to boot.

Sheryl told Shelley she was sure that Mom and John would supply some of the necessary ingredients for their new nest—surely they wouldn't have to buy everything themselves. And, they each had a complete bedroom set that they could take with them. They would have such fun shopping around at garage sales for miscellaneous living room furniture and some type of table to use for meal times. A united front emerged.

When the two girls sat down with us to tell us about their plans, both John and I were skeptical. Not about Shelley, we had no doubt that she was ready to go out on her own. It was Sheryl. This was the kid who had completely messed up 3 different bank accounts within a short period of time. The only solution was to close them and start all over, because none of us could figure out what she had done.

We were primarily concerned about their schooling. Both girls assured us that we had nothing to worry about on this score. They would both be working part time and they had each applied for student loans. We finally decided to give it a go, and the primary factor in our decision was that Shelley was a capable and responsible young adult. John and I actually fantasized that it would nice to be alone at last—an end in sight to the day in, day out responsibilities of parenting.

The girls managed to make it work for six months. Their life style and their choice of friends didn't seem to mesh. And, I suspect that the biggest problem evolved from the difference in their individual approach to making the joint venture work smoothly. Sheryl was driving Shelley nuts with an attitude of, "The first time is not always the charm," both of the girls got new roommates. Shelley stayed in the original apartment. Sheryl moved, renting a room in a co-op house.

Today, 15 years later, after a few more roommate candidates, some ups and downs, both are responsible adults. They pay their bills on time and, yes, they still have their opposite personalities. Sheryl's philosophy is still—bless this mess. And, Shelley's is—what mess?—they're not allowed!

Our Rules

Long before the girls took their leave of our home for one of their own, we had set out some guidelines, anticipating their (and our) eventual desire for emancipation. We told the 3 kids that, when they graduated from high school and/or turned 18, they had some options if they wanted to continue to live at home with us. Continued attention to their family member/ household responsibilities would be required, regardless of their choice. And, they would pay for their extra personal items through allowance and outside earnings.

- ♦ Choice #1   They could go to school full time and we would cover their room and board at home and we would cover their tuition.
- ♦ Choice #2   They could attend school and work part time, but they would have to pay rent.
- ♦ Choice #3   They could work full time, to pay a larger rent, and would also have to help pay for the food and utilities they used.
- ♦ Choice #4   Sit on their jobless duff, and get out of contributing to their upkeep and use of household space. This choice, one that so many kids seem to manipulate, was not an option in our household. If selected, it was immediate grounds for expulsion.

Shelley understood the concept perfectly well. During her first three years of college, she had worked part time, and covered all her personal expenses including clothing and her choices of entertainment. In addition, she was able to save.

Our son Frank was another story. He graduated from high school a year before he died. Frank had no enthusiasm about going to college, at least not yet. He thought working might be okay. His attitude was later, rather than sooner. Right then he was too busy hanging out with his pals and having a good time, and didn't have time to look for a job. So, he didn't have the money to pay for room and board as our household rules called for.

I used to get out the classifieds and highlight jobs from the daily newspapers and leave them on his bed. One time, I even noted a position for a chimney sweep. When he didn't respond to any of these "hints", I became more aggressive. I called the Army, Navy, Air Force and Marines for enlistment information. Frank developed quite a mailbag!

Nothing seemed to get his attention. We warned him twice and he ignored us.

The Household "Pink Slip"

To really get his attention, I felt we had to be more innovative. I told him that we were going to have a "Last Supper," and he could choose the menu for the meal that evening. After we all had dined sumptuously, he was told he had to leave. First he laughed. You can't be serious," he said. Then it finally dawned on him that we were dead serious. He got mad and threatened us. The threat? He said that if we kicked him out of the house he would sleep in front of our house in a sleeping bag or in his truck. He'd show us—he'd embarrass us in front of the neighbors.

His threats didn't phase us; he had broken the rules and it was time for the consequences. We told him, "Sleep away."

True to his word, he camped in front of our home for three days and nights. We weren't impressed, the neighbors weren't impressed, but one of his pals was. Frank was offered the couch at his buddy's home. That night his friend's mother called about the boy on her sofa. I explained our rules to her and what had led up to Frank's ouster. I also told her that he was welcome to come home, but he had to either go to school or get a job. The choice was his. Within 24 hours, Frank had called me at my office and asked for an appointment. When he showed up that evening, he announced that he had found a job. And, he asked if he could come home.

Ah, the parent has power after all. We told him that he would be more than welcome to come home, but there would be some conditions. During the next hour we wrote up a contract to be signed by all of us, Frank and John and me. We reiterated the household rules and came up with a dollar amount that he would pay toward rent and food and utilities. In addition, I was able to get a commitment from Frank that he would save/bank half of every paycheck.

In the beginning of this chapter, I shared that Frank had died in an accident. This happened a year after we made him leave. Did/do we have any regrets with our position in handling Frank's non-work/non-school scenario? Absolutely not.

As parents, we have not a clue how long God will share his children with us. Each day must be taken one at a time. Both my husband and I are quite comfortable that we did the best job we could with the "tools" we had at the time. No one can rewrite our lives. We must learn and move on.

So, how did Frank do when he came back? Quite well. He had lined up a full-time job, grew in maturity as new responsibilities were added. He also saved money for the first time in his life—almost $2,000. When Frank died, I divided his savings between his sisters. It was the $1,000 that enabled Sheryl to buy her first home in Denver, Colorado.

Throughout this book, as in this chapter, I have shared stories of how John and I met the challenges of parenthood and grandparenthood, and how we got our youngsters ready to deal with the money maze. Your experiences won't mirror ours, but my hope is that our experiences will encourage you to be candid with your kids about money. It's a tragic mistake when parents don't talk about all the money issues that will face their kids as adults. And, give them opportunities to fail and succeed before they leave the shelter of your financial resources.

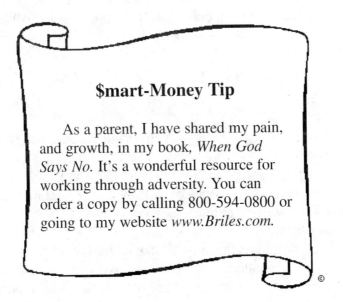

$mart-Money Tip

As a parent, I have shared my pain, and growth, in my book, *When God Says No*. It's a wonderful resource for working through adversity. You can order a copy by calling 800-594-0800 or going to my website *www.Briles.com*.

I will say it again. One of your primary roles as a parent is to propel (and sometimes you do have to push) your kid into a position where they can break away from their dependency upon you. In the latter years of teenhood, you as the parents should be actively unveiling the money maze. Teens are busy. They get distracted. And they sometimes think their parents are aliens. It's sometimes hard to get their attention.

They don't hang on every word you say like they did when they were little ones. But you must make sure you get their attention regularly about money issues, and track their progress. They need to have the opportunity to succeed and to fail while you're still in their financial picture. They won't get a rose garden out there, better they understand that sooner than later when it can really hurt.

Your New Assistant

One the smartest things I did with my kids when they hit the mid-teens was to enlist their help in paying our family bills and generally running the household. I covered this more fully in an earlier chapter. They came out of this exercise with a clear understanding of what it cost to run our household—invaluable information for their own future nest.

My kids got important, hands-on experience about checking accounts, budgets, shopping wisely, etc. And, they also learned why a savings program was imperative for those times of financial crisis that hit everyone. And, that savings are a must in reaching the goals of pleasurable events like vacations or buying a car. Even leaving home.

Money Steps

So, if your teens do not have their own checking accounts, they should. Ditto with a savings account. Granted you may have to be a co-signer depending on the requirements of the bank you deal with, but do it anyway. Then spend the time to see that they learn all the ropes by getting them to set their account(s) up on the computer. They will be able to see exactly how they spend their money and where it comes from.

There are several programs that anyone can learn. I favor the ease of Quicken by Intuit. Teens love computers and you will love their balanced checkbook. Plus, Quicken will introduce them to other types of financial reports—-such as profit and loss statements. Quicken is available for under $50 at stores that sell software.

The Dos and Don'ts of Credit

Today, just about everyone uses a credit card. And, just about everyone has a credit history when they reach adulthood. Thus, it is critical to open up the channels about credit usage—the do's and don'ts. At the age of sixteen, we added our kids onto a MasterCard account that was in my name. They became co-signers/users on the account and their social security numbers had to be given to the bank. They each got a card with their own name.

When the monthly the bill came, we broke down all the charges and tallied who owed what. Each of our teens had to pay their portion of the bill within 15 days of receipt of the statement, or their charge privileges were suspended and their card repossessed. Their privileges were reinstated only when the owed monies came forward. And, three strikes and they were out of the credit card business for six months.

Of course, I would personally pay what they owed on the due date so my credit was not undermined. And monthly, the credit grantor reported that the card was paid on time and they reported under the kids' names and social security numbers as well as mine. In our household, Shelley only charged what she could pay for and never had a problem with meeting her obligations. Sheryl had her privileges suspended several times. Today both my daughters are practitioners of paying the entire credit card balance each and every month. Smart.

Secure vs. Debit

When my kids were teens, "secured " and "debit "cards were not available. I wish they had been, because they would be the strategy I would begin with today. The "secured " credit card holder guarantees the use of the card with a type of savings account. The savings account is thus, collateral against future use of the card. In some cases the institution will allow for an inflation factor, and my thinking on this would be, steer clear.

Here's how it works. If $300 is deposited in the savings account, the bank could allow charging privileges of up to $450, for example. It could be more. Money is not drawn from the savings unless the charge account is not paid on time.

The debit card is a little bit different. It is in essence, a plastic reusable check. Money is immediately drawn against the account, either checking or savings. It is not true credit, unless a line of credit (unsecured) is attached to the account to handle overdrafts. Again, I don't advise having a credit line attached to a debit card.

This type of card could be the answer for the teen who simply can't remember to enter the payee and amount of each check written in his or her check registry. And since the debit card transactions are handled electronically, the balance of the account is usually very accurate from day to day, unlike a regular checking account. Rapid debiting of charges is another plus for the debit card and a good tool for the teen whose checking account is chronically overdrawn. You both will know sooner when the account is hungry and maybe avoid some of those heavy-duty "bad check" charges—non-sufficient funds.

The negative here is that if you have an "absent-minded" teen, not remembering to enter all transactions in the check register, they may hit a non-sufficient fund (NSF) status quickly. Banks penalize overdrawn accounts; often the charge is the same for a NSF entry. I would suggest the rule in your home to be one NSF is enough—it should be; it's not uncommon for a charge to be $20-$30 for each item. If more than one, suspend the account until you think your teen is ready to try again. We had to do this with Sheryl.

One for the Money, Two for the Show . . .

Below is the **Leaving the Nest $mart-Money Quiz**. When your son or daughter can answer yes to all 26 questions, you can be confident that your efforts to educate your teen about the money maze have been successful. You have instilled the fundamentals of a Smart-Money adult. But first, take the test yourself, giving the responses you think they are likely to give. You will have some idea of just what they know, and don't know (and maybe what you know and don't know).

Leaving the Nest $mart-Money Quiz

1. Do you know how to open a checking account?   Yes ___ No ___
2. Do you know how to balance a checkbook?   Yes ___ No ___
3. Do you know how to open a savings account?   Yes ___ No ___
4. Can you name 2 types of savings vehicles, other
   than a passbook savings account?   Yes ___ No ___

5. Would you know how to stop payment on a check if you needed to?   Yes ____ No ____

6. Do your outside earnings account for more than 15 percent of the total balance in your savings account?   Yes ____ No ____

7. When you run out of checks, do you know how to order more of them?   Yes ____ No ____

8. Do you understand all the entries on monthly bank statements for both checking and savings accounts?   Yes ____ No ____

9. Do know the difference between a bank, a savings and loan institution, and a credit union?   Yes ____ No ____

10. Do you know what interest rate is charged on the unpaid balance of your credit card or on one of your parents credit cards?   Yes ____ No ____

11. Have you been saving 10 to 25 percent of all money that you receive from parents, gifts and outside jobs?   Yes ____ No ____

12. Do you have money left over at the end of your pay period, either weekly or monthly, after all your expenses have been paid?   Yes ____ No ____

13. Do you know who to call if you lose a checkbook or a credit card?   Yes ____ No ____

14. Do you know how to use an ATM card?   Yes ____ No ____

15. Do you know how to get cash in an emergency—day, night or out of town?   Yes ____ No ____

16. Could you make up a livable spending plan for yourself without your parents' assistance?   Yes ____ No ____

17. Do you understand how to read a simple contract, such as the one found on the back of a credit card application, or the conditions of a lease?   Yes ____ No ____

18. Do you know how to get car insurance?   Yes ____ No ____

19. Do you know what penalty or penalties are assessed when you make a late payment on a credit card?   Yes ____ No ____

20. Do you know what a credit report is and how to get a copy of yours?   Yes ____ No ____

21. Savings accounts earn interest; do checking accounts?   Yes ____ No ____

22. Do you buy on impulse?   Yes ____ No ____

23. Do you know how and when to file federal and state
tax returns?   Yes ___ No ___

24. Do you know what an IRA is?   Yes ___ No ___

25. Do you know what travelers checks are and how
to get them?   Yes ___ No ___

How To Score: Give every *Yes* answer 2 points. Give *No* answers 0 points

If your teen scores:

40 to 50 points—   Help him pack his bag, he's ready to leave home or perhaps even support you.

26 to 38 points—   He's on his way, but still needs input from you. He can read this book, so get him his own copy.

24 and below—   You both need to wake up fast, otherwise he will never be ready to leave home. You may have to support him the rest of your life.

As you can see there are a lot of queries in the preceding quiz. All pertain to important money skills that will be carried with your kids throughout his or her life. As your kids gets ready to leave the nest, you want to make sure that they leave on solid footing.

Three, To Get Ready . . .

The above is just some other money and credit-related areas you should cover with your teen. Ask them if they understand how to complete applications for a new job, a loan, an apartment, car insurance, phone and utility service? Do they know how to prepare a tax return? Have they read the fine print on credit applications, apartment leases and insurance policies (no lapsing on car insurance allowed)?

Tell your teen to go out and gather up examples of each. Then, spend time with them until you feel they fully understand the terminology and the implications of their answers when they fill in the blanks. Have them brush up on their resume writing skills. Talk to them about the deposits that are required when renting an apartment and for the phone and utilities for this apartment. They must know when and under what conditions these deposits are returned. Many young adults who are conscientious about their credit and their money get cheated by the system, simply because they didn't have all the facts and know how to use them.

As your son and daughter get ready to fly, now is the time to set up a realistic spending plan (AKA the budget). Below is a sample that you can use as a guideline. The objective is to help your soon-to-be-emancipated kid get a firm grip on the concept that outgoing monies can't exceed incoming monies.

Leaving the Nest Spending Plan

Income:
Jobs _____
Investments _____
Money gifts _____
Parental Assistance _____
Other _____

Total Income _____

Expenses:
Food _____
Rent _____
Clothing _____

Utilities:
Gas _____
Electric _____
Water _____
Trash _____
Cable TV _____
Phone _____
Other _____

Transportation:
Car payment _____
Car Insurance _____
Gasoline _____
R & M _____
Misc. Expense _____

(Traffic tickets, Deductible/accidents)
Bus/mass transportation
Bicycle _____
Other _____

Medical:
    Insurance _____
    Doctor _____
    Dentist _____
    Medicine _____
    Other _____

Education Expense:
    Tuition _____
    Books _____
    Fees _____
    Supplies _____
    Other _____

Entertainment:
    Food _____
    Movies _____
    Sports _____
    Vacations _____
    Other _____

Gifts _____

Church & Charities _____

Total Expenses _____

What else should your about-to-leave child know about? Everything. Everything that I have put down and everything I haven't. Think about how you spend your time and money. Consider spreading out what a typical week looks like for you. How you spend your time—work, visiting with friends and family, community activities, church, cleaning, errands, shopping—what obligations you incur.

I strongly suggest you have your son or daughter read the following chapters in this book: *The Introduction; Money Talks Within the Family; Your Insurance IQ; Creating A Wall Street Wizard; The Will of Your Way; Savings . . . Creating a Habit for the New Millennium;* and *The Boomerangers Are Back.* When it comes to buying a car, review *Look Out . . . My Kid Wants Wheels* and if a wedding appears, *A Wedding to Remember.*

As a parent, your goal is to launch a responsible and self-reliant adult into his or her community. *$mart-Money Moves for Kids* is meant to help you launch yours. If you follow the guidelines suggested within this chapter, as well as the entire book, you should have no problem. You have done the best you could with the tools you have. Good luck.

. . . And Go!

Chapter Eighteen

The Boomerangers Are Back!

When I speak publicly, there is one subject about kids that always pops up. A comment on this topic that I have used, in a kidding manner, covers my feelings about keeping the nest empty once all the kids have left home. Sell the house and get one that is too small for them to move back to. This comment always gets a big laugh from my audiences, and some have commented to me that they wish they had thought of this a long time ago. Many newly adult children of the 90's appear on their parent's doorstep, bags in hand. And, some appear with their *own* children in tow. This happens just about the time parents have settled into a peaceful existence that offers them time for themselves—at last.

Boomerang kids—you did your job as a parent, taught them how to fly the nest and now life has broken one of their wings. Now, they want to come home. One of the most common reasons that kids boomerang is immediately following college graduation. The perfect job hasn't been found yet, or they might have decided to pursue a graduate study program. Surveys of young adults between the ages of 20 and 29 show that 50 percent of them live with their parents. And depending on which studies you look at, between 30 to 40 percent adult children return to living under their parent's roof at least once.

Most parents will experience a time when their kids are anxious to be on their own. And sometimes it's only because they want their own "place", free from parental direction. Freedom, they think, will be so wonderful—no one to answer to, but themselves. And to this end, they have found the perfect job and the perfect place to begin their own life of freedom. The cost of living becomes, for some of these newly emancipated kids, a rather stark reality. A case in point is the roommate who was sharing the rental costs in the perfect "place" (an exorbitantly expensive apartment), and has now moved out.

Each year, the major magazines such as *U.S. News & World Report, Forbes, Newsweek* and *Time* publish articles about the best places to live in America. There are many qualifiers used to crown a city or state as "The Best", and two of them are the availability of affordable housing and affordable base living costs. A reasonable and growth oriented economy is usually tied to overall affordable living costs.

I now live in Colorado, but I lived in my native state of California for 44 years. The last 18 of these years were spent in the Bay Area of northern California. Anyone familiar with the Bay Area knows that this is not an inexpensive area to live in. In fact, it is not uncommon for a one bedroom apartment (with a carport) to rent for $1300 per month. Hopefully, your kid doesn't live in an area as costly as this.

No matter where you and your kids live, when they decide to leave home, post high school or post-college, there will be a rude awakening when they face the cost of housing themselves. In particular, the cost of the deposits required. They can't have a phone or utilities without a deposit and the landlord will require at least two months rent in advance, plus, in some cases, a damage deposit for pets and kids.

They will hopefully have done the math that shows what they can afford, from their present earnings, to spend on the monthly costs to live on their own. But, they rarely have a nest egg to cover all the front-end costs required to move into their own place. Here's where the "6-Ps" come in—Prior Planning Prevents the Probability of Poor Performance.

Your family spending plan sessions of the past has laid the foundation for your kid's first full-blown adult spending plan. So, *before* they commit to the time they will officially leave the nest, call a family pow-wow. Help them prepare for successful emancipation with some *in depth* prior planning.

Ask these questions:

- First, and most importantly, what dollars do they anticipate each month from their job? This is their net, after tax, income.
- What are the fixed costs of living on their own? Rent, phone, utilities, car insurance (maybe they also have a car payment), any debt from

student loans (these animals rear their heads after graduation and must be paid on a monthly basis) or credit cards and, oh yes, there's food.

♦ What do they plan to spend for non-fixed costs? Entertainment (an item that often "blows the budget"), clothes, haircuts, gasoline, auto repair and maintenance (new tires can break their bank), gifts, vacations and dry cleaning and laundry of their clothes. They will probably not think of renter's insurance. But, they should at least consider it, if they have costly audio and visual equipment and computers they are taking with them to their new place.

♦ What about savings, church and charity? Where do these items, from their earlier spending plans, fit in?

Hello Mom, I'm Your New Tenant

Let's admit it, once the kids are gone, your life changes! And, you love a lot about it. The benefits include laundry duty that doesn't take a whole day, grocery tapes that aren't a yard long (new challenge: can you make spaghetti sauce for *only* one or two?), one page phone bills, no base speakers vibrating you awake at 1 AM and you can sleep—no more need to wait up and worry where they are and when they will be home.

But, some kids do ask to come back home. The reasons are myriad; the "6-Ps" didn't take, the roommate vamoosed, a marriage has failed, a job was lost,

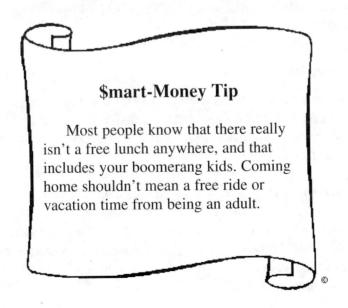

$mart-Money Tip

Most people know that there really isn't a free lunch anywhere, and that includes your boomerang kids. Coming home shouldn't mean a free ride or vacation time from being an adult.

illness took it's toll. The kid is wounded in some way and wants to lick these wounds under your roof. And then, your life changes again if you say *Yes*.

One of the biggest mistakes, related to me by parents of boomerang kids, is that they haven't set guidelines for the new life with their adult child under their roof. And, it's tough to do. These "kids' are used to their autonomy by now and don't respond to parental authority in the same way they used to. And, this kid may be a parent to one or more children.

Additionally, when your kid announces "Mom, I'm coming home" there is often the stress of immediacy involved. They need (or think they need) your help NOW. You may be tempted to react emotionally in such a situation and take them in your arms and put no parameters on the move-in. Don't do it! They can have your unlimited love and emotional support in their time of need, but not your unlimited or unrestricted financial support.

Some kids solve the problem(s) that brought them home and some really never had a problem in the first place. But the fact is that they are living in your home now. The rationale may then become—why leave a great, comfortable place, why take on another possibly problem roommate, where else can I get such a good financial deal that I get from Mom and Dad?

Granted, moving back home can be hard on your kid, her grand life style is gone. She has to move into her old room that still has the flowered wallpaper and the stuffed animals of yesteryear. These issues are light, when considering the ones that you as parent are forced to deal with in redefining the relationship with your now, very adult child. Sticky issues pop up in the area of privacy, sex, life style and money.

Before They Move In

The best formula for success is to hammer out the guidelines and the agreements you will have with your kids, before they officially move in. Talk over the following issues with your adult kid and make a contract (you may want to put it in writing and sign it):

- *What is your financial situation now and what do you anticipate it to be over the next few months?* If the kid is unemployed, what is being done to find new work must be discussed, and re-discussed weekly.
- *What options do you have, if any, for living accommodations besides the parental residence both now and in the future?* Your home may not be the best choice after all.

- *How long do you need to live at home and when can you leave again?* Pin this one down, i.e. is it two months from now that they will be gone, no matter what.
- *What space in your home will you to surrender to your adult child?* This is a crucial question. You like your life as it is and this is *your* home now. Don't give them carte blanche, even if they bring your grandchildren home with them. You want them to be comfortable, of course, but not so comfortable that they want to stay forever.
- *What will you charge them for living in your home?* You must keep the reality of life in front of your adult child by charging them for rent and food, even if they have to pay you back at a later date. This doesn't mean that you should charge the "market" rate for rent—be reasonable. Consider either a percentage of present income or a sliding scale, in case they get a raise or better job.

A side note about this rent income and the tax implications: The IRS considers this to be under the same roof and with parents only and, you are not required to declare, as income, any rental money received from your child. By charging for living expenses, they will be more eager to spend *their* money on *their* place and will do it, hopefully sooner rather than later.

- *What household duties will you require of them while they live with you?* They must help with the extra work they create and should not be "on vacation" in your home. This is not the "old days"; they will not get paid for the required duties. For example, you have every reason to expect them to keep their areas in the type of condition, that were normal for you (i.e., their use of your guest bath requires "apple pie" order at all times). Be specific if you expect them to assist you with any cooking or house cleaning activities. If they don't do it, don't do it yourself. Consider hiring it done and charge it to their account.
- *What about expenses other than food and rent?* You are not an ATM machine. You may have an unemployed kid at home or some emergency could arise for an employed kid that he can't cover. Keep a ledger of all money expended and let them know that these are loans that are to be paid back within a very short period of time and, before they treat themselves to any new toys or entertainment.
- *What are the rules about phone and automobile (if applicable) usage?* If your kid will be living with you for more than month and they are

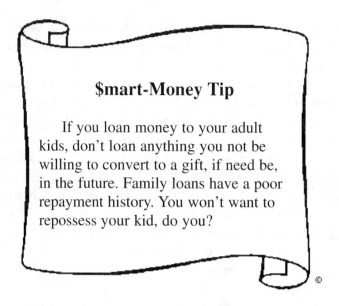

$mart-Money Tip

If you loan money to your adult kids, don't loan anything you not be willing to convert to a gift, if need be, in the future. Family loans have a poor repayment history. You won't want to repossess your kid, do you?

working, you could have them install their own phone line, at their own cost now and in the future. If they use your automobile, they must share in all costs—insurance, car payments, gasoline and repairs. Or you could look at the lowest rate for a rental car and charge him a reasonable per diem rate. Guaranteed, this will get his attention.

♦ *What about your kid's kid(s)?* You will be sorry later if you don't set rules at the outset in this special case of grandchildren living in your home. Don't become a full time baby-sitter and learn about your child's parenting philosophy—hands off are usually best. But if the grandchild is out of line a lot of the time, your philosophy should take over, it's your home and your sanity, after all.

♦ *And finally, what time do each of you need alone in the home?* You both need your space because you both have been used to it. Set times for each of you to entertain friends at home without the other present, you need your life and they need theirs. You know your rules for behavior of guests in your home; your adult child's friends must adhere to them too. Do you allow overnight stays?—your choice not theirs.

Managing Their Money During a Financial Time-out

When queried about their reasons from returning to the homestead, most kids will respond—money. When they do move back home, promises are made

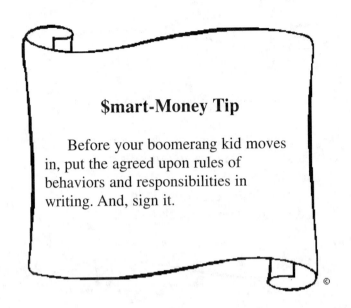

$mart-Money Tip

Before your boomerang kid moves in, put the agreed upon rules of behaviors and responsibilities in writing. And, sign it.

to you and to themselves that, in a very short period of time, they will be back on their feet and ready for living on their own again. It all sounds good, but it is easy to get side tracked. You both want to avoid turning a short term move back into a long-term stay.

Sit down with them and get a firm grip on a financial plan of action as was suggested earlier in this chapter. Believe it or not, parents who charge rent and require their kid's contribution to routine household expenses are doing the best thing possible for these move home kids. They are once again encouraging their kid's future independence, both financially and emotionally.

In this effort to get them back out on their own, don't overlook the possibility of "sweat equity" or bartering. There are ways for them to live rent-free and these can be very much in line. For example, if your daughter is going to law school and is also working part-time at a law firm, she may be covering her tuition, health insurance and personal expenses. She can do some chores around the house or the yard in lieu of paying rent. And pat yourself on the back that she is paying her own tuition and other expenses.

When kids suddenly are relieved of the obligation to pay for their own living expenses, amounting to many hundreds of dollars, they might begin to "treat" themselves to more goodies than they could afford when they were on their own—entertainment, clothing and toys. It's time, parents, to blow the whistle. They moved back because they needed a financial time-out.

I'm sure that their move back home—whether it was welcomed with open

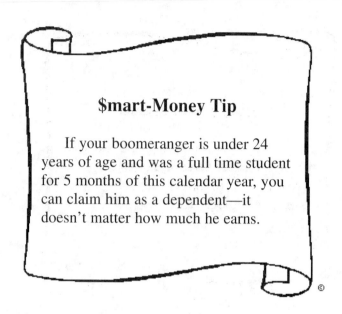

$mart-Money Tip

If your boomeranger is under 24 years of age and was a full time student for 5 months of this calendar year, you can claim him as a dependent—it doesn't matter how much he earns.

arms or reluctantly allowed—was not done under the auspices that they would be allowed to redirect their money into "fun" endeavors. If this occurs, a not so gentle reminder should be forthcoming from you. Tell them you agreed to a temporary stay and that a pass on expensive hair-do's/haircuts, weekend trips, dinner out and the like is expected from them.

Put It in Writing. . Setting Up a Lease

If you have adult kids at home, either Boomerangers or Misfires (adult kids who have never ventured out on their own), it makes sense to have a different set of ground rules. Adult kids living at home should have responsibilities and behaviors that reflect their adult status. They aren't "just the kids" anymore.

Below are a series of questions intended to serve as a guide to setting up a room-and-board status for your boomeranger. There are no right and wrong answers to these questions. Rather, they are meant to probe into both sides of the issues involved and get them to the surface. Believe, there's going to be plenty of times that they rear their heads; you might as well attempt to do a little planning.

Parent's Lease Worksheet

Should rent be charged?   Yes ___   No ___

How much should be paid per month? $ _____

Should there be a different charge if your kid is employed or unemployed?

Yes ___   No ___

If employed—how much per month? $ _____

If unemployed—how much per month? $ _____

How long will the lease term be (weeks, months, years)? _____

Is it renewable?   Yes ___   No ___

Will your son get his own phone, or use yours? Yours ____

Get his own _____

Will you charge for utilities?   Yes ___   No ___

How will you allocate utility charges, by percentage (i.e. 25% of each bill)
   or a fixed dollar amount? I won't charge ____   Fixed amount ___ % ____

How much will the utility charges be (or are they now)?

   Phone _____Water _____

   Trash Collection _____Gas & Electricity _____

Does your son own his own car?   Yes ___   No ___

Will he use your car?   Yes ___   No ___

Who will pay the insurance, maintenance and gas? I will ____   He will ____

If he has a car, where will it be parked?(garage, street, driveway) _____

What household chores will your son be responsible for? (do an inside and
outside list) _____

How often do want chores done? Include it on the list.

Is your kid allowed to have pets of his own in your home?   Yes ___   No ___

If yes, who will care for them? I will ____   He will ____

Will he eat only the food he buys, or will he consume yours?

His only ____   Parents ____

If he eats yours, will he reimburse you or contribute to the food bill?

   Give a percentage ____   Other ____

If your kid eats at home, will he assist with preparations?   Yes ___   No ___

Will he do his own laundry?   Yes ___   No ___

301

Can he use your TV and other equipment?   Yes ___ No ___
If yes, will there be any time or program restrictions?   Yes ___ No ___
Will he be allowed to entertain friends in your home?   Yes ___ No ___
If yes, what types and what number of guests? _____
Are there to be any curfew rules?   Yes ___ No ___
Will overnight guests be allowed?   Yes ___ No ___
If yes, how long can a guest stay? _____
If he ignores or violates his agreement with you, what are
the consequences? _____

Now, after you have gone through the worksheet, draft your lease and the two (or three) of you sign it. Most parents will go out of their way to help and support their kids. But roles begin to shift when the adult-to-adult relationship becomes a reality. I strongly encourage you to set this new adult-to-adult relationship in motion when your son or daughter graduates from high school. It doesn't matter if college is in the picture or not. Your flexibility and good negotiating skills (theirs too) are important factors in the parent/child tenant agreement.

Lease Violations

If your rules are ignored or violated, what will your policy be? By now, most parents know that their kids can be master manipulators (We grand parents know it too!). Yours are probably no different. The last thing you need is open warfare in your own home.

So, from the start, set out the consequences of noncompliance, just as you did when your son or daughter was little. Cause and effect are the issues—then be sure you stick to them! Here's my two bits—

- ♦ When a first-time infraction occurs, a verbal warning is in order.
- ♦ The next time, a written and/or financial penalty should be levied.
- ♦ The third time, get out the eviction notice. If your kid, and his stuff, are not gone from your home in your given number of days, put them into storage or on the front lawn.

This may sound a tad harsh. But, by now, your kids are supposed to be grown-ups, yes? The advance planning that you created before they moved in

302

$mart-Money Tip

If your kid comes home and brings
bill collectors home with him too,
refer him to CCCS (Consumer Credit
Counseling Service) at 800-388-2227.

has set the stage. Your house, your rules, which part isn't understood? It's called performance and accountability.

Protecting Their (and Your) Privacy

You may, just may, want to close your doors once in a while, but this kid of yours has moved home. For that matter, so will they. And, if your son or daughter is receiving their mail at your home, it's difficult not to know more than either of you would like about their business. You both deserve more privacy than was present when they were living with you when they were younger. They are adults now and you are no longer a full time parent, you were also emancipated. The lack of needed privacy can cause tempers to flare on both sides. Hone up on your negotiating skills, you may need them.

If your kids' attitudes and/or behavior "bug" you, that seem inappropriate under your roof, you should tell them. It is critical for your kids to know, up front, what you can and cannot accept. If you feel negatively about what they do or say in your home, tell them. Touchy areas are their friends—male and female, love interests could bring out the worst reaction in you; their finances— if they are not model citizens, you will probably "see red "; their personal habits—loud music and smoking, make you crazy; their kids (or their pets)—a set bedtime is a must, you as a grandparent can have the fun of reading a bedtime story but you've earned your stripes already in enforcing the bedtime regime.

Make it very clear what you can and cannot accept. A lot of unnecessary negative transactions with your adult child can be avoided if they adhere to three simple rules:

1. Keep your area and areas you use—Neat,
2. Sex is private—keep it that way, and
3. Think before you speak or act—Don't upset your Mom and Dad.

When kids move home, the bottom line is—it's your home and you have the final word. If your kids don't agree with the final word on any subject, they should pack up now. And, return your keys.

Part Five

The Internet

Chapter Nineteen

Making Money on the Net

One thing that most kids do better than their parents is working with cyberspace. Your budding stock investor can tap into an arsenal of web-sites that offer information galore. Accounts can be opened (with you if they are under 18); magazines and newspapers read and games played online. Everyday, new features and websites are being added. Because of that, it's impossible to identify all the places to go. But, I can offer a few to get you started. Have fun.

Let's Play

Starting with games makes sense. Most of the money sites are neutral—they don't lean toward girls or boys. You will be amazed at the variety of visuals offered and the creative energy that has gone into some of these websites. Some of them offer contests—

- *E*Trade's Stock Game* is open to the 18 year and up crowd and offers real money (versus virtual bucks for play money) as a prize at *www.etrade.com.*
- *The Stock Market Game* is designed for kids in the nine and up range. Players try to increase the value of their stock portfolios over a ten-week period, starting with $100,000. The game is sponsored by the

Securities Industry Foundation for Economic Education. The SMG website is *www.smg2000.com.*

♦ *Student Stock Tournament* is run by CNBC. Its format is a student investment club for grades 4-12 (clubs range from 4-25 members each). Each club (team) gets $100,000 virtual dollars to invest. The tournament runs twice a year—top prize is 200 shares of GE stock and an appearance on CNBC. Its website is *www.cnbc.com.*

♦ *Lava Mind* offers education games for kids 8 and up. Some of the games are fairly simple (Gazillionaire) and become more complicated as the player advances. Its website is *www.lavamind.com/edu.*

♦ *Cash University* presents a format that's quite familiar to most kids— arcade games. Its website is *www.beseen.net/cashuniversity/home.*

♦ *Liberty Financials Young Investors Website* is a game room for just about everyone. Puzzles, brainteasers, quizzes, you name it—there's something here for all your kids (including you). Their website is *www.younginvestor.com.*

Most of the sites are geared to junior high and above, but don't let that stop your kids from exploring, even if they are only 7 or 8. Financial firms have discovered the web, with almost all of them having their own sites today. Within the sites, are sites designed for kids. I'd suggest you merely do some exploring yourself with names that you are familiar with—i.e. Charles Schwab is *www.schwab.com*—and put a "www." in front of the name, then a ".com" after it and see what pops up.

Below are a variety of topics and their websites. The list is definitely not all encompassing, but it's a start to get you surfing for information.

Need to Know About	Website
Budgeting	www.finitycorp.com/hazam
	www.mastercard.com/cgi-bin
Cars	www.cars.com
	www.autoweb.com
	www.carpoint.msn.com
	www.carsdirect.com
	www.priceline.com
	www.kellybluebook.com
Collecting	www.kovels.com
	www.eBay.com

www.Shopgoodwill.com
www.bejeanie.com
www.yahooAuction.com
www.bejeanie.com
www.tomart.com

College Loans
www.fastweb.com
www.savingforcollege.com
www.collegeboard.com
www.ed.gov
www.fastweb.com
www.finaid.org
www.synet.org

Consumer Credit
www.nfcc.org
www.cfcministry.org

Consumer Information
www.consumerreports.com

Credit Cards &
General Information
www.creditnet.com
www.bankrate.com
www.championmortgage.com
www.creditchoice.com
www.creditreportsite.com
www.firstusa.com
www.college-vias.com
www.consumeraction.org

Credit Reporting
www.experian.com
www.equifax.com
www.transunion.com

Entrepreneurship
www.kidsway.com
www.deca.org
www.4h-usa.org
www.ja.org
www.youngandsuccessful.com

Games
www.cnbc.com
www.smg2000.com
www.lavamind.com/edu
www.younginvestor.com

Insurance—Low Cost
www.quotesmith.com
www.selectquote.com
www.iquote.com

Investing	www.makingsense.com
	www.younginvestor.com
	www.fool.com
	www.plan.ml.com/family.kids
	www.better-investing.org
	www.netstockdirect.com
	www.valueline.com
Mutual Funds (Minimal $)	www.janus.com
	www.seinroe.com
	www.usaa.com/beta
	www.invesco.com
Mutual Find Info	www.morningstar.com
Newspapers	www.wsj.com
	www.usatoday.com
Parenting	www.parenting.com
	www.newdream.org
	www.parentsoup.com
	www.familyeducation.com
Savings Bonds	www.savingsbonds.com/chart/html
	www.savings-bond.gov
	www.ed.gov
	www.ustreas.gov/opc/opc0035.html
Stocks, etc. Discount	www.etrade.com
	www.schwab-worldwide.com
	www.fidelity.com
	www.discoverbrokerage.com
	www.seibert.com
Taxes	www.irs.ustreas.gov

About the Author

Judith Briles, MBA, PhD

Dr. Judith Briles is the founder of The Briles Group, Inc, a Colorado based research, training and consulting firm. She is internationally acclaimed as a speaker and recognized as an expert in solutions to workplace and women's issues. Her audiences range from 50 to 5000. Over 20,000 women and men hear her speak each year.

She is an award winning author of twenty books including *10 Smart Money Moves for Women, Woman to Woman 2000, The Confidence Factor, Money Sense, The Money Sense Guidebook, Financial Savvy for Women, Judith Briles' Money Book, When God Says NO, The Confidence Factor, Raising Money Wise Kids, The Dollars and Sense of Divorce, GenderTraps, Woman to Woman, The Workplace, Faith and $avvy, Too!, Money Phases, The Woman's Guide to Financial Savvy* and *The Dollars of Divorce*.

She has been featured on over 1000 radio and television shows nationwide and writes a column for *Colorado Woman News* and the *Denver Business Journal. Her work has been featured in The Wall Street Journal, Time, People, USA Today and the New York Times. She's a frequent guest on MSNBC, CNNfn* and *CNN*.

Dr. Briles is a director of the WISH List, serves on the Advisory Boards of Colorado Woman News, Zenith magazine, is a past director of the National Speaker's Association, the Woman's Bank of San Francisco and Colorado Women's Leadership Coalition.

For information of Judith Briles' availability for speeches and workshops, participation in her annual Confidence Working Cruise or to obtain her newsletter, The Woman's Voice, contact her at:

The Briles Group, Inc
PO Box 460880
Aurora CO 80046
Email DrJBriles@aol.com
www.Briles.com
Fax 303-627-9184
303-627-9179

Where to Find It . . .

A Final Word

No single book about such a broad topic for a huge age span can hope to cover everything a parent needs to know. *$mart-Money Moves for Kids* is just the beginning of a long journey in learning the *$mart-Money* approach to your and your kids financial well-being.

The money maze can be quite exciting. It can also be terrifying. How will you prepare for the trip? How will you negotiate the many and inevitable detours and obstacles that block your path? Your actions and answers will be the determining factors in whether your kids turn out to be money wise or money dumb.

I've shared with you my many years of success (and failures). It's now time for you to create your family's *$mart-Money* legacies. The work won't be easy. But do your best. And if you falter or make some mistakes, forgive yourself. Most of all, have fun.